Cataloging Sound Recordings

A Manual with Examples

About the Author

Deanne Holzberlein, PhD, MLS, Associate Professor of Library Science at Northern Illinois University, teaches cataloging and classification. When *AACR1* was published, she taught school media specialists at Southern Illinois University in Edwardsville. Realizing the students' needs for more information on nonbook cataloging, she developed a cataloging manual for her classes. Since the publication of *AACR1* and its amplified rules for nonbook cataloging, she has enjoyed teaching this subject.

Cataloging Sound Recordings

A Manual with Examples

Deanne Holzberlein
with the assistance of
Dolly Jones

The Haworth Press
New York • London

Cataloging Sound Recordings: A Manual with Examples is monographic supplement #1 to *Cataloging & Classification Quarterly*. It is not supplied as part of the subscription to the journal, but is available from the publisher at an additional charge.

The Haworth Press, Inc., 12 West 32 Street, New York, NY 10001
EUROSPAN/Haworth, 3 Henrietta Street, London WC2E 8LU England

Library of Congress Cataloging-in-Publication Data

Holzberlein, Deanne.
    Cataloging sound recordings

    (Monographic supplement # 1 to Cataloging & classification quarterly, ISSN 0898-008X)
    Bibliography: p.
    Includes index.
    1. Cataloging of sound recordings — Handbooks, manuals, etc. 2. Anglo-American cataloguing rules. I. Jones, Dolly. II. Title. III. Series: Monographic supplement ... to Cataloging & classification quarterly ; # 1.
ML111.5.H59   1987   025.3′482   87-31082
ISBN 0-86656-790-9

CONTENTS

CHAPTER 1

Introduction:
The Basics
for Cataloging Sound Recordings

THE REASON FOR THIS MANUAL

This manual is designed to assist in cataloging sound recording. It assumes the user will have some familiarity with cataloging and the *Anglo-American Cataloguing Rules*, 2nd edition, called the AACR2 rules, minimal experience with cataloging sound recordings and no background as a musician. This manual provides numerous examples of catalog cards for different types of sound recordings, so that the rules and Rule Interpretations from the Library of Congress[1] can be seen with specific applications. The examples presented in this manual show the full level of descriptive cataloging.

The manual begins by literally stepping through the thought-process used in cataloging a sound recording, beginning with what to use as the source for the title, through the physical description and series information. General information about notes are given in the first chapter, while details about notes are given in an appendix. The examples begin in the second chapter with 20th century music which is relatively easy to catalog. This is the longest chapter and includes rock music, country music, blues, orchestral music, etc. This is followed by a short informational chapter on the use of uniform titles and how to construct them for musical material. The following chapter returns to the detailed example format dealing with classical music and uniform titles. This chapter is arranged according to the cataloger's needs: by single composer with a single work; a single composer with multiple works; multiple composers with multiple works; and under performer, when the recording's purpose is to display the virtuosity of the person or group.

The next six chapters provide examples of different types of recordings: musicals and motion picture music, children's records, special

1

music, which includes band and Christmas music, spoken records, compact discs, and records with numbers at the beginning of either title or author. The last chapter examines the level of descriptive cataloging that might be needed in accord with patron needs and collection policy, as well as suggestions for cataloging short cuts.

The Appendixes are intended to make this a worker's manual. Help with general cataloging problems is provided in the chapters, while the appendixes assist when one wants to see more detail or to explore the reasons behind the examples. The appendixes include: order and content of cataloging notes, order of parts in a uniform title, a glossary of musical terms as well as acronyms used in this manual, a list of basic reference books and thematic indexes, a complete set of catalog cards, and the Library of Congress rule interpretations for sound recordings. As with any book intended for use rather than reading, it has a detailed index down to three levels prepared by the author.

Included throughout the manual are references to *Anglo-American Cataloguing Rules*, 2nd edition, *Cataloging Service Bulletin*, and *Music Cataloging Bulletin*, current to the time of publication. Should this manual appear clean and unused a year after purchase, it will have failed in its mission. It is sent forth to be used, marked up, and perhaps provoke inquiry. Cataloging should be fun, and it is hoped that the examples in this manual will take the chore out of cataloging sound recordings and return the joy to that work. The author is happy to answer questions, as well as acknowledge errors which can be corrected in a hoped for next edition. Please address questions to:

Deanne Holzberlein
Department of Library and Information Studies
Adams Hall-Northern Illinois University
DeKalb, IL 60115
Phone: 815-753-1733 (departmental office)

THE BASICS FOR CATALOGING SOUND RECORDINGS

The *Cataloging code* followed for cataloging sound recording is the *Anglo-American Cataloging Rules*, 2nd ed.[2] with rule changes by the Joint Steering Committee for Revision of AACR and rule interpretations by the Library of Congress, both the changes and interpretations[3] given quarterly in *Cataloging Service Bulletin*,[4] and music cataloging decisions, given monthly in *Music Cataloging Bulletin*.[5]

Selecting the Chief Source of Information

According to AACR2, the permanent labels[6] are used for cataloging sound recordings. The labels, jacket, and accompanying material are examined for a common[7] or collective title,[8] and *in that order*. When the title used on the bibliographic record comes from elsewhere than from the labels, the source of the title is given in a Note 3.

Title

The cataloger chooses as the title the words in the largest, or most outstanding typeface. In some instances, this means slightly rearranging the words as given on the label, as is seen with *Dueling Banjos*[9] which gives Curtis McPeake as the beginning words on the label, but these words were moved by the cataloger to the statement of responsibility position. When the record label gives the performer's name in large letters and there is no other title, such as the recording for *Ink Spots*,[10] these words need to be taken as the title, because librarians consider everything cataloged should have a title. Some titles have statements of responsibility grammatically linked as an inseparable part of the title, as in *Bernard Shaw speaks*,[11] *Join Bing and sing along*[12] and *John Denver's greatest hits*.[13]

Noncollective Titles

When the cataloger cannot find a single, all inclusive title, then the different, individual titles are listed as given on the label. Two extreme examples of noncollective titles are given in this manual:

one composer with different titles

    Haydn, Joseph, 1732-1809.
        [Symphonies, H.I. 82, C major]
        Symphony no 82 in C : l'ours = the bear ; Symphony no. 83 in G
        minor : la poule = the hen [sound recording] / Franz Joseph
        Haydn.[14]

many composers, many titles

    Loewe, Frederick, 1904-1988
        [My fair lady. Selections]

My fair lady / music of Lerner and Loewe. The king and I / music of Rodgers and Hammerstein [sound recording].[15]

no composer or composer unknown

Title : other title information. Title. Title : other title information [sound recording].

If there is no collective title, the recording cannot be entered under a principal performer.[16]

General Material Designation

The general material designation is [sound recording], as given in AACR2, 1.1C1. This is used when the material being cataloged is primarily a recording. When the material is a filmstrip, a sound recording and a book or booklet, it is likely the primary material may be the filmstrip. Some consider that if there are three diverse materials, then the designation should be "kit." Following this line of thinking will simply lead to labeling most nonbook material as "kit."

Statement of Responsibility

This area is used for meticulously copying the information relative to who was responsible for the recorded material which is given on the label. This area is not machine searchable[17] and is *not* the area to write the correct "form" of the name. The correct "form" of the name will be given later in either the main entry or a tracing.

Choosing the Main Entry

The AACR2 rules for determining whether the work is entered as a work of personal authorship,[18] a work of corporate authorship[19] or is entered under title[20] are used here, just as they are with anything being cataloged. The same consideration is given with this as with other works:

a. can personal authorship be established?
b. can corporate authorship be established within the very narrow limits now imposed?
c. can it be named conference, and thus corporate authorship?
d. when none of the above, it is a title main entry.

For any work with a personal or corporate main entry, the "form" of the name is checked in the authority files. The usual places to check these authority files are on a national database, such as OCLC or RLIN, or by using the microfiche edition of the National Union Catalog, *Name Authority Records*,[21] or by examining the local authority file at the home library, which contains names of regionally prominent people and corporations not yet listed in the national database. After the correct "form" of the personal or corporate name is established, either by finding it, or through the more difficult task of establishing it,[22] then this "form" is put into the main access point, which, for a catalog card, is the top line of a main entry record. A name will need the same careful checking if it is to be added to the tracings.

Place, Publisher, Date

The name of the city of publication, taken from the label or the jacket, box, etc., is given on the catalog entry. The province or state is added if it is also available from these sources. The province or state is added in square brackets [] if the name of the city is relatively unknown and the cataloger knows this information. For sound recordings where only the country is known, then this information, by itself, is given in the bibliographic record as the place, followed by the name of the publisher or distributor. When the place of publication is assumed, then the name of the place is placed in square brackets with the place given, followed by a question mark:

[London?][23]

When the cataloger does not have any idea of the place of publication, then the Latin words, Sine loco, meaning "without a place" are given in their abbreviated form:

[S.1.][24]

Address of Publisher

The address of the publisher is given for sound recordings if all three of these conditions are met:

a. it was issued by a United States publisher, distributor, etc., whose address is given in the item being cataloged;
b. it was issued within the current three years;
c. it does not have an ISSN or an ISBN number.[25]

In order to develop familiarity with this instruction to add the address, some examples in this manual include the address.[26]

The publisher's or distributor's name is given in the shortest form readily understood by library patrons.[27] The publisher's name may come from the container, accompanying material, or even a logo. Just as an unknown place of publication can be identified by a Latin abbreviation which means: I don't know, so an unknown publisher's name also has an abbreviation:

[s.n.]

which means "without a name."

The copyright date is given with a small "p" if the material gives a p within a circle, or says Phonoright. The copyright date is given with a small "c" if the material gives a c within a circle, or says copyright. Sometimes the label says the material is copyrighted, but no date is given. In that case, record it as a questionable date, and give the date as accurately as possible.[28] For example:

c[198-?]

Physical Description

The physical aspect of what is cataloged is divided into four parts: the extent, other characteristics, size and accompanying material.

1st: Extent. This describes the number and type of material. Time, if given, is included here.[29]

EXAMPLES:
   6 sound discs (326 min.)[30]
   1 sound cassette (3 min., 15 sec.)[31]
   10 piano rolls (105 min.)

2nd: Other characteristics.

a. Analog or digital <Analog is common>
b. Speed
c. Monographic, stereophonic, or quadrophonic

EXAMPLES:
   2 sound discs (ca. 80 min.) : analog, 33 1/3 rpm, stereo.
   1 sound disc (31 min.) : digital

3rd. Size, which is record height. The size for sound cassettes is omitted when it is the "standard" size.

EXAMPLES:
    1 sound disc (360 min.) : digital, stereo. ; 4 3/4 in.
    1 sound disc (50 min.) : analog, 33 1/3 rpm, stereo. ; 12 in.
    1 sound cassette : analog, stereo., Dolby processed.

4th. Accompanying material. Only include generic material meeting these qualifications:

—without a special title
—without a different author
—published at the same time as the record

EXAMPLE:
    3 sound discs (121 min.) : analog, 33 1/3 rpm, quad. ; 12 in. + 1 libretto (19 p. : ill. ; 29 cm.)

Notes

The *first* note for sound recordings gives the short form of the publisher's name and then the record number. The number is unique with each publisher and is used in a manner approaching desperation because publisher's have not generally adopted any standard numbering system. Yet there are many records that appear to be the same as another record until one examines the publisher's record number.

Because this note is usually known as Note 19 and has been moved up to the first position when cataloging sound recordings, it is listed in this manual as Note Super 1. This leaves the regular numbering of notes intact with AACR2 numbers, since notes *must* be given in the correct order.[32]

Notes provide the space for catalogers to add information they consider might be important to patrons. The order of the notes begins with general information about the recording as a whole, and then follows the order of the bibliographic description.

Notes also provide a place to give the reason for listing someone or something in the tracings, if the reason is not already obvious from the main part of the catalog entry. For example, an orchestra might be listed in a tracing, while not given in the main part of the catalog entry. Then Note 6 could give the name of the orchestra.

BRIEF GUIDELINES FOR MAKING ADDED ENTRIES: 2ND PART OF THE TRACINGS

The following represent the added entries most frequently used when cataloging music. The guidelines for these will be found in AACR2 and in the LCRIs.

Adaptors, arrangers, etc. (21.18 and 21.9)
Added accompaniments, which means giving the name of the person who changed the music from its original form into the form given on the sound recording (21.21)
Added entries in general (21.29-30)
Ballet music (21.20)
Collections (21.7)
Librettos (21.19)
Liturgical music (21.22)
Music adaptors, arrangers, etc. (21.18 and 21.9)
Sound recordings (21.23)

Given below are some highlights of these guidelines
Analytical added entries are listed by author plus uniform title. This is called a name-title tracing. Follow the instructions for constructing uniform titles, since the title part of this entry is always the uniform title.[33] There is more information about this in Chapter 3.

A *collection* of 25 musical works, exclusive of pop, folk, ethnic, jazz, recitals, or incomplete collections, may have analytical added entries for each work.[34]

Composer as principal performer: If the composer is the main entry, and is also the principal performer, then give an added entry for him as performer. This is done so the person may be located as a performer in the catalog, and may be located as the author.[35]

Librettist is given a tracing if the total work is included.[36]

Noncollective title entries have name-title tracings for each work named in the main body of the catalog record.[37]

Principal performers have added entries, except for performers listed as the main entry.[38] If the sound recording has no collective title, but does have principal performers, do not give the main access point to the performer(s). The performers can be listed in the tracings.[39]

Order for the Added Entry Tracings[40]

1. Personal name.
2. Personal name-title.

3. Corporate name.
4. Corporate name-title.
5. Title.
6. Title traced differently.
7. Series.
8. Series traced differently.

HOW TO STAY CURRENT

For those cataloging sound recordings, the following periodicals provide current information about changes in the cataloging practice. Some of the periodicals contain general, all-purpose cataloging information, useful for sound recordings, books, slides, and other materials. Some of the periodicals are specifically designed for the needs of the music cataloger, and are given here because a large part of most sound recording collections is musical.

Cataloging Service Bulletin.[41] Includes current information on rule interpretations and major subject heading changes for cataloging all types of material. For those on a small budget, this is an essential purchase.

LC Rule Interpretations of AACR2, 1978-1985, 2nd cumulated ed. Sally S. Tseng, comp. Metuchen, N.J.: Scarecrow, 1985. This is a reprint, in loose-leaf form, of AACR2 and the Rule Interpretations. Cost: $49.50.

Library of Congress Rule Interpretations for AACR2.[42] This is useful, but arrives about 3 months after the *CSB* issue. It is a loose-leaf cumulation of the Rule Interpretations from *CSB*, beginning with *CSB*, issue 11, the first issue dealing with AACR2. This contains only Rule Interpretations, and hence does not contain all the information found in *CSB*.

MARC for Library Use: Understanding the US-MARC Formats. Walt Crawford, White Plains, NY: Knowledge Industry Publications, 1984. This shows the US-MARC format, what it looks like now, how it has changed, and what its history has been. "The records illustrate actual use of USMARC, and are not intended to show correct or desirable cataloging practice, an area outside the scope of this book." The examples are all from RLIN.

Music Cataloging Bulletin.[43] This gives information for cataloging music and sound recordings. The rule interpretations under consideration are discussed at length in *MCB*. This also gives LC classification changes in the M schedule, LCSH changes related to music, and lists cataloging record changes for records and music material.

There is at least one online music catalogers group: Music OCLC Users Group, and they publish an occasional newsletter. Their address is: c/o Judy Weidow, Treasurer, P.O. Box 8272, Austin, TX 78713-8272. Cost: $5.00/year.

CHAPTER 2

20th Century Music

In order to illustrate the easiest cataloging of sound recordings, and not use the uniform title,[1] some 20th century music will be presented first. In addition to careful consideration of AACR2 21.1 for assigning the main access point for 20th century music, AACR2 21.23[2] needs to be used. The following is paraphrased from the rule and Rule Interpretation:

1. For *one work* on a sound recording:
   give the author or composer as the main access point
2. For *two* or more *works* on a sound recording, all having the *same author* or composer:
   give the author or composer as the main access point
3. *Collections with a collective title:*
   give the first named *principal performer*
4. *Collections with no collective title*, even on the jacket:
   give the performer as main access if he is responsible for the creation of the work. Or, more commonly, *give the author* or composer[3] of the first work[4] if the performer only performed the work.

For comments on new subject headings, see *Music Cataloging Bulletin* 16(May 1985):2-4.

Example 2.1. BLUES : UNDER PERFORMER

```
Belafonte, Harry
   Belafonte sings the blues [sound recording] /
[sung by] Harry Belafonte. -- [New York] : RCA
Victor, [1958?].
   1 sound disc (33 min.) : analog, 33 1/3 rpm,
stereo. ; 12 in.
   RCA: LSP-1972.                                    Note Super 1
   Produced by Ed Welker.                            Note 6
   Recorded: New York, Jan. 29, 1958, Alan Greene,   Note 7
leader : Mar. 29, 1958, Bob Corman, leader --
Hollywood, June 5, 7, 1958, Dennis Farnon, leader.
   Contents: A fool for you / Ray Charles (3:38) --
Losing hand / Charles Calhoun (4:16) -- One for my
baby / Johnny Mercer, Harold Arien (4:34) -- In
                            (Continued on next card)
```

```
Belafonte, Harry.
   Belafonte sings the blues [sound recording]...
[1958?]. (Card 2).
the evenin' mama / C.C. Carter (3:29) --
Hallelujah I love her so / Ray Charles (2:53) --
The way that I feel / Fred Brooks (4:29) -- Cotton
fields / C.C. Carter (5:17) -- God bless' the
child / Billie Holiday, Arthur Herzog, Jr. (5:03)
-- Mary Ann / Ray Charles (2:41) -- Fare thee well
/ Fred Brooks (4:37).
   1. Blues (Music)--1951-1960. 2. Jazz music--1951
-1960. 3. Jazz vocals. I. Title.
```

Main entry: This disc has a collective title, and will be entered under 21.23C, under the principal performer.

Title and statement of responsibility: Belafonte is repeated in small print at the bottom of the label, so his name can be repeated in the statement of responsibility area.

Note 7: This record told on the jacket about its recording history.[5]

Note 18: The duration for each piece is added,[6] and came from the jacket.[7]

Added entries: Belafonte is not traced[8] as a performer because he is given in the main entry as the leading performer.

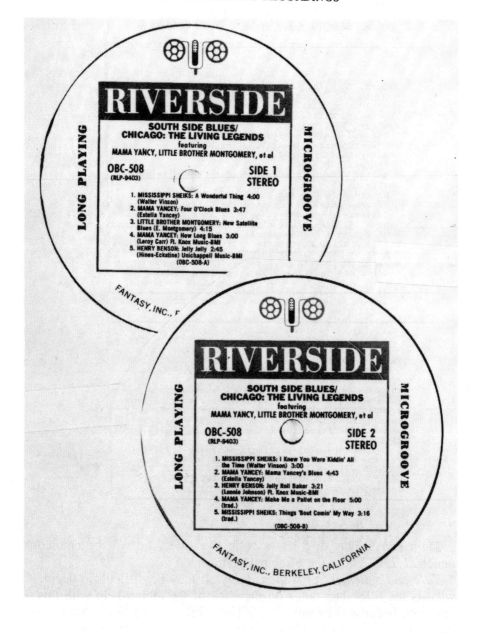

Example 2.2. BLUES : UNDER PERFORMER

```
Yancey, Estella.
   South side blues [sound recording] / featuring
Mama Yancey, Little Brother Montgomery, et al. --
[Berkeley, Calif.?] : Riverside ; Distributed by
Fantasy, Inc., c1984.
   1 sound disc : analog, 33 1/3 rpm, stereo. ; 12
in. -- (Chicago, the living legends)
   Riverside: RLP-9403.                             |Note Super 1
   Fantasy: OBC-508.                                 |Note Super 1
   Walter Vinson is accompanied by the Mississippi  |Note 6
Sheiks.                                              |
   Recorded in Chicago, Sept. 6 and 8, 1961.        |Note 7
   Program notes on container by Chris Albertson.   |Note 11
   Contents: A wonderful thing / sung by Walter     |Note 18
Vinson (4:00) -- Four o'clock blues / sung by Mama|
Yancey (3:47) -- New satellite blues / sung by    |
Little Brother Montgomery (4:15) -- How long blues|
/ sung by Mama Yancey (3:00) -- Jelly, jelly /    |
sung by Henry Benson (2:45) -- I knew you were    |
kidding all the time / sung by Walter Vinson      |
                     (Continued on next card)      |
```

```
Yancey, Estella.
   South side blues [sound recording]... c1984.
(Card 2).
(3:00) -- Mama Yancey's blues / sung by Mama
Yancey (4:43) -- Jelly roll baker / sung by Henry
Benson (3:21) -- Make me a pallet on the floor /
sung by Mama Yancey (5:00) -- Things 'bout comin'
my way / performed by the Mississippi sheiks
(3:16).
   1. Blues (Music)--Illinois--Chicago--1961-1970.
2. Jazz music--1961-1970. 3. Jazz vocals. I.
Montgomery, Little Brother, 1906-    . II. Vinson,
Henry. III. Mississippi Sheiks. IV. Title. V.
Series.
```

Main entry: This disc has a collective title, and will be entered under 21.23C, under the principal performer.[9]

Title and statement of responsibility: It may be difficult to decide what is the title. The notes on the back of the album help with this decision, because they say, ''. . . This album is part of an extensive group of recordings of traditional jazz as played today made by Riverside in Chicago during September, 1961, and issued under a general series title, "Chicago: The Living Legends.''

Place, publisher, date: The address of the distributor is clearly given, and this place is given as the possible place for the publisher. The distributor's name is given in the main body of the card because it needs to be repeated again in the Note Super 1 area, and the activity of each needs to be clear to the patron. The date for this came from the "spine" of the record album, a most unusual place.

Note 7: This note is always given if the information is readily available about its recording history.[10]

Note 11: For those wondering what else can be stated in Note 11, there are numerous examples given in Appendix A of this manual.

Note 18: The duration for each piece is added,[11] and came from the labels.[12]

Subject headings: Information about the date and location are given in *Music Cataloging Bulletin* (May, 1985), p. 1.[13] The geographical subdivision is added because this is a recording of the Chicago blues, not just a recording in Chicago of American blues.

Added entries: Yancey is not traced[14] as a performer because she is given in the main entry as the leading performer. Since there were only four main performers, all four were traced, since in today's cataloging it is considered best to be full and complete. It is also easier to add these entries during the initial process of cataloging the disk rather than discovering the need to add these names at a later time. Revising a record is never the fun that the initial cataloging is, it is postponed, and susceptible of a higher error rate than the initial catalog records.

Example 2.3. COLLECTION : UNDER PERFORMER

```
Crosby, Bing.
    Join Bing and sing along [sound recording] : 33
great songs / Bing Crosby and Friends. -- [Camden,
N.J.] : RCA Victor, c1960.
    1 sound disc : analog, 33 1/3 rpm, stereo. ; 12
in. + 1 pamphlet (5 p. ; 28 cm.)
    RCA: LSP-2276.                               Note Super 1
    Contains mostly medlies.                      Note 18
    Contents: Take me out to the ball game, Meet me  Note 18
in St. Louis, Peggy O'Neil / Pease, Nelson, Dodge
-- K-K-Katy / O'Hara ; Mairzy Doats / Drake, Hoff-
man, Livingston -- Old Mac Donald had a farm --
Aura Lee, Cuddle up a little closer / Harbach,
Hoschna -- Daisy Bell, The bowery after the ball
                    (Continued on next card)
```

```
Crosby, Bing
    Join Bing and sing along [sound recording] ...
c1960. (Card 2). '
-- Long, long ago on the banks of the Wabash, I
was seeing Nellie home -- Shoo fly, don't bother
me, Oh them golden slippers, On the road to
Mandalay -- Give my regards to Broadway / Cohen
; Mary's a grand old name, You're a grand old
flag -- When you wore a tulip / Mohoney, Wenich ;
You were meant for me / Freed, Brown -- Good-bye,
my lady love / Howard -- Linger awhile / Owens,
Rose ; Heart of my heart / Ryan -- Doodle doo doo
/ Kassel, Stitzel ; All I do is dream of you /
Freed, Brown -- Alice blue gown / McCarthy,
                    (continued on next card)
```

```
Crosby, Bing
   Join Bing and sing along [sound recording] ...
c1960. (Card 3).
Tierney -- I love you truly, When I grow too old
to dream / Hammerstein, Romberg -- A hot time in
the old town tonight, Toot, Toot, tootsie
goodbye / Kahn, Erdman, Russo -- Ta ra ra boom der
e.
   1. Popular music--1951-1960. 2. Popular music--
1941-1950. I. Title. III. Sing along.
```

Main access: This is a collection with a collective title, and is entered under the principal performer, according to AACR2, 21.23C.

Title and statement of responsibility: The title and statement of responsibility might be considered linked, but a separate statement of responsibility can be found at the bottom of the label: Bing Crosby and Friends.

Main access point: Mr. Crosby is the major performer and main entry under him follows LCRI 21.23C.

Place, publisher, date: Neither the place nor the address was given on the label or the jacket, so the place was given in brackets and the address omitted. The date was given on the jacket.

Notes: A note telling the recording contained medleys was given because the contents note has the pieces grouped, not separated into individual listings, and this first Note 18 helps to explain these groupings to the patron.

Example 2.4   COLLECTION   :   UNDER PERFORMING GROUP

```
Ink Spots (Musical group).
    Ink Spots [sound recording]. -- [United States]
: Pirouette Stereo, [196-?]
    1 sound disc : analog, 33 1/3 rpm, stereo. ; 12
in.
    Pirouette: FM-51.                                   |Note Super 1
    Contents: If I don't care -- Whispering grass -- |Note 18
With my eyes wide open -- Frankie & Johnny --
Sweet sixteen - We'll meet again -- It's a sin to
tell a lie -- You tell me your dream -- When the
saints go marching in -- I love you truly.
    1. Popular music--1961-1970. I. Title.
```

Main entry: This is a collection with a collective title and entered under 21.23C, under principal performer.

Title/statement of responsibility: Are the words "Ink Spots" the title or the statement of responsibility? LCRI 1.1B3 answers: "[if in] doubt whether the . . . name [is] a collective title proper or a statement of responsibility, treat the name as the title proper."

Place, publisher, date: When the place of the publisher is not given and cannot be easily determined, then 1.4C6 says to add the country [United States]. [S.l.]. The date was a probable date for a decade (1.4F7).

Note 18: The contents are listed.

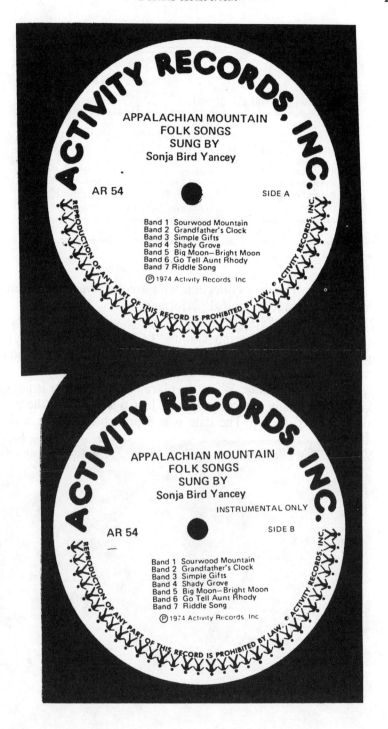

Example 2.5. COUNTRY MUSIC : UNDER PERFORMER

```
Yancey, Sonja Bird
    Appalachian mountain folk songs [sound
recording] / sung [and played] by Sonja Bird
Yancey. -- Freeport, N.Y. : Activity Records,
p1974.
    1 sound disc : analog, 33 /1/3 rpm ; 12 in.
    Activity: AR 54.                              Note Super 1
    Words given on jacket.                        Note 11
    Contains songs on one side, instrumental only on Note 18
the other side.
    Contents: Sourwood mountain -- Grandfather clock Note 18
-- Simple gifts -- Shady grove -- Big moon, bright
moon -- Go tell Aunt Rhody -- Riddle song.
                    (Continued on next card)
```

```
Yancey, Sonja Bird
    Appalachian mountain folk songs [sound
recording] ... p1974. (Card 2).
    1. Folk music--United States--Appalachian
mountains. I. Title.
```

Main entry: This is a collection with a collective title and entered under 21.23C, the principal performer.

Title and statement of responsibility. The cataloger supplied the information that Ms. Yancey played, as well as sang the songs.

Example 2.6. COUNTRY MUSIC : UNDER PERFORMER

```
Starcher, Buddy.
   Country, soul & inspiration [sound recording] /
[sung by] Buddy Starcher. -- Nashville, Tenn. :
Heart Warming Records : Processed by RCA Victor,
[1954?].
   1 sound disc (29 min.) : analog, 33 1/3 rpm,
stereo. ; 12 in.
   HWS: 1954 ; UR 3S-2411.                          |Note Super 1
   Contents: Beyond the sunset / narrated by Albert|Note 18
Kennedy Rowswell ; [composed by] Brock-Kerr (3:57)|
-- I talk to the shepard / Mercer (1:46) -- Have a|
seat close to Jesus / Starcher (2:30) -- They tore|
the old country church down (old Uncle Andy) /     |
Fralix-Starcher (5:32) -- It is no secret /         |
               (Continued on next card)
```

```
Starcher, Buddy.
   Country, soul & inspiration [sound recording]
[1954?]. (Card 2).
Hamblen (2:52) -- Ladder to the sky / Payne-Beck
(1:50) -- What then / Starcher-Glaser (2:46) --
When payday comes / Rambo (2:50) -- How great thou|
art / Hine (3:03) -- Mamma's teaching angels how
to sing / Rambo (2:02) -- Beyond that last long
mile / Starcher (2:55) -- What'll we tell our son
/ Starcher-Powell (2:00).
   1. Country music--1951-1960. I. Title. II.
Title: Country soul and inspiration.
```

Main entry: This is a collection with a collective title, and entered under the principal performer, according to AACR2, 21.23C.

Title/statement of responsibility: This is taken directly from the label, with a comma inserted in the title to make the reading easier for the patron. This follows 1.1B1. It will not change the filing, either in an online or in a manual file.

Note Super 1: The numbers of Heart Warming Records were listed first, followed by the other numbers found on the label.

Note 18: When the durations for the individual pieces are given, they are listed with the contents (LCRI 6.7B10).

Added entry tracing: The title is first traced the way it is given in the main body of the bibliographic record, and then traced again, spelling out the ampersand as "and" (LCRI 21.30J(14)).

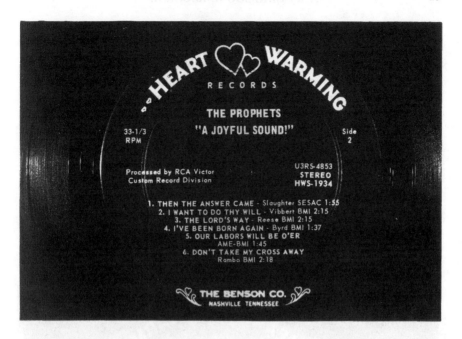

Example 2.7. GOSPEL MUSIC : UNDER PERFORMING GROUP

```
Prophets (Musical group).
   A joyful sound! [sound recording] / the
Prophets. -- Nashville, Tenn. : Heart Warming
Records, [196-?].
   1 sound disc (23 min.) : analog, 33 1/3 rpm,
stereo. ; 12 in.
   Heart Warming: HWS 1934.                       |Note Super 1
   Contents: He's a personal saviour / Abernathy  |Note 18
(1:35) -- The family Bible (2:43) -- I know that
this is true / Mercer (1:53) -- Marvelous grace /
Rambo (2:13) -- Close to the master / Hughes,
LeFevre (2.25) -- A house of love / Sutton,
Sherrill (1:40) -- Then the answer came /
Slaughter (1:55) -- I want to do thy will (2:15)
              (Continued on next card)
```

```
Prophets (Musical group).
   A joyful sound! [sound recording] ... [196-?].
(Card 2).
-- The Lord's way / Reese (2:15) -- I've been born
again / (Byrd) (1:37) -- Our labors will be o'er
(1:45) -- Don't take my cross away / Rambo (2:18).
   1. Gospel music. I. Title.
```

Main access point: The troupe is named: The Prophets, but "the" is omitted. This is a collection entered under a collective title, and so the main entry is under the principal performer, according to AACR2, 21.23C. The quotation marks are removed from the title, according to 1.1B1.[15] The exclamation mark at the end of the title can remain without endangering the retrieval of this record in an online search. This shows a transposition of the title, according to 1.1A2, where the title is given first, and the statement of responsibility is listed next on the catalog record, although the disk label gives them in the opposite sequence.

Note 18: The durations were given adjacent to the title and statement of authority. If the disc label or accompanying material does not include the statement of authority, the cataloger will not take the time to look this up for every title, but will merely give the title without a statement of authority, as shown with *No Strings*.[16]

Example 2.8. HYMNS : UNDER PERFORMER

```
Ford, Tennessee Ernie.
   Tennessee Ernie Ford [sound recording] : hymns /
Tennessee Ernie Ford. -- Hollywood, Calif. :
Capital, [1960?].
   1 sound disc : analog, 33 1/3 rpm ; 12 in.
   Capital: T 756.                                  Note Super 1
   Orchestra and chorus, Jack Fascinato, conductor. Note 6
   Contents: Who at my door is standing / M.B.C.    Note 18
Slade, A.B. Everett -- Rock of ages / adapt. and
arr. by J. Fascinato, Ernest J. Ford -- Softly and
tenderly / adapt. and arr. by J. Fascinato, Ernest
J. Ford -- Sweet hour of prayer / adapt. and arr.
by J. Fascinato, Ernest J. Ford -- My task /
Ashford, Pickup, Ray -- Let the lower lights be
                         (Continued on next card)
```

```
Ford, Tennessee Ernie.
   Tennessee Ernie Ford [sound recording] ...
[1960?] (Card 2).
burning / adapt. and arr. by J. Fascinato, Ernest
J. Ford -- The ninety and nine / adapt. and arr.
by J. Fascinato, Ernest J. Ford -- Old rugged
cross / George Bennard -- When they ring the
golden bells / adapt. and arr. by J. Fascinato,
Ernest J. Ford -- In the garden / C. Austin Miles
-- Ivory palaces / Henry Barraclough -- Others /
Arthur A. Penn, C.C. Meigs.
   1. Gospel music. I. Title. II. Title: Hymns.
```

Main entry: This sound recording was a collection with a collective title, and entered under the principal performer, according to AACR2, 21.23C.

Example 2.9.   INSTRUMENTAL POPULAR MUSIC : UNDER PERFORMER

```
McPeake, Curtis.
    Dueling banjos [sound recording] : [as from the
motion picture Deliverance] / [played by] Curtis
McPeake. -- [S.l. ] : Power Records, [197-?]
    1 sound disc (23 min.) : analog, 33 1/3 rpm,
stereo. ; 12 in.
    Power: POW-MOE-210.                              Note Super 1
    Added title from jacket.                         Note 5
    Contents: Dueling banjos / Trad. ; arr. by Eric  Note 18
Weissberg (1:55) -- Worried man / Trad. ; aarr. by
T. Hill (2:04) -- Brassy bluegrass / Curtis
McPeake and Larry Morton (1:55) -- Home sweet home
/ Trad. ; arr. by T. Hill (2:10) -- Fireball /
Trad. ; arr. by T. Hill (2:26) -- Sally Goodin' /
                        (Continued on next card)
```

```
McPeake, Curtis.
    Dueling banjos [sound recording] ... [197-?]
(Card 2).
Trad. ; arr. by T. Hill (3:43) -- Doolin' Banjos
; part 1 / Trad. ; arr. by T. Hill. (1:32) -- Red
dress / Curtis McPeake (1:43) -- Black mountain
rag / Trad. ; arr. by T. Hill (1:55) -- Old Joe
Clark / Trad. ; arr. by T. Hill (2:12) -- Ruby /
Trad. ; arr. by T. Hill (2:11) -- Doolin' banjos :
part 2 / Trad. ; arr. by T. Hill (2:00).
    1. Bluegrass music--1971-1980. 2. Bluegrass
music 1961-1970. 3. Banjo music (Jazz). I. Title.
Title: Deliverance (Motion picture).
```

Main entry: This was a collection with a collective title, and entered under the principal performer, according to AACR2, 21.23C.

Title/statement of responsibility. The other title information was taken from the jacket. The quotation marks were removed, according to 1.1B2.[17] This shows the title transposed, according to 1.1A2. The label gives the statement of responsibility first, but the cataloger takes the title first, and the statement of responsibility second.

Place, publisher, date: Only the name of the record company was given on the label and the jacket, so the unknown information was placed in brackets, according to AACR2 1.4C6 and 1.4F7.

Note 5: The source of the bracketed other title information is given here.

Note 18: The duration for each piece is added, according to AACR2, 6.7B18.

Example 2.10.   INSTRUMENTAL MUSIC : UNDER PERFORMER

```
Alpert, Herb.
   What now my love [sound recording] / Herb Alpert
and the Tijuana Brass. -- Hollywood, Calif. (8255
Sunset Blvd., Hollywood) : A&M Records, [196-?]
   1 sound disc (31 min.) : analog, 33 1/3 rpm, 12
in.
   A&M: LP 114.                                        Note Super 1
   Contents: What now my love / Becaud, Sigman        Note 18
(2:18) -- Freckles / Ervan Coleman (2:12) --
Memories of Madrid / Sol Lake (2:28) -- It was a
very good year / Ervin Drake (3:37) -- So what's
new? / John Pisano (2:07) -- Plucky / Alpert,
Pisano (2:21) -- Magic trumpet / Bert Kaempfert
(2:18) -- Cantina blue / Sol Lake (2:34) --
                          (Continued on next card)
```

```
Alpert, Herb.
   What now my love [sound recording] ... [196-?]
(Card 2).
Brasilia / Julius Wechter (2:30) -- If I were a
rich man / Harnick, Bock (2:333) -- Five minutes
more / Styne, Cahn (1:53) -- Shadow of your smile
/ Mandel, Webster (3:28).
   1. Trumpet music. I. Tijuana Brass (Musical
group). II. Title.
```

Main entry and added entries: This is a collection, with a collective title, and entered under the principal performer, according to AACR2, 21.23C. However, there were two 'principally named' performers: Herb Alpert, and the Tijuana Brass. Since Mr. Alpert was listed first, he was given as the main entry[18] and Tijuana Brass was given in the tracings.

Example 2.11.   OPERETTA AND ORCHESTRA MUSIC : UNDER PERFORMER

```
Mantovani, Henry.
    Operetta memories [sound recording] / Mantovani
and his orchestra. -- England : London Records,
[c196-?]
    1 sound disc : analog, 33 1/3 rpm, stereo. ; 12
in.
    London: PS.202                              Note Super 1
    Title from jacket.                          Note 3
    Contents: Merry widow : waltz / Lehair -- My Note 18
hero : [from] the Chocolate soldier / Strauss --
Play gipsies, dance gipsies : [from] Contess
Maritza / Kalman -- O maiden, my maiden : [from]
Frederica / Lehair -- Gipsy love : waltz / Lehair
-- Gipsy baron : waltz / Strauss ; arr. Mantovani
                 (Continued on next card)
```

```
Mantovani, Henry.
    Operetta memories [sound recording] ... [c196-?]
(Card 2).
Die Fledermaus : overature / Strauss ; arr.
Mantovani.          .
    1. Operetta music. 2. Orchestra music. 3. Big
band music. I. Title.
```

Main entry: This is a collection, with the collective title given on the jacket. Because it has a collective title, it can be entered under AACR2, 21.23C, under the name of the principal performer.

Title/statement of responsibility: The jacket gave a collective title, and this was used for the bibliographic entry, with a source for this title given in Note 3.

Example 2.12.   POPULAR MUSIC : UNDER COMPOSER

```
Ellington, Duke, 1889-1974.
    The best of Duke Ellington [sound recording] :
and his famous orchestra. -- [Hollywood, Calif.]
: Capitol, p[1977?]
    1 sound disc (33 min.) : analog, 33 1/3 rpm,
mono. ; 12 in.
    Capitol: SM-1602.                                   Note Super 1
    Recorded 1953-54. Released as Capitol: T-1602      Note 7
in 1961.
    Contents: Warm valley / Ellington (3:21) --        Note 18
Rockin' in rhythm / Ellington, Mills, Carney
(4:31) -- Prelude to a kiss / Ellington, Gordon,
Mills (2:59) --.Satin doll / Ellington (2:55) --
Caravan / Ellington, Tizol, Mills (4:28) --
                    (Continued on next card)
```

```
Ellington, Duke, 1889-1974.
    The best of Duke Ellington [sound recording]
... p[1977?] (Card 2).
Flamingo / Grouya, Anderson (3:40) -- In a
sentimental mood / Ellington, Mills, Kurtz (2:27)
Black and tan fantasy / Ellington, Miley (5:10) --
Passion flower / Strayhorn, Raskin (3:01) --
Bakiff / Tizol, Schwartz, Gallet (5:41).
    1. Jazz music--1951-1960. I. Ellington, Duke,
1889-1974. II. Title.
```

Main access: This is a collection of two or more works, all by the same composer, so it is entered under Mr. Ellington as the composer, under AACR2, 21.23B.

Title/statement of responsibility: Duke Ellington's name is given only once on the record label. Since the words are used as the title, they cannot be repeated as a statement of responsibility.

Note 7: This record has an interesting history. Ellington fans who want to listen to new music from his baton will need to know this recording contains 'nothing new,' that it is just a re-issue of an old recording.

Added entries: Duke Ellington is traced[19] as a performer. The main access is for his activity as a composer.

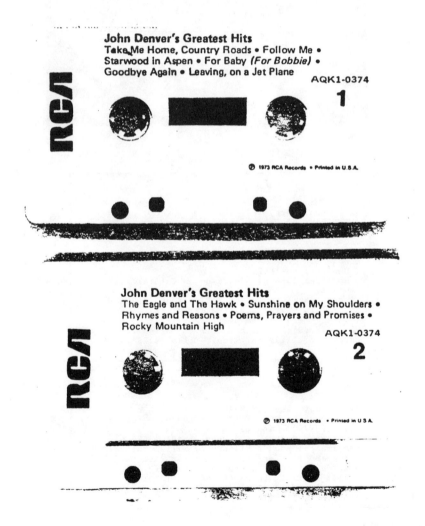

Example 2.13. POPULAR MUSIC : UNDER COMPOSER

```
Denver, John.  •
    John Denver's greatest hits [sound recording] /
[composed and sung by John Denver]. -- [New York]
: RCA Victor, c1973.
    1 sound cassette : analog
    RCA : AQK1-0374.                                    Note Super 1
    Contents: Take me home, country roads -- Follow   Note 18
me -- Starwood in Aspen -- For baby, for Bobbie --
Goodbye again -- Leaving on a jet plane -- The
eagle and the hawk -- Sunshine on my shoulders --
Rhymes and reasons -- Poems, prayers and promises
-- Rocky mountain high.
    1. Popular music--1971-1980. I. Denver, John.
II. Title.
```

Main access: This is a collection from one composer, and is entered under Mr. Denver as the composer, according to AACR2, 21.23B.

Title/statement of responsibility: The information in the statement of responsibility was added. Otherwise the patron might think this is just music, without vocals.

Added entries: John Denver is both the composer and performer. He is given an added entry for his performing activity.

LOS DOS REALES
Por ningún motivo ● Tampico hermoso ● Puñalada
trapera ● Los cerros de Chihuahua ● Amigos de
acuerdo

CSC
83
1
℗ 1972

Hecho en México

LOS DOS REALES
Paloma piquito de oro ● Polvo y olvido ● Caminos
de la vida ● El aguitado ● Línea divisoria ●
Aquel amor

C
3
2
℗ 1972

Hecho en México

Example 2.14. POPULAR MUSIC : UNDER PERFORMER

```
Vargas de Tecalitlan.
  Los dos reales / Vargas de Tecalitlan, con el
mariachi. -- Mexico : RCA Camden, p1972.
  1 sound cassette : analog, stereo.
  Camden: CSC-83.                              |Note Super 1
  Contents: Por ningun motivo -- Tampico hermoso |Note 18
-- Punalada trapera -- Los cerros de Chihuahua --
Amigos de acuerdo -- Tres dias -- Paloma piquito
de oro -- Polvo y Olvido -- Caminos de la vida --
El anguitado -- Linea Divisoria -- Aquel Amor.
  1. Popular music--Mexico--1961-1970. 2. Hispanic
Americans--Music. I. Title.
```

Main access: This has a collective title. The name of the principal performer, "Vargas de Tecalitlan," appears only on the wrapper, which is the equivalent of the disk's jacket. This is when the information on the jacket is used, along with the information given on the label, so it is entered under performer, according to 21.23C.

Title/statement of responsibility: The title came from the upper portion of the label.

Place, publisher, date: The place of publication was just: "Hecho en Mexico"[20] on the label, with the date given on the label.

Tracings: No analytical added entries are made for the individual titles listed in the contents since this contains popular music.[21]

Example 2.15. ROCK MUSIC : 8 TRACK

```
Ace (Musical group).
   No strings [sound recording] / [performed by]
Ace. -- [Sunnyvale, Calif.?] : Anchor Records :
Manufacted/Printed by GRT, p. 1976.
   1 sound cartridge (41 min.) : analog, 8 track ;
4 x 5 3/8 in.
     GRT: 3808 -- Anchor: 2020 H.                   |Note Super 1
     Produced by Trevor Lawrence.                   |Note 6
     Contents: Rock and roll singer -- C'est la vie |Note 18
-- Found out the hard way -- You're all that I
need -- Why did you leave me -- Crazy world --
I'm not takin' it out on you -- Let's hang on --
Movin' -- Gleaming in the gloom.
   1. Rock music--1971-1980. I. Title.
```

Main access: This is a collection with a collective title, and entered under the principal performer, according to AACR2, 21.23C. Also, LCRI 24.4B(3) says that (Musical group) is to be added if the name for the performing group does not indicate it is a musical group.

Title/statement of responsibility: "Performed by" was added for the patron's benefit.

Place, publisher, date: See AACR2, 1.4E1 for an example of both a publisher and a distributor listed, with a single date. The above is an instance when the cataloger does not know if Anchor Records is the publisher, but the cataloger follows the likely pattern.

Subject headings: The date for the subject heading came from the information given in *Music Cataloging Bulletin* (May, 1985) p. 1.[22]

Example 2.16. ROCK MUSIC : UNDER PERFORMER

```
Sugarloaf (Musical group).
   Sugarloaf [sound recording] / [played and sung
by] Sugarloaf. -- Los Angeles, Calif. : Liberty,
[197-?]
   1 sound disc (38 min.) : analog, 33 1/3 rpm,
mono. ; 12 in. ·
   Liberty: LST-7640.                              Note Super 1
   Jerry Corbetta, organ, piano, clavichord and    Note 6
vocals ; Bob Webber, guitar and vocals ; Bob
Raymond, bass ; Bob MacVittle, drums.
   Contains on medley.                             Note 18
   Contents: Greeny-eyed lady / Jerry Corbetta,    Note 18
J.C. Phillips, David Riordan -- Train kept a-roll'
/ Relf, Page, Beck, Drega -- Bach doors man /
                       (Continued on next card)
```

```
Sugarloaf (Musical group).
   Sugarloaf [sound recording] ... [197-?] (Card 2)
... p[1977?] (Card 2).
Jerry Corbetta, Bob Webber, Bob Raymond, Myron
Pollock; [and] Chest fever / J.R. Robertson --
West of tomorrow / Jerry Corbetta, Bob Raymond,
J.C. Phillips -- Gold and the blues / Jerry
Corbetta, Myron Pollock, Bob Raymond, Bob Webber
-- Things gonna change some / Jerry Corbetta, Van
Dorn, Bob Raymond, Bob Webber.
   1. Rock music--1971-1980. I. Title.
```

Main entry: The word "Sugarloaf" was taken as the collective title. This allowed it to be entered under principal performer, according to 21.23C.

Title/statement of responsibility: The word, Sugarloaf, appears twice in a prominent place on the label, so one instance is considered the name of the group, and the other as the title.

Note 6: The names of the four members of this performing group are given on the inside of the jacket.

Added entries: The people performing in Sugarloaf are not traced, since they are not prominently named on the record label.[23]

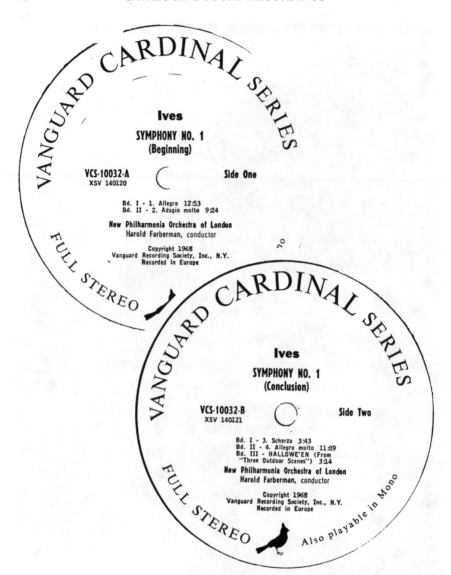

Example 2.17. 20th CENTURY SYMPHONY : UNDER COMPOSER

```
Ives, Charles Edward, 1874-1954.
    [Symphonies, no. 1-4]
    The four symphonies [sound recording] / Charles
  Ives. -- New York, N.Y. : Vanguard Recording
  Society, c1968.
    3 sound discs (136 min.) : analog, 33 1/3 rpm,
  stereo, Dolby processed ; 12 in. -- (Cardinal
  series)
    Vanguard: VCS-10032--VCS-10034.                    Note Super 1
    Title from container.                              Note 3
    Ambrosian Singers, John McCarthy, director ; New   Note 6
  Philharmonia Orchestra of London, Harold Faberman,
  conductor.
    Recorded October, 1968 at Bishopsgate Institute,   Note 7
  London.
    Program notes on container by Harold Faberman.     Note 11
    Contents: Symphony 1 (35:24) -- Symphony 2         Note 18
  (40:05) -- Symphony 3 (23.09) -- Symphony 4
  (34:38) -- Hallowe'en (3:14).
    1. Symphonies. 2. Orchestral music. I. Faberman,
  Harold, 1929-  . II. Ives, Charles Edward, 1874-
  1954. Hallowe'en. 1968. III. New Philharmonia
  Orchestra. IV. Title.
```

Main access: This is a collection from one composer, and is entered under Mr. Ives the composer, according to AACR2, 21.23B.

Uniform title: This 20th century recording needs a uniform title, which will be explained in Chapter 3, and illustrated in Chapter 4. This is just presented as a reminder that it is occasionally needed with 20th century music.

Title/statement of responsibility: Since a collective title is preferred, the title from the container was used. This requires a Note 3 to state where the title came from, when it does not come from labels.

Notes: These are more fully explained by the examples given in Chapter 4 of this manual.

Added entries: The added entry for Mr. Ives is a name-title tracing, and uses the uniform title in the name. Again, these are more fully explained by the examples given in Chapter 4 of this manual.

Example 2.18. TWENTIETH CENTURY MUSIC : TITLE MAIN ENTRY

Million dollar memories [sound recording] : 30
  years of great hits from the top stars. --
  [Pleasantville, N.Y.] : Reader's Digest ; [New
  York] : Made by Columbia Special Products,
  p1973.
  4 sound cassettes (300 min.) : analog + 1
  booklet (6 p. ; cm.)
  Reader's Digest: RD 5 196-8 (on container: KRD   Note Super 1
  196-A1--4).
  CBS: C2T 10994 (on container).   Note Super 1
  Partial credits: [Sung by] Tony Bennett, Doris   Note 6
  Day, Judy Garland, Harry James, Frankie Laine,
  Johnny Mathis, Patti Page, Johnnie Ray, Barbara
  Streisand, and others.
  (Continued on next card)

```
Million dollar memories [sound recording] ...
   p1973. (Card 2).
   "Electronically re-recorded to simulate stereo."  Note 10
   Contents: Hits from 1941-1971. Songs included    Note 18
are listed on each side of cassette, and in
booklet.
   1. Popular music--To 1961. 2. Popular music--
1961-1970. I. Reader's Digest Association. II.
Title: 30 years of great hits from the top stars.
III. Title: Thirty years of great hits from the
top stars.
```

Main entry: While this has a collective title, there is no principal performer. So it is entered under a title main entry, according to AACR2, 21.23 and 21.1C.

Publication, distribution area: The set of cassettes is sold by *Reader's Digest*. The labels give *Reader's Digest* as publisher.[24] "Made by" is indicated the same way as "Manufactured by."

Note Super 1: There were two sets of publisher's numbers on the containers, with a slightly differently number on the individual cassettes. The other identification number was given in a separate note with an explanation in parenthesis as to where the number was found.

Note 6: Not all the singers were listed because no one was given a predominant position and there were too many to list. This is not a 'show case' for any performer, but is merely a collection of popular songs. Listing some of the singers in a note gives the patron an idea of the contents.

Added entry tracings: Because there was no predominant performer, no one was listed in the tracings.[25] The other title information was traced. Since the other title begins with a number "30," it was traced again, with the number spelled out.[26]

Example 2.19. COLLECTION OF POPULAR SONGS : NO PRINCIPLE
PERFORMERS

```
All time favorites [sound recording]. -- New York,
   N.Y. : Golden Tone, [195-?]
   1 sound disc : analog, 33 1/3 rpm, mono. ; 12
in.
   Golden Tone: C4011.                           Note Super 1
   George Lewis and his all-star orchestra.      Note 6
   Contents: Lisbon antigua -- I can't give you  Note 18
anything but love -- Melody of love -- Adios
muchachos -- Frenes! -- Touch of your lips -- All
or nothing at all -- Humoresque.
   1. Popular music--To 1961. I. Lewis, George.
```

Main entry: While this has a collective title, there is no principal performer. So it is entered under a title main entry, according to AACR2, 21.23 and 21.1C.

Title/statement of responsibility: The title was taken from the upper portion of the label. George Lewis, etc., did not appear prominently, so his name was put into the note area.

Place, publisher, date: The date was not given on the label or the jacket, but is deduced.[27] No analytical added entries are made for the individual titles listed in the contents since this contains popular music.[28]

Note 6: This lists the credits.

Note 18: This gives the contents.

Added entries: An added entry was made for the conductor's name given in Note 6.

CHAPTER 3

Overview of Uniform Titles

WHY A UNIFORM TITLE MAY BE NEEDED

Although a uniform title is given in AACR2 as an option,[1] its use will be considered a necessity in this manual.

A uniform title is used[2] to provide unity and cohesion, and also to separate and provide distinction. A uniform title is defined in the LCRI for Appendix D as:

> 1. The particular title by which a work is to be identified for cataloguing purposes. 2. The particular title used to distinguish the heading for a work from the heading for a different work. 3. A conventional collective title used to collocate publications of an author, composer, or corporate body containing several works or extracts, etc., from several works, e.g., complete works, several works in a particular literary or musical form.

As a unifier it collects into one place in the catalog all the known forms of a work, no matter what the language, nor how the publishers have reworded the title. All copies[3] of Beethoven's *Ninth Symphony* can be found in the catalog in one place, regardless of whether the title was in Hungarian, whether the work was given a fancy title by the publisher or even if the composer embellished upon his original title with a later title for the same work.

Librarians construct uniform titles[5] using the first title given by the composer. When this original title is distinctive and unique, little else is done to the title, unless there are conflicts and a different work also has the same title. When this happens, the uniform title is constructed to separate works that have the same title and is formed by using the unique title and some distinguishing feature, such as publisher, first three or four words of the libretto, if this makes it distinctive, etc. If

the original title is "generic," and in music this often means a name of
a type of composition and then a composition number or key, such as:

Symphony in D   D minor Concerto
Third Symphony   Concerto No. 6

then a generic term in the plural[4] is given for the title. For the above
titles they might look like:

Symphony in D   =   [Symphonies, D major]
Third Symphony   =   [Symphonies, K. 331, no. 3]
D minor Concerto   =   [Concertos, bassoon, orchestra,
                                        D minor]
Concerto No. 6   =   [Concertos, no. 6]

A generic title, formulated by the cataloger,[5] has other elements added
to the generic label, and is in a specific order.

Conventions Used with Uniform Titles

Several conventions have developed through years of use with uniform titles:
1. The uniform title is added above the bibliographic title.

EXAMPLE:
Normal cataloging look like:
      Rodgers, Richard, 1902-1979.
            Selections from Oklahoma and other standard hits [sound
recording] . . .
      A *uniform title,* given in brackets just above the bibliographic
title, looks like:
      Rodgers, Richard, 1902-1979.
      --->> [Oklahoma. Selections]
            Selections from Oklahoma and other standard hits [sound
recording] . . .

2. When the uniform title is given under a personal or corporate
main entry, then it is placed in square brackets.

Brunhoff, Jean de, 1899-1937.
[Babar en famille. English]
Babar and his children . . .

3. When both a uniform title and a bibliographic title are given, the uniform title is the one used for filing.

> Strauss, Johann, 1825-1899.
> [Waltzes, orchestra. Selections]
> Strauss waltzes [sound recording] . . .

When the filer is filing the entries for Strauss, Johann, he will file this under "Waltzes, orchestra. Selections," and will ignore "Strauss waltzes."

4. When the uniform title is the main access point, it does not have square brackets.

> -- > Hot chocolates. Selections.[6]
> Souvenirs of Hot chocolates [sound recording].

5. When the uniform title appears in a tracing, it does not have square brackets.

> II. Bond, Michael. More about Paddington, 1979. III. Bond, Michael. Paddington helps out. 1979.[7]

"More about Paddington" and "Paddington helps out" are both uniform titles.

With a uniform title, the patron has only one place to look for a work which has variant bibliographic titles. Uniform titles have proven so useful they are employed in cataloging other than music and religious works. The "Title" listed in the tracing always refers to the bibliographic title. When added entries are constructed by the cataloger for a tracing, the added entry name-title entry uses the uniform title[8] in the title segment of the entry.

HOW TO CONSTRUCT A UNIFORM TITLE FOR MUSIC

General Information

When constructing a uniform title, the cataloger consults standard reference sources to locate the original title:

1. By verifying the original title in a generally approved bio-biblio-graphical work. For music this is generally a thematic index.[9] A general bio-bibliographical work will present a complete list of the author's works under the original titles.
2. By verifying the title by checking at least three modern reference works such as music or literature dictionaries in the language of the composer or writer.
3. By consulting a national trade bibliography in the language of the author or composer.
4. By consulting trade publications listing current and forthcoming works. For authors, *Publisher's Weekly*, and its family of publication may be consulted. However, the information in *Publisher's Weekly* is taken from the MARC[10] database, so checking an online database with current MARC records would accomplish the same purpose. *World Literature Today* is useful for tracing the output of current writers outside the U.S. For sound recordings, *Schwann's Record and Tape Guide, Phonolog Reports*, or *Billboard* may be consulted.
5. By checking this with the standard cataloging practice of the past for this author or composer. Usually this is done by checking the National Union Catalog and the MARC database. The current practice is to add uniform titles to the online name authority files, so the cataloger checks there also. Since bibliographic control is still weak for sound recordings, the cataloger may have to take the work in hand to be the only known publication, and will follow AACR2 25.27B, and the LCRIs for this and construct his own uniform title.

A cataloger must trust his own judgment. If he learns later that a correction is needed, it can be made. But changes, or corrections, are costly, so catalogers work to keep changes to a minimum.

Below are selected examples of the uniform titles used for Mozart's works[11]

Adagios, violin, orchestra, K. 261, E major -	Generic
Bacio di mano	Unique
Concertos, bassoon, orchestra, K 191, B^b major -	Generic
Cosi fan tutte. Selections	Unique
Cosi fan tutte. Come scoglio	Unique
Deutsche Tanze	Unique
Don Giovanni. Selections	Unique
Duets, violin, viola, K. 424, B^b major -	Generic

Nozze di Figaro. Deh vieni, non tardar		Unique
Piano music, 4 hands. Selections	-	Generic
Symphonies, K. 319, B♭ major	-	Generic
Zauberflote. Libretto. English & German		Unique

GENERIC TITLES

A generic title is used for works with titles consisting solely of the name of one type of composition[12] or which are a type of composition for which a generic term is most frequently used.[13] Further identifying elements are added *in this order*:

1. *Medium of performance*[14] is given next, if this has not been implied in the title.[15] For listing the medium of performance, the cataloger uses a list of terms and their cataloging definitions.[16]

EXAMPLE:
Tchaikovsky, Peter Ilich, 1840-1893.
    [Concertos, piano, orchestra, no. 1, op. 23]
    Piano concerto no. 1 in B-flat minor, op. 23
    [sound recording] . . .
The medium of performance is omitted when:

— the medium is that which is expected with this generic title. For instance, with a symphony, one expects to hear an orchestra. This list of generic titles and implied media are given in AACR2 25.29A2.
— the media are so diverse that it is difficult to list them all, according to 25.29A(2)d.
— the works are generally those of the Renaissance period and intended for performance by voices and/or instruments, or the medium is not clearly defined, according to 25.29J.
— no medium is designated by the composer, see 25.29A(2)c.
— another method provides better file organization, according to 25.29A(2)d.[17]
— the instruments, or the medium is not clearly defined, according to 25.29J.

2. *Serial number*[18] if available. The example given above for Tchaikovsky illustrates this.
3. *Opus*, or *thematic index numbers*[19] if available.
4. *Key*[20] if available.
5. Other identifying elements in this order[21]

a. year of completion of the composition
b. year of original publication
c. any other identifying elements (e.g., place of composition, name of first publisher).

UNIQUE TITLES

Unique titles present a very different method for the cataloger. The unique titles are taken from the composer's original title[22] in the original language, with the following deletions:

1. remove the beginning a, an, or the.[23]
2. remove subtitles, and alternative titles.[24]
3. remove separable statements of responsibility.[25]
4. shorten lengthy titles. The first five words always remain intact.[26]

ADDITIONS FOR BOTH GENERIC
AND UNIQUE TITLES

The following can be added to generic and unique uniform titles:

1. Part.[27] This is added when a distinctly titled part of the work is given, or consecutive, distinctly titled parts of the work are included. The name of the part is not given when the sound recording contains nonconsecutive but distinctly titled parts of the work, nor is this used for just abridgements of the work. See "Selections"[28] for other ways to solve this need.

EXAMPLE:
    Schumann, Robert
       [Album fur die Jugend. Nr. 30]
       Pictures for the young [sound recording] . . .

2. Altered work. If alterations to a musical work include a different title, the uniform title is constructed in the normal manner, with the altered title added at the end in parentheses.

EXAMPLE:
    Strauss, Johann
       [Fledermaus (Gay Rosalinda). Selections]
       Selections from Gay Rosalinda [sound recording] . . .

3. Language.[29] This is added when it is a liturgical text, or is textual matter and is a translation from an original language.

EXAMPLE. See Hesse just below. The original *Steppenwolf* is in German.

4. Selections. This is used for 3 or more nonconsecutive parts, or for an extract, abridgement, etc., in a medium.[20]

EXAMPLE OF AN EXTRACT:
Hesse, Hermann, 1877-1962.
[Steppenwolf. For madmen only. English. Selections]
Steppenwolf [sound recording] : for madmen only . . .

EXAMPLE OF 3 OR MORE NONCONSECUTIVE PIECES:
Rodgers, Richard, 1902-1979.
[Oklahoma. Selections]
Selections from Oklahoma and other standard hits [sound recording] . . .

5. Sketches.[31] If the work is only sketches for either a single work or a group of works, then formulate the uniform title for the completed work, and add (Sketches).

Gershwin, George
[Selections. (Sketches)]
Sketches from Gershwin's notebook [sound recording] . . .

6. Arr. (for arrangements)[32] If the work is an arrangement, it is listed under the main entry for the original composer, and the uniform title, followed by a semicolon and "arr." For a cataloger to use this terminology, the work must be changed from the medium of performance written for the original piece into another medium of performance.[33]

EXAMPLE:
Schubert, Franz
[Octets, woodwinds, horn, strings, D. 803, F. major; arr.]
Grosses Octett, op. 166
(now arranged for four hands at a piano)

7. Date. This is used only when there is a conflict *and* for analytical added entries. Date is also added to the generic title "Works" because conflicts are expected with this broad title.[34]

EXAMPLES FOR CONSTRUCTING A UNIFORM TITLE

Special Information

[Title. Chapter 6-8]	The part is added when it is not the whole of the work.
[Works. 1987]	This refers to the whole body of the author's, or artists, works.[35] Also use "Works" when it contains 3 or more pieces of various genre.[36] Add date for "Works," since more than one are expected in this category.[37]
[Works. Selections. 1987]	This is used when 3 or more pieces from different types of the author's works are included.

Always check the authority records for author-uniform title information.

UNIFORM TITLES IN TRACINGS
(AS ADDED ENTRIES)

With the advent of online cataloging, added entries are made for anything the cataloger considers might have current or future relevance to patrons using the bibliographic information. If a disk or cassette has two works on it, then the first work will be given in the main entry and the second work will be given in a tracing. Looking at the cataloging for the Haydn cassette,[38] there are two works given without a collective title. The first work, Symphony no. 82 in C has the uniform title given in square brackets just above it. This uniform title says, in very abbreviated form, Haydn's works, symphonies form, Hoboken's volume one, number 82, in C major. Hoboken is the thematic index for Haydn's works. To provide a tracing for this, everything will be repeated. However, the form will change, because in a tracing it should be short. Let's look at an abridged form of this Haydn work:

Example 3.1

```
Haydn, Joseph, 1732-1809.
  [Symphonies, H. I, 82, C major]
  Symphony no. 82 in C : l'ours = the bear ;
Symphony no. 83 in G minor : la poule = the hen
[sound recording] / Franz Joseph Haydn. --
Minneapolis, Minn. ...................... p1981.
  Program notes on container by Ekkehart Kroher.     |Note 11
  1. Symphonies. I. Haydn, Joseph, 1732-1809.
Symphonies, H. I, 83, G minor. 1981. II. Maier,
Franzjosef. III. Collegium Aureum. IV. Title. VI.
Series.
```

The first added entry traced is for the second symphony, and employs the uniform title. The date, 1981, refers back to the date of the sound recording (never to the date the composer wrote the piece), and indicates that this recording *contains* this work. When the date is missing, it indicates that the piece is *related* to this work, and that the work in the tracing is not contained in the recording.

This added entry card can be given in several ways, but usually is given thusly:

Example 3.2

```
Haydn, Joseph, 1732-1809.
  Symphonies, H. I, 83, G minor. 1981.
Haydn, Joseph, 1732-1809.
  [Symphonies, H. I, 82, C major]
  Symphony no. 82 in C : l'ours = the bear ;
Symphony no. 83 in G minor : la poule = the hen
[sound recording] / Franz Joseph Haydn. --
Minneapolis, Minn. ...................... p1981.
  Program notes on container by Ekkehart Kroher.     |Note 11
  1. Symphonies. I. Haydn, Joseph, 1732-1809.
Symphonies, H. I, 83, G minor. 1981. II. Maier,
Franzjosef. III. Collegium Aureum. IV. Title. VI.
Series.
```

A complete set of cards for one bibliographic record is given in Appendix F of this manual, to show how tracings are formatted. The current emphasis is to make added entries for all parts the cataloger considers important. Generally added entries are made for the following:

—*Analytical added entries* are listed by author plus uniform title, called name-title tracings.[39] Follow the information given earlier for constructing uniform titles.

—A *collection* of 25, or less, musical works, exclusive of pop, folk, ethnic, jazz, or incomplete collections, may have analytical added entries for each work.[40]

—*Collections which are entered with a noncollective title.* These have name-title tracings for each work named in the main body of the catalog record.[41]

CHAPTER 4

Classical Music and Uniform Titles

Statement of responsibility area: For classical music, the composer and librettist usually go into the statement of responsibility area. Performers' names go into Note 6.[1]

Simple name-title added entries: Added entries referring to a previous work,[2] are given a simple name-title added entry. *Il Trovatore* by Verdi has an example of a simple added entry in the tracing: "Gutierrez, Anatonio Garcia. Trovatore." This added entry relates to the author of the drama upon which this opera by Verdi is based. The title used in this added entry for Gutierrez is the uniform title for Gutierrez' work.[3]

Analytical name-title added entries: Added entries that bring out items contained on the recording are analytical added entries[4] and also follow the prescribed name-title form:[5]

Personal Name (from authority files). Uniform title. + date (of publication).

For a work that is a translation, the prescribed name-title is:[6]

Personal Name (from authority files). Uniform title. Language. + date (of publication).

Many of the name-title examples in this manual are examples of analytical added entries which refer to something contained in the recording.

Example 4.1. CLASSICAL MUSIC : ONE WORK
Entered under 21.23A: One work

```
Tchaikovsky, Peter Ilich, 1840-1893.
   [Concertos, piano, orchestra, no. 1, op. 23,
      Bᵇ minor]
   Piano concerto no. 1, in B-flat minor, op. 23
[sound recording] / Tchaikovsky. -- Camden, N.J. :
RCA Victor, [196-?]
   1 sound disc : analog, 33 1/3 rpm, stereo. ; 12
stereo. ; 12 in.
   RCA Victor: LSC 2252.                            |Note Super 1
   Van Cliburn, piano ; Symphony Orchestra, Kiril  |Note 6
Kondrashin, conductor.
   1. Concertos (Piano). I. Kondrashin, Kirill
Petrovich, 1914-    . II. Cliburn, Van, 1934-     .|
III. Title.
```

Main entry: This is a single work by a single composer, and is entered under AACR2, 21.23A, under the name of the composer.

Uniform title: Since Mr. Tchaikovsky is a pre-twentieth-century composer, the key is added in the uniform title.[7]

Title/statement of responsibility: A generic title includes the medium, key and number in the title proper.[8]

Note 6: This note gives the principal performers. For classical music, the performers are not given in the main body's statement of responsibility area.

Example 4.2. CLASSICAL MUSIC : ONE WORK
Entered under 21.23A : One work

```
Stravinsky, Igor, 1882-1971.
   [Vesna sviashchennaia]
   Le sacre du printemps [sound recording] / Igor
Stravinsky. -- New York : Nonesuch Records,
[196-?]
   1 sound disc (42 min.) : analog, 33 1/3 rpm,
stereo. ; 12 in.
   Nonesuch: H-71093.                              Note Super 1
   First work a ballet.                            Note 1
   Orchestre National de la R.T.F., Pierre Boulez, Note 6
conductor.
   Also contains: Four etudes for orchestra.       Note 18
   1. Ballets. 2. Orchestral music. I. Boulez,
Pierre, 1925-     . II. Stravinsky, Igor, 1882-
1971. Etudes, orchestra. III. Orchestra National
de I'O.R.T.F. IV. Title.
```

Main entry: This is a single work by a single composer, and is entered under AACR2, 21.23A, under the name of the composer.

Physical description: The durations were found on the labels and added to give the total playing time.

Subject heading: Many libraries have a local policy to omit such subject headings as "Orchestral music," because there are so many works using this subject heading that it is virtually useless. However, for a cataloger entering this work onto a national bibliographic database, the highest level of cataloging is needed, so this subject heading would be given. Having this subject heading in an online catalog will provide excellent access through Boolean searching techniques.

Example 4.3. CLASSICAL MUSIC : ONE WORK
Entered under 21.23A : One work

```
Beethoven, Ludwig van, 1770-1827.
   [Symphonies, no. 6, op. 68, F major]
   Symphony no. 6 in F, op. 68 [sound recording] :
pastoral / Beethoven. -- New York : Funk &
Wagnalls, c1966.
   1 sound disc : analog, 33 1/3 rpm, stereo. ; 12
in. -- (Family library of great music ; album 1)
   Funk & Wagnalls: FW 301.                      |Note Super 1
   Royal Philharmonic Orchestra, Sir Charles     |Note 6
Groves, conductor.
   Biographical and program notes by R. Jacobson  |Note 11
(12 p. : ill.) inserted in container.
   1. Symphonies. 2. Orchestral music. I. Groves,
Charles. II. Royal Philharmonic Orchestra. III.
Title.
```

Main entry: This is a single work by a single composer, and is entered under AACR2, 21.23A, under the name of the composer.

Uniform title: A uniform title is needed.

Note 11: This is used to describe material not included in the physical description.

Verdi
IL TROVATORE

CAST

Leonora ....RENATA TEBALDI *Soprano*
Manrico ....MARIO DEL MONACO *Tenor*
Azucena ....GIULIETTA SIMIONATO *Mezzo-Soprano*
Ferrando ....GIORGIO TOZZI *Bass*
The Count di Luna ....UGO SAVARESE *Baritone*
Ruiz ....ATHOS CESARINI *Tenor*
A messenger ....ATHOS CESARINI *Tenor*
Inez ....LUISA MARAGLIANO *Soprano*
An old gipsy ....ANTONIO BALBI *Baritone*

with

CHORUS OF THE
MAGGIO MUSICALE FIORENTINO
and
L'ORCHESTRE DE LA SUISSE ROMANDE
conducted by
ALBERTO EREDE

Il Trovatore is perhaps the most typical Italian opera that has ever been written, for all the features popularly associated with that *genre* are to be found in it—a romantic and highly improbable plot, a colourful locale, simple, direct melodies, and elementary orchestral writing which nevertheless rises on occasion to great dramatic effectiveness. The second of the three great masterpieces of Verdi's middle period—the first is *Rigoletto* and the third *La Traviata*—*Il Trovatore* was first performed in Rome on January 19, 1853 and gained an immediate triumph. For many years it was reckoned to be the most popular opera in the world, and although Gounod's *Faust* later succeeded to that position, *Il Trovatore* still ranks among the first half-dozen favourites of the repertory and is sure of a hearing in every country where opera is performed.

The libretto was adapted by Salvatore Cammarano from a Spanish play *El Trovador* by Antonio García Gutiérrez, who was also the author of the drama on which *Simon Boccanegra* was based. Though the story is by no means ideally lucid, it undoubtedly appealed to Verdi's imagination, for it drew from him a flood of melody which is unsurpassed in any of his other works. This, coupled with the composer's extraordinary flair for telling dramatic strokes—the last minute of *Trovatore* is perhaps the swiftest-moving and most exciting passage of its kind in all opera—has assured the work's continued success.

The present recording is notable for containing several passages from the opera which are generally omitted in performance. Amongst these is the duet for Leonora and Manrico which follows the latter's "Ah si, ben mio" in Act 3, Scene 2; the repeat, later in the same scene, of Manrico's "Di quella pira" which enables a connecting passage with half-a-dozen bars of Leonora to be included; and the heroine's rarely heard solo "Tu vedrai che amore" in Act 4, Scene 1.

ACT 1 *Scene 1:*

The story of *Il Trovatore* is set in mediaeval Spain during a civil war between the court of Aragon and the followers of the Pretender of Urgel. The first act takes place in the palace of Aliaferia, a residence of the court of Aragon, and when the curtain rises after a brief orchestral introduction soldiers are seen resting in a hall of the palace. The veteran Ferrando warns them to rouse themselves, for the Count di Luna, one of the Aragonese commanders, is shortly due to return from his lonely watch beneath the window of a lady with whom he is in love. The Count, it appears, is a prey to jealousy, for he has a rival for the lady's favours—a certain troubadour.

Ferrando now tells the soldiers the gruesome story of di Luna's family. The old Count had two sons. As infants, one of them, the present holder of the title, thrived, but the other grew pale and sickly after a gipsy-woman had been found near its cradle in suspicious circumstances. The gipsy was captured and burned at the stake, but she left a daughter who swore to avenge her. Shortly afterwards the sickly child disappeared, and the subsequent discovery of a charred infant corpse led all to believe that the revenge had been carried out.

But the old Count would never believe that his child had perished and on his deathbed made his other son swear never to give up the search for him. The gipsy's daughter also, vanished, but Ferrando declares that he remembers her features clearly and, even now could identify her if she were found. He reveals that the old gipsy's spirit still haunts the neighourhood—recently a serving-man of the palace who encountered it died of fright. At this the soldiers are stricken with terror and invoke curses on such diabolical sorcery.

Scene 2:

The Scene changes to the gardens of the Palace, where Leonora (with whom di Luna is in love) is seen with her attendant, Inez. She speaks of her passion for an unknown knight whom she first saw at a tournament. Though he had no de···

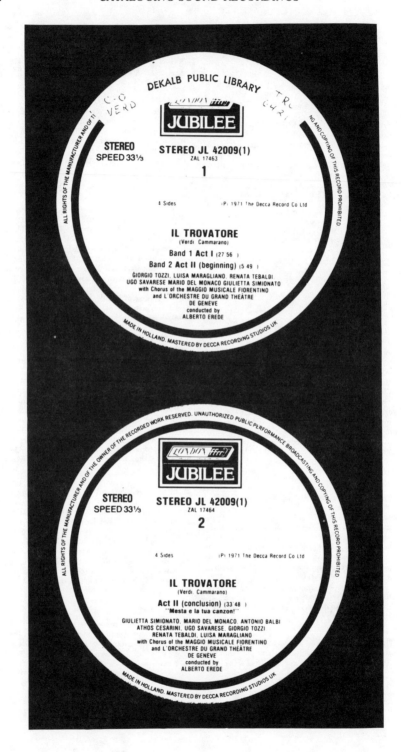

Example 4.4.   CLASSICAL MUSIC : ONE WORK
Entered under 12.23A: One work

```
Verdi, Giuseppe, 1813-1901.
     Il trovatore [sound recording] / Verdi ;
[libretto adapted by] Cammarano. -- New York, N.Y.
: London, p1971.
     2 sound discs (128 min.) : analog, 33 1/3 rpm,
stereo. ; 12 in.
     London: JL 42009.                               |Note Super 1
     Opera in 4 acts.                                 |Note 1
     Mario Del Monaco, tenor (Manrico) ; Ugo Savarese|Note 6
baritone (Count di Luna) ; Giorgio Tozzi, bass
(Ferrando) ; Renata Tebaldi, soprano (Leonora) ;
Giulietta Simionato, mezzo-soprano (Azucena) ;
Athos Cesarini, tenor (Ruiz) ; Antonio Balbi,
baritone, (Gipsy) ; Athos Cesarini, tenor
(Messanger) ; Luisa Maragliano, soprano (Inez) ;
                          (Continued on next card)
```

```
Verdi, Giuseppe, 1813-1901.
     Il trovatore [sound recording] ... p1971.
(Card 2).
The Chorus of the Maggio Musicale Fiorentino ;
L'Orchestre de la Suisse Romande, conducted by
Alberto Erebe.
     Recorded in England.                            |Note 7
     In container, automatic sequence.               |Note 10
     Synopsis (20 p.) ; libretto with Italian and the|Note 11
English translation laid in container.
     1. Operas. I. Del Monaco, Mario, 1915-    . II.
Tebaldi, Renata. III. Simionato, Giulietta. IV.
Tozzi, Giorgio. V. Cammarano, Salvatore, 1801-
1852. VI. Erede, Alberto. VII. Garcia Gutierrez,
Antonio, 1813-1884. Trovator. VIII. Maggio
musicale fiorentino. Chorus. IX. Orchestre de la
Suisse romande. X. Title.
```

Main entry: This is a single work by a single composer, and is entered under AACR2, 21.23A, under the name of the composer.

Uniform title: A uniform title is not needed. If one were given, it would be [Il trovatore], the same as the bibliographic title and redundant. The uniform title could not be: [Nabucco. Italian] since the original language was Italian — only the language of the original is given in the uniform title.

Note 18: There is *no* Note 18 because it is used only to "show . . . material not implied by the rest of the description."[9]

Added entries: Only Del Monaco, Tebaldi, Simionato and Tozzi were named on the cover, so they were the only ones considered sufficiently important to trace.

Example 4.5 CLASSICAL MUSIC : COLLECTION : BY SAME COMPOSER
Entered under 21.23B
Two or more works by the same person

```
Strauss, Johann, 1825-1899.
   [Waltzes, orchestra. Selections]
   Strauss waltzes [sound recording] / by Andre
Kostelanetz. -- [New York] : Columbia, [196-?]
   1 sound disc : analog, 33 1/3 rpm ; 12 in.
   Columbia: CL 805.                                    Note Super 1
   Performed by Andre Kostelanetz and his              Note 6
Orchestra.
   Contents: Blue Danube waltz, op. 314 -- Southern   Note 18
roses, op. 188 -- Tales from the Vienna woods, op.
325 -- Waltz from The Gypsy baron -- Waltzes from
Die Fledermaus -- Artist's life, op. 316 -- Voices
of spring, op. 410 -- Emperor waltz, op. 437 --
Vienna life, op. 354 -- A thousand and one nights,
                       (Continued on next card)
```

```
Strauss, Johann, 1825-1899.
   [Waltzes, orchestra. Selections]
   Strauss waltzes [sound recording] ... [196-?]
(Card 2).
op. 346.
   1. Waltzes (Orchestra). 2. Orchestra music. I.
Kostelanetz, Andre, 1901-    . II. Title.
```

Main entry: This is a single work by a single composer, and is entered under AACR2, 21.23A, under the name of the composer.

Uniform title: This is entered according to 25.35B, for Waltzes, orchestra, and 25.35C for "Selections."

Title/statement of responsibility: The title is taken as an integral title, and Strauss was not separated and put into the statement of responsibility area.

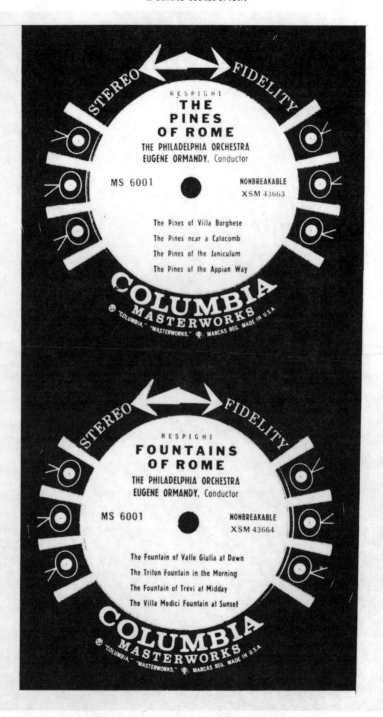

Example 4.6.   CLASSICAL MUSIC : TWO WORKS : SAME COMPOSER
Entered under 21.23B
Two works by the same person

```
Respighi, Ottorino, 1879-1936.
  [Pini di Roma]
  The pines of Rome ; The fountains of Rome
[sound recording] / Respighi. -- New York :
Columbia, c[196-?]
  1 sound disc : analog, 33 1/3 rpm, mono. ; 12
in.
  Columbia: MS 6001.                              |Note Super 1
  Symphonic poems.                                |Note 1
  The Philadelphia Orchestra, Eugene Ormandy,     |Note 6
conductor.
  1. Symphonic poems. I. Ormandy, Eugene, 1899-
   . II. Respighi, Ottorino, 1879-1936. Fontane
di Roma. III. Philadelphia Orchestra. IV. Title.
```

Main entry: This has a single composer, and is entered under AACR2, 21.23A, under the name of the composer.

Uniform title: The title is given for the first work, and The Pines of Rome was considered to be side 1 because it had the lowest number of the numbers on the right side: SCM 43663 and XSM 43664.

Note 18: This shows a unique title, with key, etc., given as "other title information."

Added entries: The added entry for The fountains of Rome follows 21.30G: a name-title added entry. The title segment is the uniform title without any square brackets. The orchestra and the conductor are traced.[10] Each of the names are checked first in the name authority records.

Example 4.7
Cassette Label

Franz Joseph Haydn
Symphony No. 83 in G minor, "La Poule" (The Hen)
Allegro   Andante
Menuet   Finale: Vivace

2   PAC-1001
                                     STEREO

            PROARTE

Franz Joseph Haydn
Symphony No. 82 in C, "L'Ours" (The Bear)
Vivace   Allegretto
Menuet   Finale: Vivace assai.

1   PAC-1001
                                     STEREO

            PROARTE

Example 4.7. CLASSICAL MUSIC : SINGLE COMPOSER : TWO WORKS
BUT <u>NO</u> COLLECTIVE TITLE
Entered under 21.23B: Two works by the same person
--- and --- 1.1G2: Items without a collective title

```
Haydn, Joseph, 1732-1809.
   [Symphonies, H. I, 82, C major]
   Symphony no. 82 in C : l'ours = the bear ;
Symphony no. 83 in G minor : la poule = the hen
[sound recording] / Franz Joseph Haydn. --
Minneapolis, Minn. (7500 Excelsior Blvd.,
Minneapolis 55426) : Intenational Arts, c1981.
   1 sound cassette : analog, stereo. -- (Proarte)
   International Arts: PAC-1001.                        |Note Super 1
   Titles transcribed from individual cassette         |Note 3
lables.
   Collegium Aureum performing on original             |Note 6
instruments, Franzjosef Maier, concertmaster.
   "Released under agreement with Deutsche-Harmonia|Note 9
                        (Continued on next card)
```

```
Haydn, Joseph, 1732-1809.
   [Symphonies, H. I, 82, C major]
   Symphony no. 82 in C : l'ours = the bear ;
Symphony no. 83 in G minor : la poule = the hen
[sound recording] ... c1981. (Card 2).
Mundi, p. 1975."
   Program notes on container by Ekkehart Kroher.      |Note 11
   1. Symphonies. I. Haydn, Joseph, 1732-1809.
Symphonies, H. I, 83, G minor. 1981. II. Maier,
Franzjosef. III. Collegium Aureum. IV. Title. VI.
Series.
```

Main entry: This recording contains two works by a single composer, and is entered under AACR2, 21.23B, under the name of the
composer.

Uniform title: This follows the instruction[11] which says to record the
titles in the order given [on the sound recording]. The first title given
needs to have a uniform title in order to be filed correctly. This uniform title is only for the first named work. This cannot be entered
under a collective title devised by the cataloger such as: [Symphonies.
Selections] because it does not have three to five works, it only has
two works.[12]

Title/statement of responsibility: There is a partial parallel title
given. Check the most current LCRIs for 5.1B1 and 5.1B1 to enter
correctly.

Place, publisher, date: The address came from the label, and was
added merely as a reminder about adding addresses to records.

Physical description: Record disks do not have a standard size, even though the norm might appear to be the 12 inch disk. Sound cassettes have a standard size, which is 10 × 6.5 cm. When a cassette is this size, the size is omitted. When the cassette is not this size, the size is given.

Tracings: The added entry for Haydn's Symphony No. 83 follows the guideline for "Related works."[13] It is an analytical entry[14] and needs a date at the end. Herr Maier and the Collegium Aureum are included because LCRI 21.29D says to make added entries for the major performers.

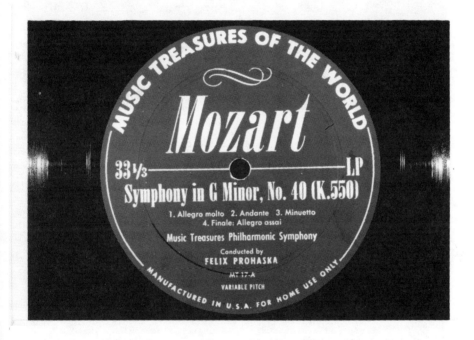

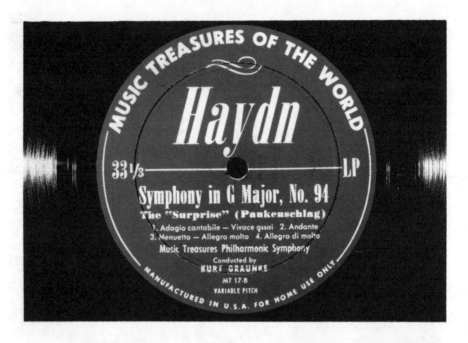

Example 4.8.   CLASSICAL MUSIC : TWO COMPOSERS : TWO WORKS
                    BUT NO COLLECTIVE TITLE
   Entered under 21.23D(2) : Works by different persons or bodies
                        No collective title
-- and --   1.1G2 : Items without a collective title

```
     Mozart, Wolfgang Amadeus, 1756-1791.
        [Symphonies, K. 550, G minor]
     Symphony in G minor, no. 40, K. 550 / Mozart.
     Symphony in G major, no. 94 : the surprise =
     Paukenschlag / Haydn [sound recording]. -- United
     States : Music Treasures of the World, [196-?]
        1 sound disc : analog, 33 1/3 rpm ; 12 in.
        Music Treasures: MT 17.                          Note Super 1
        Titles transcribed from individual disk labels.  Note 3
        Performed by the Music Treasures Philharmonic     Note 6
     Symphony. Haydn symphony conducted by Kurt Graunke
     ; Mozart symphony conducted by Felix Prohaska.
        "For home use only."                             Note 14
        1. Symphonies. I. Haydn, Joseph, 1732-1809.
     Symphonies, H.I, 94, G major. 1960. II. Graunke,
     Kurt. II. Prohaska, Felix. IV. Title.
```

Main entry: This disc has no collective title and is by more than one
composer, so it is entered under AACR2, 21.23D(2), under the name
of the composer of the first "work."

Title/statement of responsibility: First, determine which is side one,
or side A, list that title first, without the [gmd], and the statement of

responsibility, putting a period at the end. Next, list the title of the other side, the statement of responsibility and the [gmd]. There is even a partial parallel title given for one of the titles above.[15]

Uniform title: This is for the first work, only.

Note 3: Gives the source of the titles, since there is no single source.

Note 6: This lists the same orchestra with different conductors.

Note 14: This note also gives the restrictions on the material.

Tracings: Added entries are given for the second work, in the form of a name-title analytical added entry.[16]

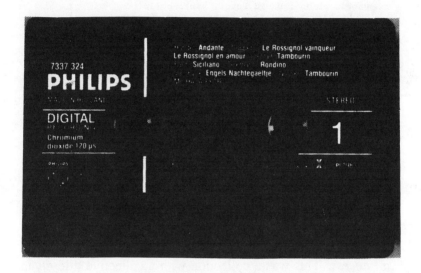

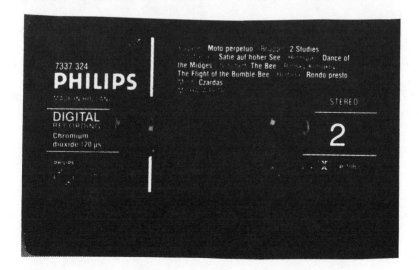

Example 4.9. CLASSICAL MUSIC : COLLECTION : DIFFERENT COMPOSERS
Entered under performer
Entered under 21.23C: Works by different persons or bodies.
Collective title

```
    Petri, Michala, 1958-
        Intermezzo musicale / Michala Petri, Hanne
    Petri, continuo. -- Holland : Philips, p1983.
        1 sound cassette : analog, stereo., Dolby
    processed.
        Philips: 7337 324.                             |Note Super 1
        Title from container.                          |Note 3
        Michala Petri, recorder ; Hanne Petri, harpsi- |Note 6
    chord, piano ; David Petri, violoncello.
        Contents: Andante / Handel -- Le Rossignol vain-|Note 18
    queur / Couperin -- Le Rossignol en amour /
    Couperin -- Tambourin / Leclair -- Siciliano /
    Bach -- Rondino / Telemann -- Engels nachtegaeltje|
    / Van Eyck -- Tambourin / Gossec -- Moto perpetuo |
    / Paganini -- 2 studies / Bruggen -- Satie auf    |
    hoher See / Christiansen -- Dance of the Midges / |
                    (Continued on next card)          |
```

```
    Petri, Michala, 1958-
        Intermezzo musicale ... p1983. (Card 2).
    Henriques -- The bee / Schubert -- The flight of
    the bumble-bee / Rimsky-Korsakov -- Rondo presto
    / Heberle -- Czardas no. 1 / Monti.
        1. Recorder music. I. Petri, Hanne. II. Petri,
    David. III. Title.
```

Main access: This was a collection with a collective title given on the container. It was entered under 21.23C, under the principal performer.

Title: The only collective title was on the container, so this title was used, and a Note 3 was given to show the source of the title.

Note 3: Whenever the title is not from the label, give the source of the title.

Tracings: The different titles in the contents were not traced, as this was a "showcase for a performer."[17]

CHAPTER 5

Musicals and Motion Picture Music with Uniform Titles

Example 5.1. MUSICAL : UNDER COMPOSER

Carmichael, Ralph.
   The cross and the switchblade [sound recording]
/ composed and conducted by Ralph Carmichael. --
Waco, Tex. : Light, [197-?]
   1 sound disc (27 min.) : analog, 33 1/3 rpm,
stereo. ; 12 in.
   Light: LS-5550-LP.   Note Super 1
   "Original sound track music;" based on the book   Note 6
by David Wilkerson ; screenplay by Don Murray and
James Bonnett.
   Contents: You gotta try / Carmichael (2:03) --   Note 18
Switchblade theme / Carmichael (1:15) -- Where is
it / Carmichael (3:21) -- I just lost /
Carmichael (2:20) -- Bright new world / Price
                (Continued on next card)

Carmichael, Ralph.
   The cross and the switchblade [sound recording]
... [197-?] (Card 2).
(3:21) -- I've got confidence / Crouch (3:00) --
The addict's psalm / adapt. by Carmichael (1:12)
-- Rumble / Carmichael (3:55) -- God loves you /
Carmichael (2:27) -- Love / Carmichael (3:26).
   1. Moving-picture music. 2. Musical revues,
comedies, etc. I. Murray, Don. II. Wilkerson,
David. Cross and the switchblade. III. Title.

Main access point: AACR 21.18C (Adaptations), and 21.19A (Musical works that include words) state this should be entered under the heading for the composer.

Note 6: Information about the book was given on the jacket.

Example 5.2. SINGLE COMPOSER : SELECTIONS FROM PRIMARILY ONE WORK

```
Rodgers, Richard, 1902-1979.
   [Oklahoma. Selections]
   Selections from Oklahoma [sound recording] : and
other standard hits. -- U.S.A. : Halo, [196-?]
   1 sound disc : analog, 33 1/3 rpm ; 12 in.
   Halo: 50114.                                      Note Super 1
   National Singers & Orchestra.                     Note 6
   Contents: Oklahoma -- People will say we're in    Note 18
love -- I cain't say no -- Out of my dreams --
Waiting for you -- Waiting afire -- My heart is
waiting -- Slaughter on Tenth Avenue -- Some
enchanted evening -- That's for me -- Surry with
the fringe on top -- Sing for your supper -- My
heart stood still -- This can't be love.
   1. Musical revues, comedies, etc.--Excerpts. I.
National Singers & Orchestra. II. Title.
```

Main access point: The composer is given the main entry, according to AACR2, 21.19A.

Tracings: Hammerstein was not given a tracing because his work is
not "fully represented," that is, it does not contain the full score from
Oklahoma, according to AACR2, 21.19A.[1]

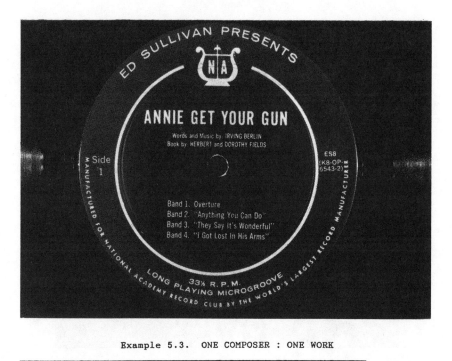

Example 5.3.   ONE COMPOSER : ONE WORK

```
Berlin, Irving.
    Annie get your gun [sound recording] / words and
music by Irving Berlin ; book by Herbert and
Dorothy Fields. -- New York, N.Y. : National
Academy Record Club ; Produced by J.J. Little &
Ives, Co., c1960.
    1 sound disc : analog, 33 1/3 rpm ; 12 in.
    National Academy: ES 8.                          Note Super 1
    "Ed Sullivan presents."                          Note 1
    Vocals by the Ed Sullivan all star cast.         Note 6
    Contents: Overture -- Anything you can do --     Note 18
They say its wonderful -- I got lost in his arms
-- The girl that I marry -- You can't get a man
with a gun -- Doin' what comes natur'lly --
                        (Continued on next card)
```

```
Berlin, Irving.
    Annie get your gun [sound recording] ... c1960.
(Card 2).
There's no business like show business.
    1. Musical revues, comedies, etc.--Excerpts. I.
Sullivan, Ed. II. Fields, Herbert. Annie get your
gun. III. Title.
```

Main entry: This is entered under the heading for the composer, see
AACR2, 21.19A and 21.23A.

Example 5.4. ONE COMPOSER : SELECTIONS FROM ONE WORK

```
Loewe, Frederick, 1904-
  [My fair lady. Selections]
  My fair lady [sound recording]. -- [Minneapolis]
: Mercury, [196-?]
  1 sound disc (ca. 20 min.) : analog, 33 1/3 rpm
; 12 in.
  Mercury: MG-20192.                             Note Super 1
  Music by Richard Hayman and his orchestra.     Note 6
  Contents: You did it (1:14) -- Wouldn't it be  Note 18
loverly (2:50) -- I could have danced all night
(2:40) -- Why can't the English (1:41) -- I've
grown accustomed to your face (2:30) -- Ascot
gavotte -- Get me to the church on time (1:50) --
On the street where you live (2:25) -- Show me
                    (Continued on next card)
```

```
Loewe, Frederick, 1904-
  [My fair lady. Selections]
  My fair lady [sound recording]. ... [196-?]
(Card 2).
(1:19) -- The rain in Spain (2:54) -- Without you
(2:54) -- With a little bit of luck (2:05).
  1. Musical revues, comedies, etc.--Excerpts. I.
Hayman, Richard. II. Title.
```

Main entry: This is entered under the heading for the composer, see AACR2, 21.18A and 21.23A.

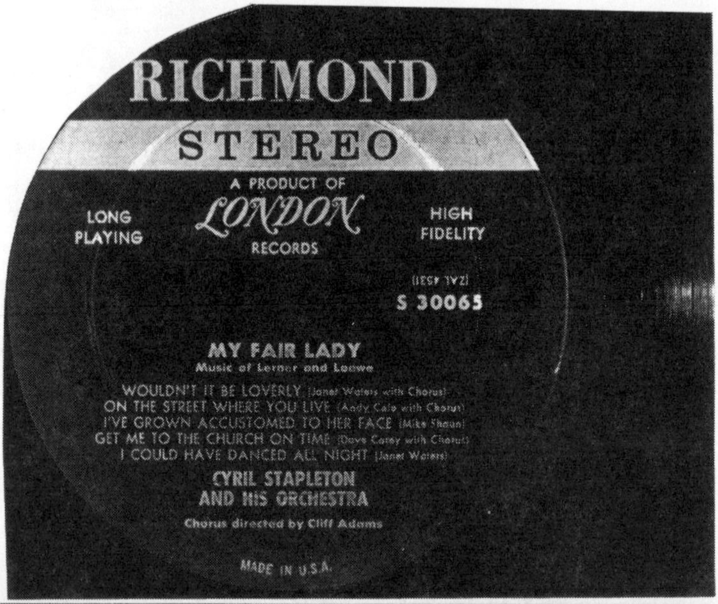
RICHMOND
STEREO
A PRODUCT OF
LONDON
RECORDS
LONG PLAYING
HIGH FIDELITY
S 30065
MY FAIR LADY
Music of Lerner and Loewe
WOULDN'T IT BE LOVERLY (Janet Waters with Chorus)
ON THE STREET WHERE YOU LIVE (Andy Cole with Chorus)
I'VE GROWN ACCUSTOMED TO HER FACE (Mike Shaun)
GET ME TO THE CHURCH ON TIME (Dave Carey with Chorus)
I COULD HAVE DANCED ALL NIGHT (Janet Waters)
CYRIL STAPLETON
AND HIS ORCHESTRA
Chorus directed by Cliff Adams
MADE IN U.S.A.

RICHMOND
STEREO
A PRODUCT OF
LONDON
RECORDS
LONG PLAYING
HIGH FIDELITY
S 30065
THE KING AND I
Music of Rodgers and Hammerstein
I WHISTLE A HAPPY TUNE (Janet Waters with Chorus)
MARCH OF THE SIAMESE CHILDREN
HELLO YOUNG LOVERS (Janet Waters)
WE KISS IN A SHADOW (Mike Shaun)
SHALL WE DANCE (June Marlowe, Dave Carey with Chorus)
CYRIL STAPLETON
AND HIS ORCHESTRA
Chorus directed by Cliff Adams

Example 5.5. TWO COMPOSERS : TWO WORKS : NONCOLLECTIVE TITLE

```
Loewe, Frederick, 1904-
   [My fair lady. Selections]
   My fair lady / music of Lerner and Loewe. The
king and I / music of Rodgers and Hammerstein
[sound recording]. -- New York, N.Y. : Richmond,
[196-?]
   1 sound disc : analog, 33 1/3 rpm, stereo. ; 12
in.
   Richmond: S 30065.                          |Note Super 1
   Chorus directed by Cliff Adams ; Cyril Stapleton|Note 6
and his orchestra.                           |
   Contents: My fair lady [and] Wouldn't it be  |Note 18
loverly / Janet Waters with Chorus -- On the
street where you live / Andy Cole with Chorus --
                      (Continued on next card)
```

```
Loewe, Frederick, 1904-
   [My fair lady. Selections]
   My fair lady [sound recording]. ... [196-?]
(Card 2).
I've grown accustomed to her face / Mike Shaun --
Get me to the church on time / Dave Carey with
Chorus -- I could have danced all night / Janet
Waters. The king and I: I whistle a happy tune /
Janet Waters with Chorus -- March of the Siamese
children -- Hello young lovers / Janet Waters --
We kiss in a shadow / Mike Shaun -- Shall we
dance / June Marlow, Dave Carey with Chorus.
   1. Musical revues, comedies, etc.--Excerpts. I.
Stapleton, Cyril. II. Adams, Cliff. III. Rodgers,
Richard, 1902-    . King and I. Selections. 1960.
IV. Title.
```

Main entry: There was no "collective" title so AACR2, 1.1G2 was followed, plus 21.23D(2). The entry was given for the first named work.

Added entries: Since neither musical was complete, the librettists were not listed in the tracings, per AACR2, 21.19A.

Vocal by Seger Ellis with his Orchestra.
Trumpet obbligato by Louis Armstrong.
Recorded for Okeh   Included by arrangement with CBS.

The Smithsonian American Musical Theater Series is an effort to research. reassemble. preserve. and offer to the contemporary listener. the songs and sounds of the American musical theater from all eras of its history.
   It is of course impossible to reconstruct a complete "original cast" album of an extended musical review like *Hot Chocolates* from surviving sources.   The selections here. both musical numbers and comedy sketches. are by the show's composer and by participants in the original New York run of *Hot Chocolates*.   We have added versions of two of the show's dance specialties recorded contemporaneously by a small group from the Ellington orchestra.

Production Coordination by Brock Holmes
Recordings from the collections of
John M. Raymond, Jr.;
Institute of Jazz Studies at Rutgers;
the State University of New Jersey at Newark;
Howard Watters; Granville Hurley; and Leon Vogel.
Master tapes prepared by Jack Towers.
Design by Staples & Charles Ltd

COLUMBIA SPECIAL PRODUCTS
A Service of Columbia Records

Example 5.6. MUSICAL : UNDER UNIFORM TITLE MAIN ENTRY

```
Hot chocolates. Selections.
   Souvenirs of Hot chocolates [sound recording].
-- New York, N.Y. (51 W. 52 St., NY 10019) :
Smithsonian collection : Produced by Columbia
Special Products, p1978.
   1 sound disc : 33 1/3 rpm ; 12 in. --
(Smithsonian American musical theater series).
   Smithsonian: 14587.                           |Note Super 1
   Vocal by Seger Ellis with his orchestra --    |Note 6
Trumpet obbligato by Louis Armstrong.
   "Recordings from the collections of John M.    |Note 7
Raymond, Jr.; Institute of Jazz Studies at Rutgers|
The State University of New Jersey at Newark;    |
Howard Watters; Granville Hurley; and Leon Vogel. |
                  (Continued on next card)
```

```
Hot chocolates. Selections.
   Souvenirs of Hot chocolates [sound recording].
... p1978. (Card 2).
   Contents: Sweet Savannah Sue / Fats Waller --   |Note 18
Sweet Savannah Sue / Louis Armstrong -- Ain't mis-|
behavin' / Fats Waller -- Ain't misbehavin' /
Louis Armstrong -- Big business / Eddie Green,
Billy Higgins & Co., -- Black and blue / Edith
Wilson -- Black and blue / Louis Armstrong -- That|
rhythm man / Louis Armstrong -- Snake hips dance /|
Harlem Footwarmers -- Jungle jamboree / Harlem
Footwarmers -- My man is good for nothing but love|
/ Edith Wilson -- Sending a wire / Eddie Green -- |
Addendum: Ain't misbehavin' / Seger Ellis with
                  (Continued on next card)
```

```
Hot chocolates. Selections.
   Souvenirs of Hot chocolates [sound recording].
... p1978. (Card 3).
Louis Armstrong.
   1. Musical revues, comedies, etc.--Excerpts. 2.
Jazz music. I. Armstrong, Louis. II. Ellis, Seger.
III. Green, Eddie. IV. Waller, Fats. V. Wilson,
Edith. VI. Harlem Footwarmers. VII. Smithsonian
Collection. VIII. Title. IX. Series.
```

Main entry: Since there is not enough information to assign an "author," it is entered under the title for the revue: Hot chocolates. This is a uniform title formulated according to 25.27A and 25.36C.

Title, etc.: Hot Chocolates was an old musical revue. The Smithsonian Institution located six copies of old recordings from this musical revue with Fats Waller and Louis Armstrong, took the best from these six sources and combined them into one record, which they named: *Souvenirs of Hot chocolates*. This record contains only part of the total musical revue.

Place, publisher, date: The address was given as a reminder that if the recording is less than 3 years old, etc., the address is given in the main body, according to LCRI 1.4C7.

Labels or Example 5.7

RAMBO * ONLY LOVE * MIAMI VICE * CAVATINA * HARLEM NOCTURNE

MERRY CHRISTMAS * AXEL F * PASSAGE TO INDIA

GODFATHER TV THEME

1   MCPS
                                                          46018

18 FAMOUS FILM TRACKS & TV THEMES

Made in Holland   Hollywood Studio Orchestra   STEREO

ST. ELMO'S FIRE LOVE THEME * CHARIOTS OF FIRE * A-TEAM

HILL STREET BLUES * GOING HOME * KILLING FIELDS * MAGNUM P.I.

ANGELA * ODE TO AMADEUS

2   MCPS
                                                          46018

18 FAMOUS FILM TRACKS & TV THEMES

Made in Holland   Hollywood Studio Orchestra   STEREO

18 FAMOUS FILM TRACKS & TV THEMES
Hollywood Studio Orchestra

SIDE ONE

1. RAMBO - First Blood Part 2 .... 2:16
2. ONLY LOVE - Theme from the TV Series 'Mistral's Daughter' 4:21
3. MIAMI VICE 2:30
4. CAVATINA - Theme from the Film 'The Deer Hunter' 3:40
5. HARLEM NOCTURNE - Theme from the TV Series 'Mike Hammei'. 3:28
6. MERRY CHRISTMAS, MR. LAWRENCE 4:43
7. AXEL F. - Theme from the Film 'Beverly Hills Cop' 2:56
8. A PASSAGE TO INDIA 3:51
9. THE GODFATHER TV THEME 3:58

SIDE TWO

1. ST. ELMO'S FIRE LOVE THEME 3:28
2. CHARIOTS OF FIRE 3:49
3. THE A-TEAM 2:45
4. HILL STREET BLUES 3:13
5. GOING HOME - Theme from the film 'Local Hero' 4:55
6. THE KILLING FIELDS 3:10
7. MAGNUM P.I. 3:08
8. ANGELA - Theme from the TV Series 'Taxi' 2:34
9. ODE TO AMADEUS 4:04

Example 5.7.   MUSICAL UNDER TITLE MAIN ENTRY

```
Hollywood Studio Orchestra.
   18 famous film tracks & tv themes [sound
recording] / Hollywood Studio Orchestra. --
Holland : MCPS, [198-?]
   1 sound cassette (63 min.) : analog, stereo.,
Dolby processed
   MCPS: 46018.                                      |Note Super 1
   Contents: Rambo, in First Blood (2:16) -- Only   |Note 18
love, theme from Minstral's daughter (4:21)  --
Miami vice (2:30) -- Cavatina, theme from Deer
hunter (3:40) -- Harlem nocturne, theme from Mike
Hammer (3:28) -- Merry Christmas, Mr. Lawrence
(4:43) -- Axel F, theme from Beverly Hills Cop
(2:56) -- Passage to India (3:51) -- Godfather
                        (Continued on next card)
```

```
Hollywood Studio Orchestra.
  18 famous film tracks & tv themes [sound
recording] ... [198-?] (Card 2).
(3:58) -- St. Elmo's fire love theme (3:28) --
Chariots of fire (3:49) -- A-team (2:45) -- Hill
Street blues (3:13) -- Going home, theme from
Local hero (4:55) -- Killing fields (3:10) --
Magnum P.I. (3:08) -- Angela, theme from Taxi
(2:34) -- Ode to Amadeus (4:01).
  1. Moving-picture music. 2. Television music.
I. Title. II. Title: Eighteen famous film tracks
and television themes.
```

Main entry: This is entered under the principal performer, according to 21.23C.

Place, publisher, date: The place, address, publisher and date were all difficult to ascertain, but the information given on the label and jacket were put on the catalog record.

Physical description: The size was omitted from the guide because it was the size expected, that is, about 12 inches, or 27 centimeters, in this case.

Tracings: There was a title traced differently, because two of the first five words in the title could be written differently: the number spelled out, and the ampersand spelled out.

Example 5.8. MUSICAL UNDER TITLE MAIN ENTRY

```
The Wiz [sound recording]. -- Universal City, CA
   (100 Universal Plaza, Universal City, CA 91606)
   : MCA Records, p1978.
   2 sound discs (80 min.) : analog, 33 1/3 rpm,
stereo. : 12 in. + 1 guide ([12] p. : col. ill.) +
1 poster (col. ill. ; 51 cm.)
   MCA: 2-14000.                                      Note Super 1
   "Original motion picture sound track" staring      Note 6
Diana Ross (Dorothy) ; Michael Jackson (Scarecrow)
; Nipsey Russel (Tinman) ; Ted Ross (Lion) ; Lena
Horn (Glinda) ; Richard Pryor (Wiz) ; Quincy
Jones, producer ; Sidney Lumet, director.
   Based on the book by William F. Brown ; screen-   Note 6
play by Joel Schumacher ; songs by Charlie Smalls.
                          (Continued on next card)
```

```
The Wiz [sound recording].  ... c1978. (Card 2).
   "A Motown production -- A Universal picture."     |Note 7
   Lyrics (12 p.) in guide.                          |Note 11
   Contents: Overture (4:37) -- Feeling that we
have (3:30) -- Can I go on? (1:56) -- Glinda's
theme (1:09) -- He's the wizard (2:52) -- Soon as
I get home/home (4:01) -- You can't win (3:14) --
Ease on down the road #1 (3:19) -- What would I do
if I could feel? (1:18) -- Slide some oil to me
(2:19) -- Ease on down the road #2 (1:30) -- I'm
a mean ole lion (2:23) -- Ease on down the road #3
(1:24) -- Poppy girls (3:17) -- Be a lion (4:04)
-- End of the yellow brick road (1:01) -- Emerald
city sequence (6:41) -- So you wanted to see the
                     (Continued on next card)
```

```
The Wiz [sound recording].  ... c1978. (Card 3).
wizard (2:48) -- Is this what feeling gets? (3:13)
-- Don't nobody bring me bad news (3:01) -- A
brand new day (7:51) -- Believe in yurself (2:54)
-- The good witch Glinda (1:10) -- Believe in
yourself : reprise (2:13) -- Home (3:27).
   1. Musical revuews, comedies, etc. 2. Motion
picture music. I. Ross, Diane. II. Jackson,
Michael. III. Russell, Nipsey. IV. Ross, Ted. V.
Horn, Lena. VI. Pryor, Richard. VII. Jones,
Quincy. VIII. Smalls, Charlie. IX. Brown, William
F. X. Schumacher, Joel.
```

Main entry: Since there is not enough information to assign an "author," it is entered under the title, according to 21.1C.

Title/statement of responsibility: This is a recording of a musical. The order of data is transposed[2] in order for the title to appear first. A uniform title is not added, because LCRI 25.32B1 says not to add "Selections," to an original cast recording if in doubt about its completeness.

Place, publisher, date: The place, address, publisher and date are all visible on the label. The address is only listed when the recording is less than 3 years old, etc.[3]

Physical description: The size was omitted from the guide because it was the size expected, that is, about 12 inches, or 27 centimeters, in this case.

Note 6: The roles of the singers are added in parenthesis after their names.[4]

Note 7: Information about the book, the screenplay and the songs was given in the booklet, and information about the production, etc., came from the labels.

Note 8: The location of the accompanying 12 pages is given in this note.

Note 18: The durations are given with the contents.[5]

Added entry tracings: The writer of the libretto is traced because it is thought this is the complete vocal score.[6]

Recordings Designed for Children

Cataloging recordings designed for children's use is really no different from other cataloging. For those who catalog solely in this area, a few examples are given.

Examples 6.1. SELECTIONS FROM ONE CHILDREN'S STORY

```
Alcott, Louisa May, 1832-1888.
   [Little women. Selections]
   Little women [sound recording] / by Louisa M.
Alcott ; read by Glenda Jackson ; music written
and directed by Kenny Clayton. -- London : Argo,
p1978.
   3 sound recordings : analog, 33 1/3 rpm, stereo.
12 in.
   Argo: ZSW 596-8.                               Note Super 1
   Read by Glenda Jackson.                         Note 6
   Extracts from: Little women.                    Note 7
   In container, automatic sequence.               Note 10
   Program notes (4 p.) by Lissa Demetriou.        Note 11
   Summary: Chronicles the humorous and sentimental Note 18
fortunes of the four March sisters as they grow
into young ladies in 19th-century New England.
   I. Jackson, Glenda. II. Clayton, Kenny. III.
Title.
```

Main entry: This is under 21.32A, a single work with a single author is entered under the main entry for the author.

Uniform title: Since this contains extracts from *Little Women* a uniform title is needed in order to add "Selections" to the title.[1]

Added entries: The two people mentioned in the main body of the catalog card were traced. It is a normal practice to trace all the people named in the main body, except for those who write introductions and forewords.

Examples 6.2. SELECTIONS FROM TWO CHILDREN'S STORIES

```
Bond, Michael.
  Paddington for Christmas [sound recording] /
read by the author Michael Bond. -- New York, N.Y.
(1995 Broadway, NY 10023) : Caedmon, p1979.
  1 sound cassette (61 min.) : analog
  Caedmon: CDL 51621.                            Note Super 1
  Read by the author ; music composed and        Note 6
conducted by Don Heckman ; notes by Alexandra
Sheedy in container.
  Extracts from: Paddington at large -- Paddington Note 7
goes to town -- Paddington takes to the air.
  Contents: Christmas stories involving the bear, Note 18
Paddington.
                    (Continued on next card)
```

```
Bond, Michael.
  Paddington for Christmas [sound recording] ...
p1979. (Card 2).
  Contains: Paddington and the Christmas pantomine Note 18
-- Everything comes to those who wait.
  1. Bears--Fiction. I. Heckman, Don. II. Bond,
Michael. Paddington at large. 1979. III. Bond,
Michael. Paddington goes to town. 1979. IV. Bond,
Michael. Paddington takes to the air. 1979. V.
Title.
```

Main entry: This contains extracts from two works by one author, so it is entered under 21.23B, under the name of the author.

Place, publisher, date: The address of the publisher was included merely as a reminder that this should be included when the following conditions are met:

1. it was issued by a U.S. publisher, distributor, etc., whose address is given on or with the item being cataloged;
2. it was issued (published) in the current three years;
3. it does not bear an ISBN or ISSN.[2]

Added entries: "Paddington for Christmas" was originally the title of a chapter. It is used here as a unique title of a sound recording. Analytical name-title added entries[3] are given for the three books from which selections were made.

Examples 6.3. SELECTIONS FROM ONE CHILDREN'S STORY

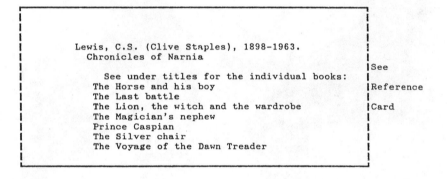

```
Lewis, C.S. (Clive Staples), 1898-1963.
   [Prince Caspian. Selections]
   Prince Caspian [sound recording] / C.S. Lewis.
-- Abridged -- New York, N.Y. (1995 Broadway, NY
10023) : Caedmon, p1979.
   1 sound recording (64 min.) : analog, 33 1/3
rpm, stereo. ; 12 in. -- (Chronicles of Narnia ;
2)
   Caedmon: TC 1503.                         Note Super 1
   Read by Claire Bloom.                      Note 6
   Extracts from: Prince Caspian.             Note 7
   Program notes on container by Walter Hooper. Note 11
   I. Bloom, Claire. II. Title. III. Series.
```

Example 6.3A

```
Lewis, C.S. (Clive Staples), 1898-1963.
   Chronicles of Narnia
                                              See
      See under titles for the individual books:
   The Horse and his boy                      Reference
   The Last battle
   The Lion, the witch and the wardrobe       Card
   The Magician's nephew
   Prince Caspian
   The Silver chair
   The Voyage of the Dawn Treader
```

Main entry: This is under 21.32A, a single work with a single author is entered under the main entry for the author.

Uniform title: Since this contains extracts from *Prince Caspian* a uniform title is needed in order to add "Selections" to the title.[4]

Place, publisher, date: The address was given as a reminder about giving addresses, although this record is more than 3 years old, and hence would not fit the guidelines for listing the address.[5]

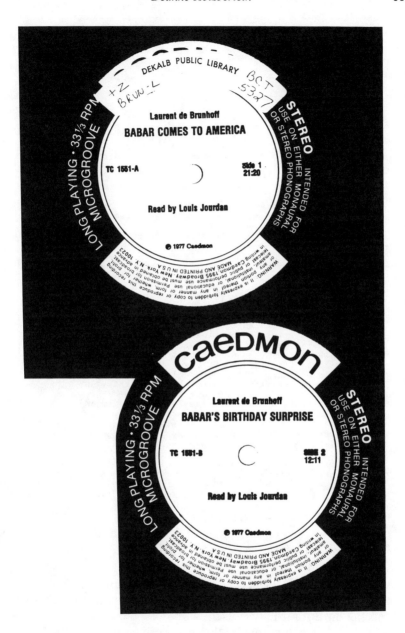

Examples 6.4. SELECTION FROM TWO CHILDREN'S STORIES
NONCOLLECTIVE TITLE

```
Brunhoff, Laurent de, 1925–
  [Babar en Amerique. English]
  Babar comes to America ; Babar's birthday
surprise [sound recording] / Laurent de Brunhoff ;
read by Louis Jourdan. -- New York, N.Y. (1995
Broadway, NY 10023), p1977.
  1 sound disc (34 min.) : analog, 33 1/3 rpm,
stereo. ; 12 in.
  Caedmon: TC 1551.                               |Note Super 1
  Translations of: Babar en Amerique -- L'anniver-|Note 3
saire de Babar.
  From: Babar comes to America. New York : Random |Note 7
House, c1965 -- Babar's birthday surprise. New
York : Random House, 1970.
                     (Continued on next card)
```

```
Brunhoff, Laurent de, 1925–
  [Babar en Amerique. English]
  Babar comes to America ... p. 1977. (Card 2)
  Program notes on container by Winifred S. Vogt. |Note 11
  Summary: Babar comes to America: Babar goes to  |Note 17
Washington, D.C. on an official visit, then tours
New York, Detroit, and Chicago. Then he meets his
family and they tour San Francisco, Carmel, Yose-
mite Park and elsewhere -- Babar's birthday sur-
prise: Queen Celeste decides to surprise King
Babar with a statute of himself for his birthday
but has trouble keeping it a secret.
  1. Elephants--Fiction. 2. Christmas stories. I.
Jourdan, Louis. II. Heckman, Don. III. Brunhoff,
Laurent de, 1925-   . Anniversaire de Babar.
English. 1977. IV. Title. V. Babar's birthday
surprise.
```

Main entry: There was no collective title. It contained two works by one author, so it was entered under 21.23B, under the author's name.

Title/statement of responsibility: This is entered under AACR2, 21.23B[6] and under 1.1G2.

Note 3: This note is needed when the uniform title indicates the work is a translation. It tells the patron the original title and thus the reason the uniform title was used.

Note 7: The punctuation for this is described in AACR2, 1.7A3, at the end of the first paragraph.

Added entries: The tracing for the second work is given in the form of the author's name, according to the authority record, and the uniform title. This is called a name-title tracing. This added entry is made only for the main author of a work, and only in this form.[7]

Examples 6.5. CHILDREN'S MUSIC

```
Sandpiper Chorus.
   A child's introduction to the orchestra [sound
recording] / the Sandpiper Chorus ; the Golden
Symphony orchestra, under the direction of Mitch
Miller. -- [New York, N.Y.] : Golden Record :
Distributed by Simon & Schuster, [196-?]
   1 sound disc : analog, 33 1/3 rpm, mono. ; 10
in.
   Golden: A198.                                  |Note Super 1
   Contents: Antoinette the clarinet / David      |Note 18
Oppenhelm -- Knute the flute / Edward Powell --
Bobo the oboe / Mitchell Miller / Muldoon the
bassoon / Harold Boltzer -- Crumpet the trumpet /
Harry Freistadt -- Poobah the tuba / William Bell
                        (Continued on next card)
```

```
Sandpiper Chorus.
   A child's introduction to the orchestra [sound
recording] ... [196-?] (Card 2).
-- Monsieur forlorn the French horn / John Barrows
-- Mike Malone the slide trombone / William
Bradley -- Lucy Lynn the violin / George Ockner --
Mello fellow the cello / Frank Miller / Nola the
viola / Bernie Ocko -- Lovelace the bass / Frank
Carroll -- Peter percussion / Terry Snyder -- Max
the saxophone / Don Hammond -- Mort the pianoforte
/ Bernie Leighton -- Lady Harp / Myer Rosen -- The
Orchestra.
   1. Symphony orchestras. 2. Musical instruments.
I. Miller, Mitch. II. Golden Symphony Orchestra.
III. Title.
```

Main entry: This is under 21.23C, under the principal performer.
   Added entries: Mitch Miller and the Golden Symphony Orchestra
are traced because of LCRI 21.29D.

Example 6.6. CHILDREN'S MUSICAL : UNDER TITLE MAIN ENTRY

```
  Walt Disney's Pinocchio [sound recording]. --
    Burbank, Calif. : Disneyland/Vista Records,
    c1980.
    1 sound recording : analog, 33 1/3 rpm ; 12 in.
  -- (Disney picture disc)
    Disneyland: 3102.                             |Note Super 1
    Title from jacket.                            |Note 3
    "Original motion picture soundtrack."         |Note 6
    Contents: When you wish upon a star -- Cricket|Note 18
  theme -- Little wooden head -- Blue fairy arrives
  -- When you wish upon a star -- Give a little
  whistle -- Pinocchio goes to school -- Hi-Diddle-
  Dee-Dee -- I've got no strings -- Whale chase --
  Turn on the old music box.
    I. Collodi, Carlo, 1826-1890. Avventure di
  Pinocchio. Selections.  II. Walt Disney
  Productions. III. Title: Pinocchio.
```

Main entry: Begin with 21.9, where it discusses when the medium of "expression has been changed," and the last sentence says to search 21.10-21.23 which in turn leads to 21.23A, where it says to "Enter a sound recording of one work . . . under the heading appropriate to that work." Referring to 21.10, it says to enter the changed version under the heading for the adapter. "If the name of the adapter is unknown, enter under title." The adapter is unknown for this recording, so it is entered under title.

Title: The title came from the jacket. Following 1.1B2, it was considered that the title could not be separated into a title: *Pinocchio*, and an author: Walt Disney, due to the grammatical construction of the title.

Note 3: This tells that the title came from the jacket, and is needed whenever the title does not come from the label.

Note 6: This is taken from the jacket, and is added because the cataloger does not know whether this is the complete sound track or not. Following 25.32B1, and lacking evidence to the contrary, the cataloger assumes it is the complete sound track.

Added entries: AACR2, 21.10 says to "Make a name-title added entry for the original work." This was considered "popular" music, and following 21.7B, no analytical added entries were made for the different songs. Because it was an inseparable title, the other title by which it might be known, *Pinocchio*, was given as a title traced differently, according to AACR2, 21.29B, under a title some user's might use.

CHAPTER 7

Special Music:
Band; Folk; Holiday

The music in this chapter is diverse, and each kind will appeal to only a limited audience.

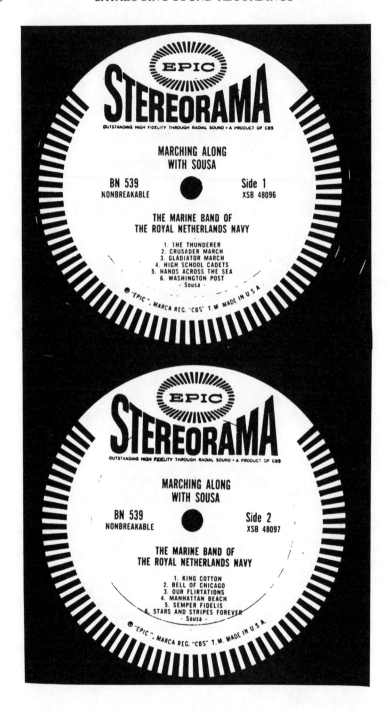

Example 7.1. BAND MUSIC : SINGLE COMPOSER : UNIFORM TITLE

```
Sousa, John Phillips.
   [Marches. Selections]
   Maching along with Sousa [sound recording] / the
Marine Band of the Royal Netherlands Navy. -- [New
York?] : Epic Stereorama, [196-?]
   1 sound disc : analog, 33 1/3 rpm, stereo. ; 12
in.
   Epic: BN 539.                                   |Note Super 1
   Contents: The thunderer -- Crusader march --    |Note 18
Gladiator march -- High school cadets -- Hands
across the sea -- Washington post -- King cotton -
- Bell of Chicago -- Our flirtations -- Manhattan
beach -- Semper fidelis -- Stars and strips
forever.
   1. Marching music--United States. I.
Netherlands. Royal Navy. Marine band. II. Title.
```

Main entry: This has a single personal author, and it is entered under this name, according to AACR2, 21.23B and 21.4A.

Since herald angels sang the first Christmas carol almost two thousand years ago, music has been an integral part of the celebration of that joyous season. Indeed, Christmas without music seems inconceivable. The music of Christmas expresses many moods—from the elation of "Joy to the World" to the solemnity of "Ave Maria." But above all it brings the message of "Peace on earth, good will toward men" to people in every land. It is my deep hope that the music presented here will contribute to your happiness and joy during the Christmas season.

Eugene Ormandy

THE SELECTIONS—PUBLISHED BY BLACKWOOD MUSIC, INC. (BMI)—ARE FOLLOWED BY THEIR TIMINGS

SIDE I	SIDE II
HARK! THE HERALD ANGELS SING 3:10	O COME, ALL YE FAITHFUL 3:15
O LITTLE TOWN OF BETHLEHEM 2:59	THE FIRST NOËL 3:33
JOY TO THE WORLD 1:50	DECK THE HALL WITH BOUGHS OF HOLLY ... 1:45
O HOLY NIGHT 2:45	O SANCTISSIMA 3:26
O COME, O COME, EMANUEL 3:31	THE WORSHIP OF GOD 3:40
GOD REST YOU MERRY, GENTLEMEN 2:46	O COME, LITTLE CHILDREN 1:47
AVE MARIA 4:39	SILENT NIGHT, HOLY NIGHT 3:15
22:10	21:11

Example 7.2.   HOLIDAY MUSIC : WITH PRINCIPAL PERFORMERS

```
Philadelphia Orchestra.
   The glorious sound of Christmas [sound
recording] / the Philadelphia Orchestra [with]
Eugene Ormandy, conductor. -- New York, N.Y. (51
W. 52nd St., NY 10019) : Columbia, c1962.
   1 sound disc (44 min.) : 33 1/3 rpm, stereo. ;
12 in.
   Columbia: MS 6369.                         |Note Super 1
   Temple University Concert Choir, Robert Page, |Note 6
director ; Arthur Harris, arranger ; Philadelphia |
Orchestra, Eugene Ormandy, conductor.
   Contents: Hark! the herald angels sing (3:10) --|Note 18
O little town of Bethlehem (2:59) -- Joy to the
world (1:50) -- O holy night (2:45) -- O come, o
come, Emanuel (3:31) -- God rest you merry
                    (Continued on next card)
```

```
Philadelphia Orchestra.
  The glorious sound of Christmas [sound
recording]. ... c1962. (Card 2).
gentlemen (2:46) -- Ave Maria (4:39) -- O come,
all ye faithful (3:15) -- First noel (3:33) --
Deck the hall with boughs of holly (1:45) -- O
Sanctissima (3:26) -- Worship of God (3:40) -- O
come, little children (1:47) -- Silent night, holy
night (3:15).
  1. Christmas music. I. Ormandy, Eugene. II.
Page, Robert. III. Temple University Concert
Choir. IV. Title.
```

Main access: This is entered under the principal performer, according to AACR2, 21.23C.

Tracings: The principal performers not given as the main access point are given in the tracings.

Example 7.3. HOLIDAY MUSIC : NO PRINCIPAL PERFORMERS

The Christmas sound of music [sound recording]. --
   Hollywood, Calif. (Hollywood & Vine Sts.,
   Hollywood) : Capitol Records, p1975.
   1 sound disc : analog, 33 1/3 rpm ; 12 in.
   Capital: SL-6996.   Note Super 1
   Includes 2 medleys.   Note 18
   Contents: Here we come a-caroling, Deck the   Note 18
hall, We wish you a merry Christmas / [sung by]
New Christy minstrels -- What child is this /
[sung by] Dinah Shore -- Pat-a-pan, While shepards
watched their flocks / [sung by] Bing Crosby --
Silent night / [performed by] Hollywood Pops
orchestra -- Angels we have heard on high / [sung
by] Dinah Shore -- Blue Christmas / [sung by]
                  (Continued on next card)

The Christmas sound of music [sound recording].
   ... p1975. (Card 2).
Glen Campbell -- Caroling, caroling / [sung by]
Nat King Cole -- I like a sleighride, Jingle bells
/ [sung by] Peggy Lee -- O come all ye faithful /
[sung by] Al Martino.
   1. Christmas music.

Main access point: There is no principal performer. The purpose of this record is to present Christmas vocal music. Under AACR2, 21.23C, when there is no principal performer for a sound recording with a collective title, the main entry is under title.

Place, publisher, date: The place, including the street address, was given on the jacket. This catalog card gives the address merely to serve as an example.[1] The address should be given when it is published in the U.S., provided the address is on or with the item, and the material being cataloged is less than three years old.

Note 18: A note stating the recording contains medleys was included because the contents note has two pieces grouped together. This note explains these groupings to the patron. Sung by is inserted in brackets, because the activity is not readily apparent.

RCA VICTOR
LPM-1623

THE WORLD OF FOLK DANCES

SEVEN JUMPS · THE IRISH WASHERWOMAN · LA RASPA · GLOW WORM
VIRGINIA REEL · POP GOES THE WEASEL · CHESTNUT TREE · SISKEN
HORA (Hava Nagila) · CHERKASSIYA · OH SUSANNA · BINGO

ALL-PURPOSE FOLK DANCES

Michael Herman's
Folk Dance Orchestra

ALL-PURPOSE FOLK DANCES

MICHAEL HERMAN'S FOLK DANCE ORCHESTRA

Dance Directions by Michael Herman, Folk Dance House, New York City

Arrangements by Walter Eriksson

126

Example 7.4. FOLK DANCE MUSIC

```
Herman, Michael.
    All purpose folk dances [sound recording] /
Michael Herman's Folk Dance Orch. -- [New York] :
RCA Victor, c1958.
    1 sound disc ; analog, 33 1/3 rpm ; 12 in. --
(World of folk dances)
    RCA Victor: LPM-1623.                          Note Super 1
    Booklet (8 p.) contains dance instructions.    Note 11
    Contents: Seven jumps (Denmark) -- Bingo (Scot- Note 18
land) -- La raspa (Mexico) -- Glow worm (America)
-- Virginia reel (America) -- Pop goes the weasel
(America) -- Chestnut tree (England) -- Sisken
(Denmark) -- Hora (Israel) -- Cherkassiya (Israel)
-- Oh Susanna (America) -- The Irish washerwoman
(Ireland).
    1. Folk dancing. 2. Dance music. I. Michael
Herman's Folk Dance Orchestra. II. Title. III.
Title: Folk dances. IV. Series.
```

Main access: This is entered under 21.23C, under the principal performer.

Title/statement of responsibility: In the statement of responsibility, "Orchestra" is abbreviated because that is exactly how it appeared on the record label.[2]

CHAPTER 8

Spoken Records

Spoken records include readings from books, recorded animal sounds, interviews, discussions and recorded talks. The first examples given below are readings from books. These are cataloged under the author of the book as the main access point, since the performer is not making an original contribution. If one or two books are read, the title entry is for the first book mentioned. When three or more books are read, a generic uniform title is used, such as: Short stories, Selections, Poems, etc. Added entries are made for the person reading the work and other major contributors.

The main access point for animal sounds, interviews, discussions and talks depends upon who makes the greatest contribution to the creation of the recording. When a person makes the greatest contribution to the creation of the recording, it is listed under the personal name. Otherwise, the recording is likely to be under title.

COMMON BIRD SONGS

Donald J. Borror

Department of Zoology and Entomology, Ohio State University

DOVER PUBLICATIONS, INC., NEW YORK

CONTENTS

Example 8.1. BIRD SONGS : RECORDED BY AN "AUTHOR"

```
Borror, Donald Joyce, 1907-
   Common bird songs [sound recording] / [recorded
by] Donald J. Borror. -- New York, N.Y. (180
Varick St., NY 10014) : Dover, c1967.
   1 sound disc : analog, 33 1/3 rpm ; 12 in. + 1
booklet (27 p. : ill. ; 29 cm.)
   Dover: 21829-5.                                    |Note Super 1
   Summary: Selections from 60 common American        |Note 17
birds are recorded to help the birdwatcher
recognize birds in the field by their calls.
booklet describes the 60 birds and their songs in
in detail.
   1. Bird-song. I. Title.
```

Main entry: The "author" and major contributor was Dr. Borror, so he was given as the main entry.

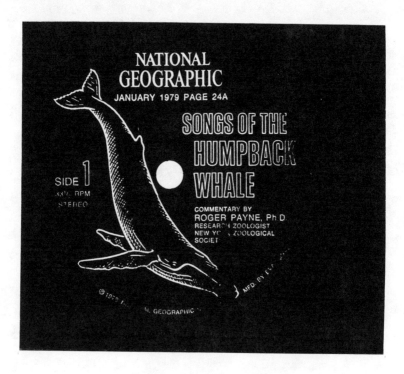

Example 8.2. ANIMAL SOUNDS : ENTRY UNDER TITLE

```
Songs of the humpback whale [sound recording] /
   commentary by Roger Payne. -- [Washington, D.C.]
   : National Geographic Society, p1978.
   1 sound disc : analog, 33 1/3 rpm, stereo. ; 7
in.
   Side 2: New York : Capital Records, p1977. Manu-
factured by Eva-Tone. Inserted in: National
geographic, Jan. 1979, page 24.
   1. Humpback whale. 2. Whales. 3. Animal sounds.
I. Payne, Roger S. II. National Geographic
Society (U.S.).
```

Main entry: It was thought this was the joint effort of many people, and so it was given a title main entry. The commentator was given a tracing.

In The Peter Principle, Dr. Peter and Mr. Hull tell you why things always go wrong. In the Peter Prescription, Dr. Peter presents proven techniques for making things go right. The world changed for the better with the publication of The Peter Principle. It is known to millions in more than 15 different languages. Business executives and educators have taken the "Principle" to heart and use the concept effectively in their own lives and in dealing with others.

Now the "Prescription" provides guidelines for achieving happiness and satisfaction in our careers. It offers remedies for bureaucratic pollution and corporate punishment. It reinforces many of the things we have been waiting to say or do something about.

Dr. Peter has dedicated his talents to developing systems to improve education and prescriptions for avoiding the pitfalls of incompetence. His modest ambition is to save mankind.

Wm. Morrow and Co. published both works in book form.

Example 8.3. SPOKEN RECORD : BOOK

```
Peter, Laurence J.
    [Peter principle. Selections]
    Peter principle [sound recording] / by Laurence
J. Peter and Raymond Hull. -- New York, N.Y. (54
W. 16, NY 110011) : Voice over Books, p1973.
    1 sound cassette (ca. 90 min.) : analog
    VOB: 00472.                                          Note Super 1
    Read by Leonard Frey.                                Note 6
    Abridgement of the book, New York : W. Morrow,       Note 7
1969.
    Summary: "Tells why most of us work, play, and       Note 17
live at a level of incompetence."
    1. Conduct of life. I. Hull, Raymond, 1919-     .
II. Frey, Leonard. III. Title.
```

Main entry: Under 21.23A enter one author with one work under the author.

Title/statement of responsibility: This area is copied exactly as it appeared in the "chief source" which was the record label, since this had a collection title on the label. "By" was included on the label and it appears on the catalog record. "And" appears on the label and it appears on the catalog record. "Dr." appears on the label and it is ignored, according to 1.1F7.[1]

Place, publisher, date: The address of the publisher was included merely as a reminder that the address is included when all the following conditions are met:

1. it was issued by a U.S. publisher, distributor, etc., whose address is given on the item being cataloged;
2. it was issued (published) within the current three years;
3. it does not bear an ISBN or ISSN.[2]

Physical description: The time came from the jacket.

Notes: The word "abridgement" was used on the jacket, so the cataloger used this term. The summary came from the jacket.

In nineteen hundred and thirty seven Bernard Shaw was eighty-one years old. The Spanish Civil War was raging and Europe was aflame with the insane declarations of a former housepainter who threatened to destroy all those who interfered with his plans for conquest. In Asia, Japan and China were locked in mass slaughter. School children in New York City innocently purchased bubble-gum cards for a penny, depicting the gory destruction in the Orient. In the midst of this chaos the voice of an old man spoke clearly once again. G.B.S. delivered a public address on war. Over short wave his voice reached out across the globe. What about this war danger? He drew a vivid verbal picture of the possibilities of destruction, of the bleak emptiness of blasted streets, of the silence of death. We cannot rely on Providence to stop war. Providence has an abundance of mankind in store and there is no danger of its running short. Nature replaces the dead. Nature regards an empire and a swarm of bees with the same indifference, judging a thousand years as we do half an hour. War is a useless waste of young lives. How many Einsteins, Newtons, Beethovens, bakers, weavers, builders, have been cut in the bud by man's inability to control war? To dislike is not a reason to destroy. The old men should carry the burden of war, should do the actual fighting, should march off, waving their sticks in the air, singing, gladly, that they will never return, never return! And he would be one of them.

BERNARD SHAW SPEAKS ON WAR is a document to be valued by all thinking people. It is controversial, but then again it is Shaw—so how could it be anything else but controversial? His weapon, Thought, is more powerful now than in Aristotle's time. In this sense progress has been made.

Notes by: Robert Arnold

Example 8.4.   SPOKEN RECORD : COMMENTARY BY AN AUTHOR

```
Shaw, Bernard, 1856-1950.
   Bernard Shaw speaks [sound recording]. -- New
York, N.Y. (17 E. 48th St., NY 17) : Heritage
Productions, c1953.
   Heritage: LP-H-0074.                              Note Super 1
   "Originally recorded from a short wave broadcast Note 7
delivered in 1937."
   Summary: Shaw speaks on war.  He pictured the    Note 17
possibilities of destruction, of bleak emptiness,
of the silence of death.  We cannot rely on
Providence to stop war.  Providence has an
abundance of mankind in store.  Nature replaces
its dead.  War is a useless waste of young lives.
To dislike is no reason to destroy.  The old men
                       (Continued on next card)
```

```
Shaw, Bernard, 1856-1950.
   Bernard Shaw speaks [sound recording]. ...
c1953. (Card 2).
should carry the burden of war.--from the jacket.
   1. War. I. Title.
```

Main entry: Under 21.23A, one author with one work, enter under the author.

Place, publisher, date: The address of the publisher was included merely as a reminder that the address is included when all the following conditions are met:

1. it was issued by a U.S. publisher, distributor, etc., whose address is given on the item being cataloged;
2. it was issued (published) within the current three years;
3. it does not bear an ISBN or ISSN.[3]

Summary: This was abridged from the jacket.

Subject heading: This heading earlier appeared as: War—Addresses, essays and lectures. But this free-floating form has been cancelled.

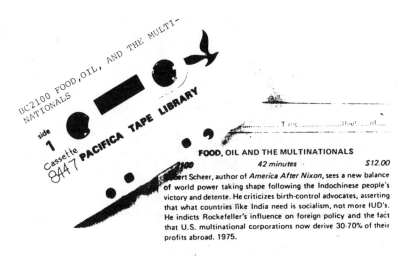

FOOD, OIL AND THE MULTINATIONALS

42 minutes *$12.00*

...rt Scheer, author of *America After Nixon*, sees a new balance of world power taking shape following the Indochinese people's victory and detente. He criticizes birth-control advocates, asserting that what countries like India need is socialism, not more IUD's. He indicts Rockefeller's influence on foreign policy and the fact that U.S. multinational corporations now derive 30-70% of their profits abroad. 1975.

PACIFICA TAPE LIBRARY

5316 Venice Boulevard — Los Angeles, California 90019
No tapes may be reproduced in whole or part without written permission

Example 8.5. SPOKEN RECORD : COMMENTARY ON CURRENT AFFAIRS

```
Scheer, Robert.
  Food, oil and the multinationals [sound
recording] / [by Robert Scheer]. -- Los Angeles,
Calif. : Pacifica Tape Library, 1975.
  1 sound cassette (42 min.) : analog.
  Pacifica: BC 2100.                         |Note Super 1
  Summary: Scheer discusses a new balance of power|Note 17
taking shape in the world following the
Indochinese victory. He criticizes birth-control
advocates, asserting that countries like India
need socialism, not more birth control. He indicts
Rockefeller's influence on foreign policy. He
contends that U.S. multinational corporations now
derive 30 to 70% of their profits from abroad.
                   (Continued on next card)
```

```
Scheer, Robert.
  Food, oil and the multinationals [sound
recording] ... 1975. (Card 2).
  1. International business enterprises--Social
aspects. 2. Corporations, International. I.
Title.
```

Main entry: Under 21.23A, one author with one work, enter under the author.

Title/statement of responsibility: Scheer's name is put in brackets because the name is not listed on the permanently attached label, but is given on the cover.

Example 8.6.   SPOKEN RECORD .: DRAMA

```
Shakespeare, William, 1564-1616.
   [Comedy of errors. Selections
   The Comedy of errors [sound recording] / by
William Shakespeare. -- New Rochelle, N.Y. :
Spoken Arts, [195-?]
   1 sound disc (ca. 50 min.) : analog, 33 1/3 rpm
; 12 in.
   Spoken Arts: 888.                                 |Note Super 1
   At head of title: Folio Theatre Players           |Note 4
production of ...                                     |
   Cast: Christopher Casson (Narrator), Charles       |Note 6
Mitchel (Solinus), John Franklyn (AEgeon), Chris
Curran (Antipholus of Ephesus and Antipholus of
Syracuse), Patrick MacLarnon (Dromio of Ephesus
and Dromio of Syracuse), Michael Mara (Angelo),
Gerry Alexander (Pinch), Christopher Casson (an
officer), Anne Clery (AEmilia), Pamela Mant
                    .       (Continued on next card)
```

```
Shakespeare, William, 1564-1616.
   [Comedy of errors. Selections
   The Comedy of errors [sound recording] ...
[195-?] (Card 2).
(Adriana), Barbara McCaughey (Luciana).
   Credits: Folio Theatre production ; director,    |Note 6
Christopher Casson and William Styles ; presentor, |
Arthur Luce Klein.                                  |
   Recorded at Stapleton Studios, Dublin.           |Note 7
   Summary: An imitation of correct Italian comedy, |
with 3 doors opening off a market place, one door . |
to Antipholus, one to the abbey and one to a        |
courtesan's house. The action takes place in a      |
single day in Ephesus. There are 2 sets of identi-  |
cal twins upon which the comedy turns.              |
   I. Casson, Christopher. II. Style, William,       |
1932-    . III. Folio Theatre. IV. Title.
```

Main entry: An interview is entered under the name of the author, AACR2 21.1A1.

Note 4: The purpose of this is to help acquisition departments and interlibrary loan know absolutely what this label stated, so they can verify if it is exactly the item wanted.

Note 6: This can list both the cast and the credits. See AACR2 7.7B6.

Note 7: A history of the recording is given in this note.

Example 8.7. SPOKEN RECORD : INTERVIEW WITH AN AUTHOR

```
Baldwin, James, 1924-
    Black man in America [sound recording] : an
interview / James Baldwin. -- Cambridge, Mass.
(102 Mt. Auburn St., Cambridge 02138) : Credo,
[1963?]
    1 sound disc : analog, 33 1/3 rpm, mono. ; 12
in.
    Credo: N08P-6397.                                    Note Super 1
    Notes on slipcase by Robert Lewis Shayon.           Note 6
    Recording of an interview by Studs Terkel for       Note 7
radio station WFMT, Chiccago, Ill.
    1. Afro-Americans. I. Terkel, Studs. II. WFMT
(Radio station : Chicago, Ill.). III. Title.
```

Main entry: An interview is entered under the name of the person being interviewed.[4]

Title/statement of authority: These are transposed, according to AACR2 1.1A2, so the title appears first on the catalog entry, and the statement of responsibility appears second.

Note 7: A history of the recording is given in this note.

Added entries: The authority record gives "Studs Terkel" as the preferred form. Tracing radio stations is described in AACR2, 24.11A.

18 872 29   j 711/1 a Institute for Black Elected Officials, c Washington, D.C., d 1969.

Example 8.8. SPOKEN RECORD : INTERVIEW WITH A POLITICIAN

Hatcher, Richard G., 1933-
    The voice of Gary [sound recording] : black
mayor Richard Hatcher analyzes Steeltown, U.S.A.
-- Tucson, Ariz. (532 Transamerica Bldg., Tucson,
85701) : Educational Research Group, Inc., p1969.
    1 sound cassette (27 min.) : analog.
    Educational Research: 13695E.   Note Super 1
    Summary: The first black man to be chosen mayor   Note 17
of a major American city tells sociologist Kenneth
Clark how he was elected and the problems he must
overcome.--From jacket.
    1. Afro-Americans--Politics annd suffrage. 2.
Cities and towns--Planning--Indiana--Gary. I.
Clark, Kenneth Bancroft, 1914-   . II. Title.

Main entry: Under 21.25, enter under the name of the person inter-viewed.

Place, publisher, date: The address was given only as a reminder that it should be given if it meets the three conditions required by LCRI 1.4C7.

E_S Phrase Dictionary and Study Guide

Chinese (Mandarin)

ISBN 0-910542-02-3

LANGUAGE/30

Educational Services
Washington, D.C.

Chinese (Mandarin)

LANGUAGE/30

E S

SIDE
1

Chinese (Mandarin)

LANGUAGE/30

E S

SIDE
3

Chinese
(Mandarin)

LANGUAGE/30

E S

SIDE
2

Chinese
(Mandarin)

LANGUAGE/30

E S

SIDE
4

Example 8.9. SPOKEN RECORD : LANGUAGE TRAINING

```
Chinese [sound recording] : Mandarin. -- Washing-
  ton, D.C. : Educational Services, p1975.
  2 sound cassettes (ca. 90 min.) : analog ; in
container, 20 x 3 x 13 cm. -- (Language/30)
  Phrase dictionary and study guide (25 p. ; 18      |Note 11
cm.) in container, in Chinese and English.
  Summary: Standard Mandarin Chinese. Contains      |Note 17
basic phrases for general expressions, personal
needs, time, numbers, colors, communications,
transportation, social customs.
  ISBN 0-910542-02-3 (phrase dictionary).           |ISBN
  1. Chinese language--Study and teaching. I.
Title: Mandarin Chinese.
```

Physical description: The time came from a sheet of paper inserted with the booklet. The physical description of the box gives the height, then width.[5]

ISBN: This was given on the phrase dictionary. ISBN numbers are always included on the catalog entry.

The U.S. government also produces and sells foreign language sound disks and cassettes from the Foreign Service Institute and the Defense Language Institute. These can be purchased from the National Audiovisual Center, 8700 Edgeworth Drive, Capitol Heights, MD 20743-3701, phone: (301) 763-1891 and (301) 763-1896. Language tapes vary greatly in price, from the one above which sells for about $20.00, to the U.S. government material, which offers greater variety and depth for close to the same unit price, to tapes from Lingaphone and Living Language selling for about 8 times these prices. Also contact bookstores specializing in native language books, as some countries are bringing into the U.S. recorded material at rather moderate prices. The large chain bookstores offer the more expensive material.

Example 8. 10.   SPOKEN RECORD   :   RADIO/TV SHOWS

```
Jack Benny (Radio program).
  The IRS pays Jack a visit [sound recording] /
the Jack Benny show. -- Minneapolis, Minn. (P.O.
Box 11041, Minneapolis 55411) : Radio Reruns,
p1980.
  1 sound cassette (ca. 30 min.) : analog.
  Radio Reruns: 252.                            Note Super 1
  "All time classic."                           Note 1
  Recorded from an original broadcast on 3/16/52.  Note 7
  ISBN 0-88676-010-0.                           ISBN
  1. Radio programs. 2. Comedy programs. I. Benny,
Jack, 1894-1974. II. Radio Reruns. III. Title.
Title.
```

Main entry: Enter under 21.1B2(e), 21.23A and 21.6B, under the corporate author. A qualifier is added to the names of radio programs.[6]

Physical description: The speed for a standard cassette need not be stated.[7]

Note Super 1: This is not required on this catalog record, because the ISBN number is given. However, since it was easily available, it was given.

ISBN: This appears on the label for side 2. If an ISBN number is found in connection with a sound recording it is always given on the catalog card.

Tracing: A tracing is given for Radio Reruns, as it may provide a link for some patrons wanting to hear the old radio programs, especially those who do not have access to the subject headings.

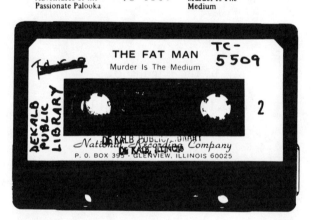

Example 8.11.   SPOKEN RECORD : RADIO/TV SHOWS

```
The Thin Man (Radio program).
   Adventures of the passionate palooka / The Thin
Man ; Murder is the medium / The Fat Man [sound
recording]. -- Glenview, Ill. (P.O. Box 395,
60025) : National Recording Co., [197-?]
   1 sound cassette (ca. 60 min.) : analog -- (Old
time radio programs)
   Caedmon: MM 6684.                                    Note Super 1
   Both programs created by Dashiell Hammett.          Note 6
   Cast: Thin Man: Les Tremayne (Nick Charles),        Note 6
Claudia Morgan (Nora Charles) -- Fat Man: J. Scott
Smart (Brad Runyon).
   1. Radio programs. 2. Comedy programs. I.
Hammett, Dashiell, 1894-1961. II. Smart, J. Scott,
1903-1970. III. Tremayne, Les. IV. Morgan,
Claudia. V. Fat Man. (Radio program). Murder is
the medium. VI. Title.
```

Main entry: Enter under 21.1B2(e), 21.23A and 21.6B, under the corporate author. A qualifier is added to the names of radio programs.[8]

Physical description: The speed for a standard cassette need not be stated.[9]

Place, publisher, date: The address would not normally be given for a record more than 3 years old, according to instructions in LCRIs for 6.4C and 1.4C7.

Modern Chinese

---◆---

A BASIC COURSE

by the Faculty of

PEKING UNIVERSITY

Dover Publications, Inc.

New York

Published in Canada by General Publishing
Company, Ltd., 30 Lesmill Road, Don Mills,
Toronto, Ontario.
Published in the United Kingdom by Constable
and Company, Ltd., 10 Orange Street, London WC 2.

This Dover edition, first published in 1971, is a
revised republication of the Introduction and the
first thirty lessons from the second, 1963, edition of
Modern Chinese Reader, originally published by
the "Epoch" Publishing House, Peking (first edition:
1958) .
This book is sold separately, and also as part of a
package (entitled *Modern Chinese: A Basic Course*)
which also contains three 12-inch long-playing
records (Dover catalog number 98832-5) .
The Publisher's note to this English edition gives
more information on the records and further
bibliographic details.

*International Standard Book Number
(text, records and album): 0-486-98832-5
International Standard Book Number
(text only): 0-486-22755-3
Library of Congress Catalog Card Number: 78-169835*

Manufactured in the United States of America
Dover Publications, Inc.
180 Varick Street
New York, N. Y. 10014

Modern Chinese: A Basic Course

99910-6   **Side One**
Band 1: Lesson 1. Band 2: Lesson 2. Band 3: Lesson 3.
Band 4: Lesson 4.

By the Faculty of Peking University

Modern Chinese: A Basic Course

99910-6   **Side Two**

Lesson 5.

By the Faculty of Peking University

Modern Chinese: A Basic Course

99910-6   **Side Three**

Band 1: Lesson 6. Band 2: Lesson 7. Band 3: Lesson 8. Band 4: Lesson 9.

By the Faculty of Peking University

Modern Chinese: A Basic Course

99910-6   **Side Four**

Band 1: Lesson 10. Band 2: Lesson 11. Band 3: Lesson 12. Band 4: Lesson 13. Band 5: Lesson 14. Band 6: Lesson 15. Band 7: Lesson 16.

By the Faculty of Peking University

Modern Chinese: A Basic Course

99910-6   **Side Five**

Band 1: Lesson 17. Band 2: Lesson 18. Band 3: Lesson 19. Band 4: Lesson 20. Band 5: Lesson 21. Band 6: Lesson 22. Band 7: Lesson 23.

By the Faculty of Peking University

Modern Chinese: A Basic Course

99910-6   Side Six

Band 1: Lesson 24. Band 2: Lesson 25. Band 3: Lesson 26.
Band 4: Lesson 27. Band 5: Lesson 28. Band 6: Lesson 29.
Band 7: Lesson 30.

Copyright © 1971 by Dover Publications, Inc. 180 Varick Street. New York, N.Y. 10014

Manufactured in the United States of America

By the Faculty of Peking University

Example 8.12.   SPOKEN RECORD   : RECORDS AS ACCOMPANYING MATERIAL.

```
Modern Chinese : a basic course / by the faculty
    of Peking University. -- New York, N.Y. : Dover,
    c1971.
    249 p. : ill. ; 22 cm. in box, 23 x 16 x 4 cm. +
3 sound cassettes (90 min.) : analog -- (Dover
foreign study guides)
    Book in Chinese and English -- Cassettes in         Note 2
Chinese.
    Based on: Modern Chinese reader. 2nd ed. Peking    Note 7
: Epoch Publishing House, 1963. First 30 lessons.
Compiled by instructors of the Chinese language
special course for foreign students in Peking -.
University.
    ISBN 0-486-9910-6                                   ISBN
    1. Chinese language--Study and teaching. I.
Modern Chinese reader. English. 1963. Lessons
1-30. 1971. II. Series.
```

Main entry: Under the title for the book, according to 21.1C.

[gmd]: There is no [gmd] for sound recording because this is cataloged for the book as the primary media, and the cassettes are included as accompanying material.[10]

Physical description: The description of "in box" follows that given in AACR2, 10.5D2 and 10.5D3.

Accompanying materials: The time was given here only because the time was obvious — it appeared on the outside of the box.

Note 2: Always give a language note if knowledge of the language is important to the use of the material, or if different from what might be expected from the title description.

POWER WRITING
BOOK 3

Example 8.13. SPOKEN RECORD : SELF-INSTRUCTION PACKAGE

Max, Robert R.
   Power writing [sound recording] / [by Robert R.
Max and Sarah Parr Cerny]. -- Mount Laurel, N.J.
(113 Gaither Drive, Mount Laurel, NJ 08054) :
Learn, Inc., c1979.
   4 sound cassettes (69 min.) : analog + 1
instruction sheet (1 p. ; 25 cm.)
   Includes: New American Webster handy college |Note 11
dictionary / Albert and Loy Morehead. Rev. ed.
New York, N.Y. : New American Library, c1973 --
New American Roget's college thesaurus. Rev. ed.
New York, N.Y. : New American Library, c1974 --
How to achieve competence in English / Eric W.
Johnson. New York, N.Y. : Bantam, c1975.
               (Continued on next card)

Max, Robert R.
   Power writing [sound recording] ... c1979.
(Card 2).
   Summary: Designed to improve business |Note 17
communications through developing skills in
analyzing letters, memos, and reports. Also
stresses preparation of competent communications.
   1. Communication in management. 2. Business
report writing. I. Cerny, Sarah Parr. II. Johnson,
Eric W. How to achieve competence in English.
1975. III. Title. IV. Title: New American Webster
handy college dictionary. 1973. V. Title: New
American Roget's college thesaurus. 1974.

Title/statement of responsibility: Mr. Max and Mrs. Cerny are listed on the printed material as the authors but their names were not given on the cassette labels, so the names are given in brackets.

GMD: The term "kit" is not accurate here because all the printed material supports the sound recordings as the key element.[11] "Kit" is reserved for nonbook material where no single media predominates.

Note 11: Accompanying materials are listed in a note and not in the physical description area because they have individual titles and authors.[12]

Note 17: This is used to give the patron the purpose of the set.

CASSETTE COMMUNICATIONS

P.O. Box 5225
Englewood, Colorado 80155
(303) 779-5965

PROGRAM NOTES

MonitoRadio Weekend Broadcast

December 19-20, 1986

This week on MonitoRadio:

* The editors of The Christian Science Monitor provide perspectives on the significant world news events of this past week.

* Despite the approach of Christmas, tighter limits on the press and increased pressure on black leaders signal a troubling new turn in South Africa's domestic problems. Monitor bureau chief Ned Temko helps sort out the latest developments from Johannesburg. (5 minutes)

* The United States can't win its "war on drugs" until public attitudes change radically. That's the position of one controversial minister who's spent years successfully counseling drug users, including one in his own family. Reporter Sara Terry visits the Rev. David Else in Pittsburgh, his home base. (6 minutes)

* Religious groups around the world will celebrate the joy of Christmas next week in many different ways. One of the more unusual will be a "birthday party" for Jesus, complete with gospel music, given by Boston's Concord Baptist Church. Pat Bodner watched the preparations. (4 minutes)

* Newly elected politicians will be sworn in across the U.S. just after the holidays, and more of them than ever before will be women. MonitoRadio's George Merry reports on why women are running for -- and winning -- so many governmental offices. (6:15 minutes)

* Home Forum page essay.

CASSETTE COMMUNICATIONS

P.O. Box 5225
Englewood, Colorado 80155
(303) 779-5965

Dear new MonitoRadio Cassette subscriber:

Welcome to the growing family of MonitoRadio Cassette listeners. Each week hundreds of tapes are sent to subscribers in nearly all 50 states...and foreign countries on all five continents! The value of MonitoRadio is being appreciated on a world-wide basis.

MonitoRadio is the award-winning weekday and weekend broadcast service of The Christian Science Monitor. MonitoRadio Cassettes bring these broadcasts to people in towns where the program is not carried or where the airtime is not convenient for listening, and to those living abroad.

Cassette Communications of Englewood, Colorado, is the authorized, international distributor of MonitoRadio Cassettes. Each Friday evening (through the courtesy of a Denver radio station), we record the weekend satellite transmission of' the MonitoRadio broadcasts. Then we rush the master tape to our duplicating service where copies are made in a matter of hours. We reach the regional Post Office -- for faster distribution into the mail stream -- a skant four hours after the end of the original program transmission.

Most U.S. continental subscribers should receive their MonitoRadio Cassette on Monday or Tuesday, close on the heels of the weekend radio broadcasts. This way the tapes are fresh, relevant and vital to all listeners.

MonitoRadio Cassettes are a product employing the best of great editorial expertise, high-speed communications technology, and first-class mail service. It's coming to you at an amazingly affordable cost of $3.27 per tape (based on the annual subscription price of $170.)

If, for any reason, you should receive a defective tape, please notify Cassette Communications and we will replace it immediately. It is recommended that you clean your cassette recorder after 10-20 hours of use for best performance.

Thank you for joining the MonitoRadio family. Let your friends know about MonitoRadio Cassettes. It's "the sound way to stay informed."

Happy listening,

Monty Hoyt

Monty Hoyt
President

Example 8.14. SERIAL ON A CASSETTE

```
MonitoRadio [sound recording]. -- June 13, 1986-
       ). -- Englewood, Colo. : Distributed by
   Cassette Communications, p1986-      .
       sound cassettes (ca. 30 min. ea.) : analog,
mono. +      program notes (28 cm.)
   Summary: MonitoRadio is a broadcast service of      Note 17
the Christian Science Monitor and these are tapes
of the weekly broadcasts heard around the world.
They contain current news, interviews with people
making the headlines that week, in depth analysis
of continuing news events and usually a literary
essay.
   1. News broadcasts. I. Christian Science
Monitor.
```

Main entry: This is cataloged as a serial first, and as a sound recording second. Enter under 21.1C, entry under title.

Numeric, chronological, or other designation area: This follows 12.3C4.

Place, publisher, date: Even though the city is not given on the cassette, the information is easy to locate.

CHAPTER 9

Compact Discs

There is nothing difficult or unusual about cataloging compact discs but they are new and some libraries are beginning to invest heavily in them. In hopes of making the cataloging of this relatively new, and still expensive medium easier and faster, this form is given in a separate chapter.

The two areas most likely to be different are the physical description and note 10, which describes the type of recording and the durations.

PHYSICAL DESCRIPTION

Let us examine the physical description for the old type of sound recording and compare this with the new compact disc:

Old Type

```
1 sound disc (51 min.)  : analog, 33 1/3 rpm, mono.     ; 12 in.
[Extant              ][: Other details                ][; Size]
```

Compact

```
1 sound disc (162 min.)  : digital, stereo.      ; 4 3/4 in.
[Extant               ][: Other details]      [; Size        ]
```

Extant

Examining this closely, it can be seen that the extant, which one is "1 sound disc (51 min.)" is almost identical for the two discs—only the period of time is longer for the compact disc.

Other Details

The method of recording the sound is stated first. The analog method is recording sound waves mechanically. In this recording the stylus, or needle, is used to "read" the mechanical pattern of the grove, and these tiny sound waves would be amplified then by the speakers and the sound waves interpreted as sound by the ear. The term analog refers to the stored sound waves having an almost infinite variation, from low to high sound and every conceivable sound in between. To play an analog recording requires a turntable, plus an arm with a stylus to follow the track and pick up the sound waves. The term digital refers to using a number as a code to generate a specific sound. With digitally encoded sound patterns, a specific sound is either "on" or "off," and there is no in-between. To play a digital recording requires each number to be read and interpreted into the specific sound by a computer. The analog records can be recorded monaurally, that is, the sound designed to come out from one speaker; it can be recorded in stereo, that is, designed to come out from two speakers; it can be recorded in quadraphonic, that is, designed to come out from four speakers; and perhaps there are or will be even more variety. If there are no words on the record or the accompanying material saying what it is, the cataloger is to omit this information. It is expected that a digital sound recording will be stereo, but only if the word or an equivalent word indicates "stereo" appears on the compact disc or accompanying material will the cataloger add the abbreviation "stereo." to the physical description. The speed to play the analog disc is vital information, whereas the speed for the digital has no meaning—the rotation of spin is greater for information stored at the center of the disc than for information stored at the periphery.

Size

There is no "standard" size for either the analog or the digital sound disc: since both have appeared in more than one size, the size for each must be given. The most common size for an analog disc is 12 inches, and the common size today for the compact disc is 4-3/4 inches. If the compact discs are part of a set or are stored in some form where the container is not the clear plastic holder slightly larger than 4-3/4 inches, then the size may appear as:
; 4-3/4 in. in box, 10 × 5 × 3 in.
The first dimension given: 4-3/4 in. refers to the size of the compact disc, while the second dimension refers to the size of the box, with the height given as the first measurement listed.[1]

Accompanying Materials

This is the last element in the physical description. A recording may be accompanied by a book or booklet, slides, microform, etc., and this is noted in the generic manner explained earlier in this manual.[2]

Note 10

The first note 10 should tell this is a compact disc. The next part of this note describes the manner in which the original recording was produced. For example, *A Little Night Music* was originally mastered as an analog, and available for purchase in that form. It has since been reproduced as a digital disc, meaning that a computer assisted mastering machine "listened" to the sound waves produced from the analog recording and rerecorded them by encoding them digitally. The objection that many have is that the range of digitally produced sound is much greater than that produced by analog recording so by taking the sound from an analog recording much of the range of sound has been eliminated before it is transferred to the digital disc. At the present, numerous productions from the "101 Strings," cataloged in this manual under: *101 Strings Play Victor Herbert Favorites* and *101 Strings Play Million Seller Hits of the 40's* are available as compact discs, but all of these began as analog recordings. The person who really wants to hear all the sound available from digital recordings will want to see the term: Digital recording in note 10, meaning that the first mastering of this disc was done digitally.

The next note 10 will give the various durations available on this compact disc. Since the compact disc player can be set to play a certain sound track, this information is noted by the cataloger on the catalog card. However, if this is the real use for this information, the patron would need this information when he has the record in hand, and not when he has the catalog card before him. The better explanation for giving the durations by themselves in note 10 is that is the way the publisher is listing the durations for compact discs. A cataloger is a copy-cat, he copies the information given into the correct "field," and also he knows when to look for additional information.

Note 11

This note may change slightly with compact discs. What was "Program notes on container by . . . " for the analog recording will likely be "Program notes by . . . " and then the pagination and illustrative information given in parenthesis, such as (4 p. : ill.) The size is expected to be 4-3/4 inches, the same as the compact disc. When the size is different, the size is given.

FELIX MENDELSSOHN (1809-1847)
Sonatas, Op.65 Nos. 2, 3 & 6
Preludes & Fugues, Op.37 Nos. 1, 2 & 3
PETER HURFORD
at the Rieger Organ in Ratzeburg Cathedral
West Germany

Sonata in C minor · ut mineur · c-moll, op.65 no.2
|1| Grave – Adagio (4.26)
|2| Allegro maestoso e vivace (2.08)
|3| Fugue (3.21)
|4| **Prelude and Fugue in G major · sol majeur · G-dur, op.37 no.2** (7.15)
Sonata in A major · la majeur · A-dur, op.65 no.3
|5| Con moto maestoso (8.06)
|6| Andante tranquillo (2.29)
|7| **Prelude and Fugue in C minor · ut mineur · c-moll, op.37 no.1** (6.15)
Sonata in D minor · ré mineur · d-moll, op.65 no.6
|8| Chorale – Andante sostenuto – Allegro molto (9.35)
|9| Fugue (2.28)
|10| Finale (2.25)
|11| **Prelude and Fugue in D minor · ré mineur · d-moll, op.37 no.3** (8.11)
DDD

Producer · Directeur artistique · Aufnahmeleiter: Chris Hazell
Sound Engineer · Ingenieur du son · Tonmgenieur: Simon Eadon
Cover · Couverture · Titelseite: Photo of Peter Hurford by Richard Holt

—2—

COMPACT
disc
DIGITAL AUDIO

MCPS
414 420-2
STEREO
Made in
W-Germany
by PolyGram

MENDELSSOHN
ORGAN WORKS
OEUVRES D'ORGUE · ORGELWERKE
SONATAS
Op. 65 Nos. 2, 3 & 6
PRELUDES & FUGUES
Op. 37, Nos. 1, 2 & 3
PETER HURFORD

(Ⓒ) 0171

Example 9.1.   CLASSICAL MUSIC : SINGLE COMPOSER

```
Mendelssohn-Bartholdy, Felix, 1809-1847.
    [Organ music. Selections]
    Organ works [sound recording] = oeuvres d'orgue
= orgelwerke / Mendelssohn ; [played by] Peter
Hurford. -- [London, England] : Argo : West
Germany : Made by PolyGram, p1986.
    1 sound disc : digital, stereo. ; 4 3/4 in.
    Argo: MCPS 414 420-2.                          Note Super 1
    Recorded at the Rieger organ in Ratzeburg      Note 7
Cathedral, West Germany.
    Compact disc -- Digital recording.             Note 10
    Durations: 9:45; 7:45; 16:50; 6:15; 14:28; 8:44. Note 10
    Notes in English by Stanley Webb, with French  Note 11
and German translations, and organ specifications
(11 p.) inserted in container.
                          (Continued on next card)
```

```
Mendelssohn-Bartholdy, Felix, 1809-1847.
    [Organ music. Selections]
    Organ works = oeuvres d'orgue = orgelwerke
[sound recording] ... p1986. (Card 2).
    Contents: Sonatas, op. 65, nos. 2, 3, & 6 --   Note 18
Preludes & fugues, op. 37, nos. 1, 2 & 3.
    1. Sonatas (Organ). 2. Organ music. 3. Canons,
fugues, etc. (Organ). I. Hurford, Peter. II.
Mendelssohn-Bartholdy, Felix, 1809-1847.
Praeludien und Fugen, organ, op. 37. 1986. III.
Mendelssohn-Bartholdy, Felix, 1809-1847. Sonatas,
organ, op. 65. No. 2. 1986. IV. Mendelssohn-
Bartholdy, Felix, 1809-1847. Sonatas, organ, op.
65. No. 3. 1986. V. Mendelssohn-Bartholdy, Felix,
1809-1847. Sonatas, organ, op. 65. No. 6. 1986.
VI. Title.
```

Main entry: This is under the single composer, according to 21.23B.

Title/statement of responsibility: The author and title were clearly given on the disc. The statement of responsibility came first on the disc label, and this was transposed to the second position, in accordance with 1.1A2.[3] The first part of the title had parallel titles, and these were transcribed before the [gmd] was included. Only the collective title was given in the main body, and the individual works were listed in a contents note.[4]

[gmd]: This was placed as instructed in LCRI 1.1E5.

JOSEPH HAYDN (1732–1809)
**Symphony No.104 in D major · ré majeur · D-dur
'London'**
**Symphony No.100 in G major · sol majeur · G-dur
'Military'**
THE ACADEMY OF ANCIENT MUSIC
*on authentic instruments · sur instruments d'époque ·
auf authentischen Instrumenten*
directed by · sous la direction de · unter der Leitung von:
CHRISTOPHER HOGWOOD, Fortepiano

Symphony No.104 in D major · ré majeur · D-dur 'London'
1. I Adagio — Allegro (8:06)
2. II Andante (7:50)
3. III Menuet & Trio: Allegro (4:36)
4. IV Finale: Spiritoso (6:21)
Symphony No.100 in G major · sol majeur · G-dur 'Military'
5. I Adagio — Allegro (7:31)
6. II Allegretto (5:45)
7. III Menuet & Trio: Moderato (5:42)
8. IV Finale: Presto (5:03)
DDD

Recording Producers · Directeur artistiques · Aufnahmeleiter: PETER WADLAND/MORTEN WINDING*
Sound Engineers · Ingénieurs du son · Toningenieure: JOHN DUNKERLEY/SIMON EADON*
Recording Location · Lieu d'enregistrement · Ort der Tonaufnahme
Kingsway Hall, London, September & November 1983
Cover · Couverture · Titelseite: Covent Garden — oil painting by John Collet (c. 1770-1780) Museum of London

— 2 —

Example 9.2. CLASSICAL MUSIC : SINGLE COMPOSER

```
Haydn, Joseph, 1732-1809.
    [Symphonies, H.I, 104, D major]
    Symphony no. 104 : London ; Symphony no. 100 :
military [sound recording] / Joseph Haydn. --
[London, England] : L'Oiseau-Lyre, p1984.
    1 sound disc (51 min.) : digital, stereo. ; 4
3/4 in. -- (Florilegium series)
    L'Oiseau-Lyre: MCPS 411 833-2.                    |Note Super 1
    Christopher Hogwood, fortepiano ; The Academy of |Note 6
Ancient Music, directed by Christopher Hogwood.      |
    Recorded at Kingsway Hall, London, Sept. & Nov. |Note 7
1983.                                                |
    Performed on authentic instruments.              |Note 7
    Durations: 26:59; 24:09.                         |Note 10
    Compact disc -- Digital recording.               |Note 10
    Program notes by Christopher Hogwood with French |Note 11
and German translations (4 p. : ill.) inserted in    |
container.                                            |
    1. Symphonies. 2. Orchestral music. I. Hogwood,  |
Christopher. II. Haydn, Joseph, 1732-1809. H.I,      |
100, G major. 1984. III. Academy of Ancient Music.   |
IV. Title. V. Series.                                |
```

Main entry: Under 21.23B, under the composer of the two works.

Title/statement of responsibility: This is entered according to 1.1G2, and is similar to the Haydn example on p. 78 of this manual in which the noncollective title appears as one title on one side of the cassette, and a totally different title on the other side. For the compact disc, both titles are given on the one side, and both titles appear to be equally prominent.

Note 10: The time for the different parts of Symphony 104 and 100 were added and given in this note. If the separate parts, such as Adagio, were other than what were expected in a symphony, then the titles of the parts would have been given in note 18, and the time listed with each separate piece, as given in *South Side Blues.*[5]

Added entries: The added entry under Haydn is a name-title analytical added entry, according to LCRI 21.30J.

Digital Recording · Digital-Aufnahme · Enregistrement numérique

412 631-2
DDD

SPIRITUALS

1	Ride on, King Jesus	2:29
2	Swing low, sweet chariot	4:34
3	Ezekiel saw the wheel	2:54
4	City called Heaven	3:58
5	Plenty good room	2:35
6	Let us break bread together	3:26
7	Go down, Moses	3:23
8	No hiding place	1:30
9	Nobody knows the trouble I've seen	4:00
10	Every time I feel the Spirit	2:39
11	Steal away to Jesus	3:48
12	Witness	2:52
13	Sometimes I feel like a motherless child	3:26
14	Standin' in the need of prayer	1:51
15	He's got the whole world in His hands	3:24

SIMON ESTES
HOWARD ROBERTS CHORALE

Arranged, orchestrated, conducted, and produced by
HOWARD A. ROBERTS

Recorded · Aufnahme · Enregistrement:
6 1984, New York

PHILIPS

Printed in West Germany   Made in West Germany

Example 9.3. FOLK MUSIC

```
Estes, Simon.
    Spirituals [sound recording] / Simon Estes ;
with the Howard Roberts Chorale. -- West Germany :
Philips : Made by Polygram, p1985.
    1 sound disc (ca. 47 min.) : digital ; 4 3/4 in.
-- (Digital classics)
    Philips: 412 631-2.                              |Note Super 1
    Arranged, orchestrated, conducted and produced  |Note 6
by Howard A. Roberts.
    Recorded in New York, June, 1984.               |Note 7
    Compact disc -- Digital recording.              |Note 10
    Durations: 2:29; 4:34; 2:54; 3:58; 2:35; 3:26;  |Note 10
3:23; 1:30; 4:00; 2:39; 3:48; 2:52; 3:26; 1:51;
3:24.
    Program notes (12 p.) by Paul Robeson in English|Note 11
with German and French translations.
                    (Continued on next card)
```

```
Estes, Simon.
    Spirituals [sound recording] ... p1985. (Card 2)
    Contents: Ride on, King Jesus -- Swing low,     |Note 18
sweet chariot -- Exekiel saw the wheel -- City
called Heaven -- Plenty good room -- Let us break
bread together -- Go down, Moses -- No hiding
place -- Nobody knows the trouble I've seen --
Every time I feel the spirit -- Steal away to
Jesus -- Witness -- Sometimes I feel like a
motherless child -- Standin' in the need of prayer
-- He's got the whole world in His hands.
    1. Spirituals. 2. Folk music, Afro-American.
I. Roberts, Howard A. II. Howard Roberts Chorale.
III. Title.
```

Main access: This is entered under performer, according to 21.23C.
Tracings: Analytics were not made for the song titles because it was folk music, according to 21.7B.

A Little Night Music

a new musical starring

Glynis Johns   **Len Cariou**   **Hermione Gingold**

with

Victoria Mallory   Laurence Guittard   Patricia Elliott   Mark Lambert
Judy Kahan   D. Jamin-Bartlett   George Lee Andrews   Despo
Barbara Lang   Benjamin Rayson   Teri Ralston   Beth Fowler   Gene Varrone

music and lyrics by **Stephen Sondheim**

book by **Hugh Wheeler**

suggested by a film by Ingmar Bergman

choreography by Patricia Birch

musical direction by **Harold Hastings**   orchestration by **Jonathan Tunick**

scenic production designed by **Boris Aronson**   costumes designed by **Florence Klotz**   lighting designed by **Tharon Musser**

music publisher
Tommy Valando

production directed by
Harold Prince

produced for records by
Goddard Lieberson

ORIGINAL CAST RECORDING
HAROLD PRINCE
IN ASSOCIATION WITH RUTH MITCHELL
PRESENTS
A LITTLE NIGHT MUSIC
MUSIC AND LYRICS BY STEPHEN SONDHEIM

COLUMBIA

CK 32265
DIDP 20438

COMPACT
disc
DIGITAL AUDIO

1 OVERTURE AND NIGHT WALTZ   2 NOW—LATER—SOON
3 THE GLAMOROUS LIFE   4 REMEMBER?   5 YOU MUST MEET MY WIFE
6 LIAISONS   7 IN PRAISE OF WOMEN   8 EVERY DAY A LITTLE DEATH
9 A WEEKEND IN THE COUNTRY   10 THE SUN WON'T SET
11 IT WOULD HAVE BEEN WONDERFUL   12 PERPETUAL ANTICIPATION
13 SEND IN THE CLOWNS   14 THE MILLER'S SON
15 FINALE (REPRISE SEND IN THE CLOWNS)
AND NIGHT WALTZ

℗ 1973 CBS Inc

COLUMBIA ··· ARE TRADEMARKS OF CBS INC

Example 9.4. MUSICAL : WITH A COMPOSER

```
Sondheim, Stephen.
     A little night music [sound recording] /
[presented by] Harold Price in association with
Ruth Mitchell ; music and lyrics by Stephen Sond-
heim. -- New York, N.Y. : Columbia, p1973.
     1 sound disc (52 min.) : digital ; 4 3/4 in.
     Columbia: CK 32265.                              |Note Super 1
     "Original cast recording" of the musical staring|Note 6
Glynis Johns, Len Cariou, Hermione Gingold ;
Harold Hastings, conductor.
     Compact disc -- Analog recording.                |Note 10
     Durations: 3:39; 10:22; 3:48; 2:21; 4:04; 5:56; |Note 10
3:19; 2:24; 6:38; 1:46; 4:23; 0:55; 3:24; 4:24;
3:06.
     Program notes (11 p. : ill.) by William Evans.   |Note 11
                    (Continued on next card)
```

```
Sondheim, Stephen.
     A little night music [sound recording] ...
p1973. (Card 2).
     Contents: Overture and night waltz -- Now, later|Note 18
soon -- The glamorous life -- Remember -- You must|
meet my wife -- Liaisons -- In praise of women --
Every day a little death -- A weekend in the
country -- The sun won't set -- It would have been|
wonderful -- Perpetual anticipation -- Send in the|
clowns -- The miller's son -- Finale (reprise:
Send in the clowns) -- Night waltz.
     1. Musical revues, comedies, etc. I. Johns,
Glynis. II. Cariou, Len. III. Gingold, Hermione,
1897-     . IV. Wheeler, Hugh. Little night music.
V. Title.
```

Main access: This was entered under the composer, according to 21.23A.

Uniform title: This is not needed, because "Selections" was not added, according to LCRI 25.32B1.

Title/statement of responsibility: Some material was transposed, according to 1.1A2.[6]

Note 10: The durations were given on the back of the container.

Tracings: Tracings were not made for all the titles, since this was popular music, according to 21.7B. A tracing was made to the book upon which this musical was based, namely, *Little Night Music*, according to 21.30G. All the principal performers were traced, according to 21.29.

Example 9.5. MUSICAL : WITH A COMPOSER

```
Herbert, Victor, 1859-1924.
   Fall of a nation / Victor Herbert. Gloria's
romance / Jerome Kern [sound recording]. --
Washington, D.C. : Library of Congress, Recording
Laboratory, [1986].
   1 sound disc (55 min.) : digital ; 4 3/4 in. --
(Our musical past ; v. 2)
   Library of Congress: OMP-103.                    Note Super 1
   "Two silent film scores."                        Note 1
   MusicCrafters Orchestra, conducted by Frederick  Note 6
Harold Hastings, conductor.
   Fall of a nation based on the book: Fall of a    Note 7
nation / by Thomas Dixon. New York : D. Appleton,
1916.
   All selections are in the public domain.         Note 9
   Compact disc -- Digital recording.               Note 10
   Durations: 3:45; 1:55; 2:00; 1:54; 1:40; 1:16;   Note 10
1:01; 2:19; 2:18; 3:00; 2:28; 2:43; 1:20; 5:09;
2:03; 2:21; 1:53; 1:15; 2:33; 1:28; 1:17; 0:54;
2:43; 5:24.
   Program notes (10 p. : ill.) by Wayne D. Shirley Note 11
                (Continued on next card)
```

```
Herbert, Victor, 1859-1924.
   Fall of a nation [sound recording] ... [1986].
(Card 2).
and John McGlinn.
   Contents: Fall of a nation: Main title ; Heroine|Note 18
; Hero ; Immigrants : Hand organ ; Demestic scene
; Rag ; Invaders' march ; Battle music ; After the
battle ; Entr'acte: Love theme ; Death of the kid
; Love and danger ; Uprising ; Victory parade --
From Gloria's romance: Little Billie ; Villainy ;
Automobile ride ; Gloria serious ; Conflict ;
Society march ; Treachery ; Gloria's father ;
Overature.
   1. Motion picture music--1911-1920. 2. Popular
music--1911-1920. I. Fennell, Frederick. II. Kern,
Jerome. 1885-1924. Gloria's romance. III. Dixon,
Thomas, 1864-1946. Fall of a nation. IV. Music-
Crafters Orchestra. V. Title. VI. Series.
```

Main access: This was entered under the composer, according to 21.23A.

Uniform title: This is not needed, because "Selections" was not added, according to LCRI 25.32B1.

Title/statement of responsibility: Some material was transposed, according to 1.1A2.[7]

Note 10: The durations were given on the back of the container.

Series: See AACR2 2.B1, the last example, for a similar series title.

Tracings: Tracings were made for the two works.

CHAPTER 10

Numbers in Titles:
Statements of Responsibility

Numbers offer an interesting challenge to catalogers when they are at the beginning of the title, or even in the first five words of the title. In addition, some musical groups have numbers in their names. LCRI 21.30J(9) states:

> When a number occurs as one of the first five words filed on in a title proper or other title for which a title added entry is made, make an additional title added entry . . . [1]

To explore the methods of handling these situations, the following examples have been provided.

Example 10.1.   NUMBER IN TITLE

```
25 all time family favorites [sound recording]. --
    [USA] : ALL DISC Production, [196-?]
    1 sound disc : analog, 33 1/3 rpm, stereo. ; 12
in.
    All Disc: ADS-1.                                    Note Super 1
    Contents: Traumeral / Schumann -- Loch Lomand /    Note 18
Anon. -- O sole mio / di Capua --'Oh promise me /
Scott, DeKoven -- Andantino / LeMare -- Oh Sussana
/ Foster -- Hora staccato / Dinicu -- Drink to me
only with thine eyes / Johnson -- Piano concerto
#1 / Tchaikovsky -- Ninth symphony / Beethoven --
Silver threads among the gold / Danks, Rexford --
Semper fidelis / Sousa -- After the ball / Harris
Scheherazade / Rimsky-Korsakov -- Minute waltz /
                        (Continued on next card)
```

```
25 all time family favorites [sound recording].
    ... [196-?] (Card 2).
Chopin -- Greensleeves / d'Urfey-Hoak -- Prelude /
Chopin -- Farandole / Bizet -- Eugene Onegin /
Tchaikovsky -- Ich liebe dich / Greig --
Cavalieria rusticana / Mascagni -- Orpheus in
hades / Offenbach -- Les preludes / Liszt -- The
rustle of spring / Sinding -- Largo / Handel.
    I. Title: Twenty five all time family favorites.
```

Main access: This is entered under 21.23C: since there is no principle performer, it is entered under title.

Title: The title begins with a number, so the title will be written exactly as it appears.[2]

Added entries: The title will be repeated in the tracings with the number spelled out.[3] This recording was not oriented toward the musical repertoire, so analytical entries were not made for the contents, per 21.7B.

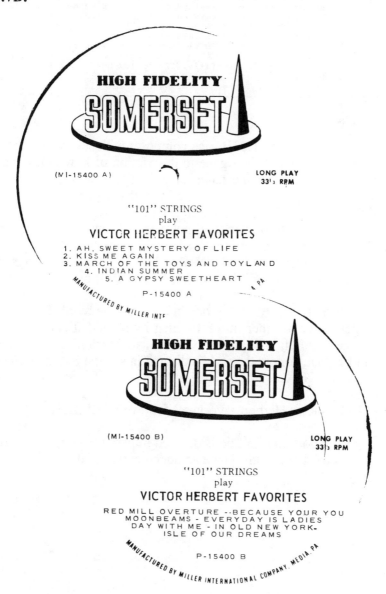

Example 10.2. NUMBER IN TITLE

```
Herbert, Victor.
   [Violin music. Selections]
   101 strings play Victor Herbert favorites
[sound recording]. -- Media, Penn. : Somerset,
[1958?]
   1 sound disc : analog, 33 1/3 rpm ; 12 in.
   Somerset: MI-15400.                              |Note Super 1
   Contents: Ah, sweet mystery of life -- Kiss me  |Note 18
again -- March of the toys and toyland -- Indian
summer -- Typsy sweetheart -- Red mill overture --
Because your you -- Moonbeams -- Everyday is
ladies day with me -- In old New York -- Isle of
our dreams.
   1. Violin music. I. Title. II. Title: One
hundred and one strings play Victor Herbert
favorites. III. Title: Victor Herbert favorites.
```

Main entry: Under 21.23B, one composer with several works.

Title: "101 strings" is a generic description of how many violins are playing rather than the name of a group. The title information given in large type is traced as an added title entry.[4]

Added entries: This is a recording with an orientation toward the presentation of violin music, and not oriented toward musical repertoire.[5] Therefore no analytical added entries were traced.

Title added entries: "II. Title: One hundred and one strings play Victor Herbert favorites" follows LCRI 21.30J(9) quoted earlier:

> When a number occurs as one of the first five words filed on in a title proper or other title for which a title added entry is made, make an additional title added entry . . . In spelling out numbers in English, follow the style indicated in section 8.4 of *A Manual of Style*, University of Chicago Press . . .

"III. Title: Victor Herbert favorites" follows LCRI 21.30J(3):

> When a portion of a title is deemed important enough to warrant a special title search, make an added entry for it . . .

Example 10.3. NUMBER IN TITLE

```
101 strings play million seller hits of the 40's
   [sound recording]. -- Media, Pa. : Sommerset,
   [195-?]
1 sound disc : analog, 33 1/3 rpm ; 12 in.
Somerset: P-21100.                                  |Note Super 1
   Contents: Some enchanted evening / Rodgers,      |Note 18
Hammerstein -- This love of mine / Sinatra, Parker|
Sanicola -- June is bustin' out all over / Rodgers|
Hammerstein -- Fools rush in / Bloom, Mercer --   |
Weekend pass / Lowden -- Now is the hour / Kaihan,|
Scott, Stewart -- Serenade in blue / Gordon,      |
Warren -- Sentimental journey / Green, Brown,     |
                     (Continued on next card)     |
```

```
101 strings play million seller hits of the 40's
   [sound recording]. ... [195-?] (Card 2).
Homer -- Mam'selle / Gordoli, Goulding -- Run-
away hear / Lowden -- To each his own / Livingston|
Evans -- People will say we're in love / Rodgers,
Hammerstein.
   1. Popular music--1941-1950. 2. Violin music. I.|
Title: One hundred and one strings in a symphony
for lovers.
```

Main entry: No principal performers were found, so it was entered under title, according to 21.23C.

Title: "101 strings" is a generic description and not the name of a group. The title information given in large type is traced as an added entry.[6]

Added entries: This recording was oriented toward the popular music, and not toward musical repertoire. Therefore no analytical added entries were made for the contents.[7]

Example 10.4. NUMBER IN TITLE

```
Locklin, Hank.
   3 Country gentlemen [sound recording] / [sung
by] Hank Locklin, Hank Snow, Porter Wagoner. --
[New York] : RCA Victor, c1963.
   1 sound disc : analog, 33 1/3 rpm, mono. ; 12
in.
   RCA: LPM-2723.                              Note Super 1
   Contents: Sung by Locklin: Ivory tower / Jack
Fulton, Louis Steele -- Followed closely by my
teardrops / Fred Tobias, Paul Evans -- Sweet
temptation / Travis, Stone -- It keeps right on
a-hurtin' / Johnny Tillotson. Sung by Snow: Laredo
Don McKinnon -- Call of the wild / Billy & Buddy
Mize -- Black diamond / Stuart Hamblen -- I went
                        (Continued on next card)
```

```
Locklin, Hank.
   3 Country gentlemen [sound recording] ... c1963.
(Card 2).
to your wedding / J. Robinson. Sung by Wagoner:
False true lover / arr. by Ann Bybee -- They
listened while you said goodbye / H. Howard --
Keeper of the key / Howard, Devine, Guynes,
Stewart -- Eat, drink and be merry / Celia &
Sandra Ferguson.
   1. Country music--1961-1970. I. Snow, Hank. II.
Wagoner, Porter. III. Title. IV. Title: Three
country gentlemen.
```

Main access: Under 21.23C.

Title/statement of responsibility: The title[8] was prominently listed at the top of the recording. Since the three singers did not perform together as a group called "3 Country Gentlemen," the names of the performers were listed in the statement of responsibility area, with the first one being given as the main access point.[9]

Note 18: There were 4 songs sung by each of the 3 singers. It was easier for the cataloger to group the songs sung by each singer in the note and then list the four songs under each singer's name. This also helped show the patron that this was not a performing group, but three individuals recording their music on one record.

ABM 1106
(ABM 1106 SA)
℗ 1972 Arista
Records, Inc.

SIDE 1
33⅓ RPM

THE 5th DIMENSION
THE GREATEST HITS ON EARTH

1. **(LAST NIGHT) I DIDN'T GET TO SLEEP AT ALL** 3:12
   (Tony Macaulay)
2. **STONED SOUL PICNIC** (Laura Nyro) 3:23
3. **ONE LESS BELL TO ANSWER** 3:29
   (Burt Bacaharach - Hal David)
4. **MEDLEY: AQUARIUS/LET THE SUNSHINE IN** 4:49
   (THE FLESH FAILURES)
   (James Rado - Gerome Ragni - Galt MacDermot)
5. **WEDDING BELL BLUES** (Laura Nyro) 2:42

Production and Sound by Bones Howe
Unauthorized duplication is a
violation of applicable laws.
Manufactured by Arista Records, Inc. 6 W 57th St. N.Y. N.Y 10019

ABM 1106
(ABM 1106 SB)
℗ 1972 Arista
Records, Inc.

SIDE 2
33⅓ RPM

THE 5th DIMENSION
THE GREATEST HITS ON EARTH

1. **SAVE THE COUNTRY** (Laura Nyro) 2:39
2. **LOVE'S LINES, ANGLES AND RHYMES** 3:57
   (Dorothea Joyce)
3. **PUPPET MAN** (Neil Sedaka - Howard Greenfield) 2:58
4. **UP, UP AND AWAY** (Jim Webb) 2:40
   Produced by Johnny Rivers & Marc Gordon
5. **NEVER MY LOVE** (Don Addrisi - Dick Addrisi) 3:55
6. **TOGETHER LET'S FIND LOVE** 3:30
   (J.W. Alexander - Willie Hutchison)

Production and Sound by Bones Howe except for *
Unauthorized duplication is a
violation of applicable laws.
Manufactured by Arista Records. Inc. 6 W 57th St. N.Y. N.Y 10019

Example 10.5.   NUMBER IN AUTHOR'S NAME

```
5th Dimension (Musical group).
   The greatest hits on earth [sound recording] /
the 5th Dimension. -- New York, N.Y. (6 W. 57th,
NY 10019) : Arista, p1972.
   1 sound disc (38 min.) : analog, 33 1/3 rpm ; 12
in.
   Arista: ABM 1106.                                   Note Super 1
   Production and sound by Bones Howe.                 Note 6
   Previously issued as Bell 1106.                     Note 7
   Contents: Last night I didn't get to sleep at       Note 18
all / Macaulay (3:12) -- Stoned soul picnic / Nyro
(3:23) -- One less bell to answer / Bacaharach,
David (3:29) -- Medley: Aquarus ; Let the sunshine
in ; Flesh failures / Rado, Ragni, MacDermot
(4:49) -- Wedding bell blues / Nyro (2:42) --
                          (Continued on next card)
```

```
5th Dimension (Musical group).
   The greatest hits on earth [sound recording] ...
p1972. (Card 2).
Nilsson, Bill Martin (3:09) -- He's a runner /
Laura Nyro (3:26) -- The singer / Elliot
Willensky, Lamonte McLemore (3:55) -- Every night
/ Paul McCartney (3:58).
   1. Popular music--1961-1970. I. Title.
```

Main access point: This is made for the name of the group as a whole.[10]

Added entries: No added entry is made for the individual members of the group.[11] Also no added entry is made for "Fifth Dimension (Musical group)," as a variant form of the name. This variant form would appear only in the authority record for the 5th Dimension (Musical group).

CHAPTER 11

For Cataloging Sound Recordings into a Local Database

One cannot take short cuts when cataloging sound recordings into a national database. But it is possible to take short cuts when cataloging into a local database. The first item to consider is what is the library's collection policy for sound recordings. After that is written, then the cataloging can follow the needs of this collection policy with the best, and most economical cataloging policy.

HOW COLLECTION DEVELOPMENT POLICY AFFECTS BOTH PURCHASE AND CATALOGING

Recordings Used to Entice Patrons to Library

Collection Policy

The collection development policy of the local library does and should influence the cataloging of the sound recordings. If the sound recordings are purchased only as an adjunct to an informational and recreational collection, or if recordings are purchased as an enticement to draw patrons into the library, then minimal cataloging will suffice. The objectives to be served by this cataloging are to: (1) define the name of the recording so library personnel can distinguish if the record is checked out, is it in the library, or is positively lost, and (2) answer the question: what does the library have, so the patron can see if any of the titles look interesting.

Cataloging Activity

This will require the least amount of cataloging, and a list of the recordings will probably be just as useful as more detailed cataloging. The list should include the title, taken from the label only, the company name and record number,[1] and the date of the recording, but the date may often be missing or approximate.

Recordings Used in Collection Policy but Specific Works and Conductors Not Required

Collection Policy

If the collection development policy incorporates recordings as an integral part of the total picture, but does not try to keep specific titles or composers in the collection, that is, when certain musicals become lost or damaged, it may or may not be reordered. Reordering would depend upon patron demand, as well as anticipation of future demand. The current demand for the Beatles may be low, but it appears there will always be some appreciation for their works, so replacements will be considered, but will be selected from the recordings easily available, and perhaps least expensive.

Cataloging Policy

For cataloging these recordings, some degree of sophistication with cataloging sound recordings is needed. In addition to the policy given in "Recordings Used to Entice Patrons to Library" above, the following information needs to be added to a cataloging record: the place of publication, and Note 7, which gives the performers. With this information, it would be easy to reorder the sound recording, if it were found still in print. This would also give enough information to allow one to reorder the same recording but in a different format, for instance, as a compact disc instead of as a sound cassette. If the collection policy here also encompasses enticing the patrons, then the cataloging policy should include Notes 17 and 18.

Scholarly or Archival Collection

Collection Policy

When the collection development policy supports a scholarly or archival type of collection, then full and complete cataloging is required. The philosophy behind this is that once the sound recording is added to the collection it will remain a permanent part of the collection, and every effort will be made to replace a lost or damaged recording, either in the same or in a slightly different format.

Cataloging Policy

Nothing but the full level of cataloging, as described in this manual, will suffice. Some libraries will even go a step beyond and make analytics, which are only hinted at in this manual by the name-title trac-ings.

Publicity of Sound Recordings

Some libraries take the information and prepare a booklet listing their sound recordings, and have the booklet available at the check-out desk for patrons to purchase for a minimal amount, such as one or two dollars. This is an excellent public relations device, and is not an eco-nomic drain on the library, although the staff time is not repaid. Other libraries keep the channels open for gifts of records and tapes. The usefulness of this idea appears to depend upon the community.

Libraries have hesitated to publicize recordings because of their fragile nature. But the compact disc technology is removing the need for that concern. Now is an excellent time to publicize recordings and get the most use of the current collections, because the future will see less use of analog discs and cassettes.

SHORT CUTS

Given below are some general comments by this author about useful shortcuts.

Title and statement of responsibility: These should be copied di-rectly from the label, and not abbreviated. The jacket is to be used as the source for a title only when there is no collective title on the labels. Staying with one source for the title and transcribing the title com-pletely will go a long way towards eliminating questionable duplica-tion.

[gmd]: Since this is "standard operating procedure" among many libraries, it would appear strange not to have it used, but the use of this is at the discretion of the local library.

Edition statement: This should not be omitted, but it rarely appears.

Place, publisher, date area: If the library does not expect to have to reorder any of the records, but rather selects new records each time they purchase sound recordings, then listing the place of publication may be superfluous. The publisher and date are necessary, but "Made by" is not necessary.

Physical description: The special material designation, that is, de-scribing whether it is a sound cassette, a sound disc, or a sound tape is useful but listing the time is not essential. Including the speed for analog discs is useful for the patron. Including accompanying material is useful if the library is desirous of keeping all the original material together. Many libraries give an accession number to each disc or cassette and an alphabetic code to tell the library whether this is a cassette or disc. If this is done, additional physical description is not necessary, except to meet local requirements.

Series: This is just as essential to add as the bibliographic title, because this is indeed just a different title for the same record. Whether it is traced is up to the discretion of the cataloger who may have local guidelines to follow.

Notes:

Note Super 1: This is always needed.

Note 2: Language note: This is needed by most patrons and by most online bibliographical databases.

Note 3: Source of title: This is useful, and will save future questions. A patron, looking at the catalog record and at the disc label, may ask why the record was cataloged in this manner.

Note 6 and 7: Except for very minimal cataloging, this should be included.

Note 17 or 18: One or the other of these notes is useful to give a patron an idea of what the record contains. This does not mean that a tracing is needed for all the contents, it only means that the contents are listed.

Tracings: This should follow the local needs and the local policy.

Notes

Chapter 1

1. Found in the Library of Congress' *Cataloging Service Bulletin.*

2. Published by the American Library Association and the Canadian Library Association in 1978. This is referred to in this manual as AACR2.

3. These are referred to in this manual as LCRI, meaning the Library of Congress Rule Interpretations.

4. Available from Cataloging Distribution Service, Library of Congress, Washington, D.C. 20541.

5. Available from the Music Library Association, P.O. Box 487, Canton, MA 02021.

6. For sound discs and sound cassettes. "In cataloguing sound recordings, treat two or more chief sources of information as if they were a single source" from AACR2, 1.0H.

7. See page 3 of this manual.

8. A title that is an all inclusive title covering everything played on the disc, cassette, etc., is called the "collective title." AACR2 defines this in Appendix D as "Collective title: A title proper that is an inclusive title for an item containing several works."

9. See page 28 in this manual.

10. See page 19 of this manual.

11. Page 137 of this manual.

12. Page 16 of this manual.

13. Page 36 of this manual.

14. See LCRI 1.1G2. The example for this is on page 77 in this manual.

15. Use the first work for the primary title. See LCRI 1.1G2. See page 90 in this manual for this example.

16. According to LCRI 21.23C.

17. At present. Only when free text searching becomes an option will this area be opened for searching.

18. AACR2 21.1A1.

19. AACR2 21.1B2-4

20. AACR2 21.1C.

21. This comes out quarterly. These quarterly issues cumulate for

that current year, while the fifth issue is a cumulation of the entire machine readable file since 1976. The cost is approximately \$250.00/year.

22. Once a name is established, it is added to the local authority file.

23. See AACR2, 1.4C6.

24. See AACR2, 1.4C6.

25. See LCRI 6.4C7. There are some variations listed in the LCRI for these general conditions.

26. See pages 31, 78, 94 in this manual.

27. AACR2, 1.4D2.

28. See AACR2, 1.4F7. It is expected that with a sound recording the cataloger can estimate within a decade.

29. Time is omitted unless it is found listed on the label, jacket or accompanying material. Librarians do not have time to play the recording and time the duration.

30. Time is given rounded up to the next minute. See AACR2 6.5B2.

31. The seconds are given only when the time is less than 5 minutes. See AACR2, 6.5B2.

32. Appendix A, in this manual, page 199, gives the order and many examples of notes.

33. More information about this is given in LCRI 21.30M.

34. See LCRI 21.7C.

35. See LCRI 21.29D(6).

36. AACR2 21.19A.

37. LCRI 21.7C.

38. AACR2 21.29D.

39. More detail is given in *Music Cataloging Bulletin*, June 1984.

40. LCRI 21.29.

41. See details in Appendix D.

42. See details in Appendix D.

43. See Appendix D for complete information.

Chapter 2

1. Uniform titles will be used, beginning with Chapter 3 of this manual.

2. And the Rule Interpretations for this.

3. It becomes a title main entry if there is no author or composer. See AACR2, 21.1C.

4. AACR2, 6.1G.

5. See LCRI 6.4F1: "If the date of recording appears on a published sound recording, give it in a note."

6. See AACR2, 6.7B18.

7. See LCRI 6.5B2.

8. See LCRI 21.29D.

9. LCRI 21.23C " . . . If there are two or three persons or bodies represented as principal performers, enter under the heading for the first named and make added entries for the others. . . . "

10. See LCRI 6.4F2: "If the date of recording appears on a published sound recording, give it in a note."

11. See AACR2, 6.7B18.

12. See LCRI 6.5B2.

13. "Establish the following period subdivisions under the headings . . . as follows:

c) for recordings, by date of recording, or if now known, date of issue; for music performed in an older style, assign a second heading for the earlier period . . . Establish period subdivisions under the following genre headings:
Rock music: To 1961, 1961-1970, 1971-1980, 1981-   . The subdivisions will be applied under the same principles as those for popular music . . . Abandon the policy of assigning geographical subdivisions for music and sound recording of popular music based on country of publication. Instead, assign the subdivisions only to works where locality is emphasized. General trade music and sound recordings from Anglo-American countries which are intended for sale in these countries, either by one publisher or by means of separate publications of the same work in each country will not be divided by country."

14. See LCRI 21.29D.

15. The quotes are also removed from *Dueling Banjos*, in the manual on page 29.

16. See p. 39 of this manual.

17. This was also done for *A Joyful Sound*, on page 24 of this manual.

18. LCRI 21.23C: "If there are two or three persons or bodies represented as principal performers, enter under the heading for the first named and make added entries for the others."

19. According to LCRI 21.29D.

20. Made in Mexico.

21. LCRI 21.7B, sound recordings, (2).

22. "Establish the following period subdivisions under the headings . . . as follows:

c) for recordings, by date of recording, or if now known, date of issue; for music performed in an older style, assign a second heading for the earlier period . . . Establish period subdivisions under the following genre headings:

Rock music: To 1961, 1961-1970, 1971-1980, 1981-   . The subdivisions will be applied under the same principles as those for popular music . . . Abandon the policy of assigning geographical subdivisions for music and sound recording of popular music based on country of publication. Instead, assign the subdivisions only to works where locality is emphasized. General trade music and sound recordings from Anglo-American countries which are intended for sale in these countries, either by one publisher or by means of separate publications of the same work in each country will not be divided by country.''

23. Make added entries for all performers named on a sound recording . . . LCRI 21.29D.

24. See LCRI 1.4B8.

25. LCRI 21.29(3)b and 21.29D.

26. LCRI 21.30J(10).

27. AACR2, 1.4F7.

28. LCRI 21.7B, sound recordings, (2).

Chapter 3

1. AACR2, 25.1: "Although the rules in this chapter are stated as instructions, apply them according to the policy of the cataloguing agency.''

2. LCRI 25.2A.

3. Librarians would call these "manifestations," meaning that all books, scores, records, videorecordings, etc., of this title.

4. Unless the composer is deceased and only wrote one work in this medium. For modern composers, the first appearance of a specific genre will call for the generic title in the singular. This means catalogers will recatalog the first work when a second work appears in that generic form.

5. Part of LCRI 25.27B reads:

"When cataloging the first occurrence of a work of a particular type by a composer

1) If the composer is deceased, search reference sources to determine whether the composer wrote more than one work of the type, and use the singular or plural form in the uniform title according to the information found.

2) If the composer is living, use the singular form in the uniform title unless the work being cataloged bears a serial number (including 2); in that case use the plural form on the assumption that the composer has written or intends to write more works of the type.

When cataloging the second occurrence of a work of a particular type by a composer, if the singular form has been used in the uniform title for the first work of the type, revise that uniform title to use the plural form.

Note that the medium of performance is not a criterion in the application of this provision of the rule; if a composer wrote one piano sonata and one violin sonata, he or she wrote two sonatas and the plural form must be used."

6. See p. 92 of this manual.

7. See p. 107 of this manual. What is the uniform title in the tracing on p. 108 for Babar?

8. See AACR2 21.30G, last sentence, also 21.30J, especially #4, and their accompanying LCRIs.

9. A list of thematic catalogs is given in this manual in Appendix E. New and additional thematic indexes are listed in *Music Cataloging Bulletin*. Other useful reference books are listed in the Bibliography, Appendix D, but these lists are not to be construed as complete.

10. *Ma*chine *R*eadable *C*ataloging records, distributed by the Library of Congress for books since 1968.

11. This list was taken from the list compiled by Dean W. Corwin in 1984 and distributed at a Music OCLC Users Group annual meeting.

12. AACR2, 25.27B.

13. AACR2 25.27C. A composer may have given unique names to some of his symphonies, but the generic term, "Symphonies" will collocate all of the symphonies together.

14. For the Mozart titles above, "bassoon, orchestra"; "violin, viola" refer to the medium. See AACR2 25.29.

15. For example, a symphony implies an orchestra.

16. These terms can be found listed in AACR2:

25.29C (for combinations of instruments),

25.29D1 (for individual instruments),

25.29D1 (for keyboard instruments),

25.29E (for groups of instruments),

25.29H1 (for solo voices),

25.29H2 (for choral music),

25.36 (for collections of one type or in one medium).

See also the LCRIs for these same numbers.

17. Mozart's *Divertimenti* are used as the classic examples here.

18. For Mozart music, serial numbers are not used. See AACR2, 25.31A(2).

19. The K. listed above refers to the Kochel number used with Mozart thematic index number used with Mozart music. For Mozart's music, serial and opus numbers are rarely used, but the Kochel number is always used.

20. For the Mozart titles above, B♭ major and E major refer to the key.

21. Quoted from AACR2 25.31A6.

22. AACR2, 25.27A.

23. LCRI for 25.3A states:
   "If a uniform title begins with an article (definite or indefinite) and is in the nominative case (for inflected languages), delete the article in all cases, even when the uniform title is entered under a name. . . ."

24. LCRI 25.3B.

25. LCRI 25.3B.

26. See 25.27F.

27. LCRI 25.6A.

28. On the following page of this manual.

29. LCRI 25.5D. See examples for LCRI 25.32 for part and language additions to uniform titles.

30. See LCRI 25.36C and 25.9.

31. This really does belong in parenthesis. See AACR2 25.30 and the LCRIs for this.

32. See 25.31B2.

33. See the AACR2 Glossary.

34. See AACR12, 25.8(1) and 21.30M, and the LCRIs.

35. See AACR2 25.8 and 25.10 and their respective LCRIs.

36. When the item contains 3 or more pieces in one genre, use the term "Selections."

37. LCRI 25.8.

38. On page 77 of this manual.

39. AACR2, 21.30M.

40. See LCRI 21.7C.

41. LCRI 21.7C.

Chapter 4

1. LCRI 6.1F1 says that "performers who do more than perform can be named in the statement of responsibility. Accept only the most

obvious cases as qualifying for inclusion in the statement of responsibility.''

2. Upon which this work is based.

3. If a uniform title is needed. This is described in detail in LCRI 21.30M.

4. LCRI 21.30M.

5. Given in detail in LCRI 21.30M.

6. LCRI 21.30M.

7. AACR2, 25.31A5.

8. LCRI 5.1B1. A unique title has the medium, key and number included in other title information. See the same LCRI.

9. AACR2, 2.7B18.

10. LCRI 21.23C.

11. AACR2 1.1G2.

12. LCRI 25.35 and 21.7B.

13. AACR2, 21.30G.

14. AACR2, 21.30M.

15. Catalogers watch LCRI 1.1G2 for the latest information about the location of the [gmd] for noncollective titles. Parallel titles also pose a problem, and catalogers watch LCRI 5.1B1 and 5.1D1 for the latest information about stating parallel titles.

16. AACR2, 21.30G and 21.30M.

17. See LCRI 21.7: ''Do not make any analytical added entries for sound recording collections . . . 3) containing recitals with an orientation towards performer(s) or instrument(s) rather than musical repertoire.

Chapter 5

1. See *Music Cataloging Bulletin*, September 1980, p. 10, which said this meant the complete text of the whole musical works is included.

2. According to AACR2, 1.1A2.

3. According to AACR2, 1.4C7.

4. LCRI 6.7B6.

5. LCRI 6.7B10.

6. AACR2 21.19A, and its LCRIs.

Chapter 6

1. According to AACR2, 25.9.

2. LCRI 1.4C7.

3. According to AACR2, 21.30M and its LCRIs.

4. According to AACR2, 25.9.

5. See LCRI 1.4C7.

6. With particular attention to the LCRIs for this changing section.

7. See 21.30J for guidance about making additional title entries, and 21.30G, last paragraph for comments about name-title entries. See also the LCRI for 21.30J for more details about name-title entries, and the concept of only making one entry.

Chapter 7

1. See LCRI 1.4C7.

2. Following AACR2, 1.1B1.

Chapter 8

1. The part to consider is the paragraph just after 1.1F7(d).

2. See LCRI 1.4C7.

3. See LCRI 1.4C7.

4. AACR2, 21.25.

5. See AACR2 2.5D1.

6. LCRI 25.5B).

7. AACR2 6.5D5.

8. LCRI 25.5(B).

9. AACR2 6.5D5.

10. See AACR2: "If an item has one predominant component, describe it in terms of that component, and give details of the subsidiary component(s) as accompanying material . . . or in a note . . . "

11. AACR2, 1.10B says: "If an item has one predominant component, describe it in terms of that component and give details of the subsidiary component(s) as accompanying material . . . "

12. LCRI 1.5E1.

Chapter 9

1. Give the height first, see AACR2, 2.5D, especially 2.5D4. For "in box" see AACR2, 10.5D2 and 10.5D3.

2. Chapter 1, page 5, the 4th item under "physical description."

3. Third paragraph.

4. See LCRI 1.1B10: "If the chief source of information bears both

a collective title and the titles of individual works, give the collective title as the title proper and give the titles of the individual works in a contents note.

5. See this manual, p. 14.

6. And its LCRIs.

7. And its LCRIs.

Chapter 10

1. The whole of this LCRI is too lengthy to include in this manual. The most recent changes, up to the time this manuscript went to press, were in *CSB* 27.

2. AACR2, 1.1B1.

3. See LCRI 21.30J(9). "When a number occurs as one of the first five words filed on in a title proper or other title for which a title added entry is made, make an additional title added entry . . . "

4. See AACR2, 21.30J, and its LCRIs.

5. See LCRI 21.7B.

6. See AACR2, 21.30J, and its LCRIs.

7. See LCRI 21.7B for sound recordings.

8. See LCRI, 1.1B3: "The following interpretation below applies to sound recordings only:

> If the chief source shows the name of an author or the name of a performer before the titles of individual works and there is doubt whether the publisher, etc., intended the name to be a collective title proper or a statement of responsibility, treat the name as the title proper. *Exception*: If the works listed are musical compositions and the name is that of the composer of the works, treat the name as a statement of responsibility in cases of doubt. . . ."

9. AACR2, 21.7A says: "Apply this rule to:

1) collections of independent works by different persons or bodies

2) collections consisting of extracts from independent works by different persons or bodies

3) works consisting of contributions by different persons or bodies, produced under editorial direction

4) works consisting partly of independent works by different persons or bodies and partly of contributions produced under editorial direction."

This follows #1 above.

10. This follows AACR2 21.7A and 21.23C and the LCRIs. LCRI for 21.23C includes: "*Principal Performer*. In applying the rules and these interpretations, understand "performer" to mean a person or corporate body whose performance is heard on the sound recording. When a person performs as a member of a corporate body, do not consider him or her as a separate person to be a performer. . . . "

11. Applying LCRI 21.23C, given in the note above. There are many more examples given in the actual LCRI, and these are given in the Appendix of this manual.

Chapter 11

1. This is essentially Super Note 1 in this manual.

Appendixes

Notes are important because they provide the obvious **link** for the patron between what is **traced** and what is **described** elsewhere in the bibliographic record. If the name of an orchestra is given as an added entry, it should be evident somewhere, perhaps in the statement of responsibility, in a Note 6 as an added statement of responsibility, or in note 18 for the contents. Nothing should be put into the added entries without an obvious reason.

Note Number:

Super 1. The publisher's name and number is the first note given for sound recordings.[1]

    Mercury: MG-20192.

    Reader's Digest: RD 5 196-8 (on container: KRD 196-Al—4).

    CBS: C2T 10-994 (on container).[2]

1. Nature or form.

    Opera in two acts.

2. Language.

    In German.

    Book in Chinese and English—Cassettes in Chinese.

3. Source of title proper.

    Title devised by cataloger.

    Title from container.

4. Variations in title.

    Also called: To a wild rose.

5. Parallel titles and other title information.

6. Added statement of responsibility.

Use "Cast:" for nonmusical recordings.

Include characterization in parenthesis, if desired.[3]

The function, i.e., conductor, harpist, tenor, follows the personal name when cataloging sound recordings.[4]

    Cast: Christopher Casson (Narrator), Charles Mitchel (Solinus), John Franklyn (AEgeon), Chris Curran (Antipholus of

Ephesus and Antipholus of Syracuse), Patrick MacLarnon (Dromio of Ephesus and Dromio of Syracuse), Michael Mara (Angelo), Gerry Alexander (Pinch), Christopher Casson (an officer), Anne Clery (AEmilia), Pamela Mant . . .

Alfons and Aloys Kontarsky, piano (side 1 and 2); Christoph Caskel and Heinz Kongi, percussion (side 1).

Carmen Balthrop, soprano ; Joy Blackett, alto ; Vinson Cole, tenor ; John Cheek, bass ; Saint Louis Symphony Orchestra, Gunther Schuller, conductor.

Chorus directed by Cliff Adams ; Cyril Stapleton and his orchestra.

Collegium Aureum performing on original instruments, Franzjosef Maier, concertmaster.

Diana Ross (Dorothy), Michael Jackson (Scarecrow), Nipsey Russell (Tinman).

Jerry Corbetta, organ, etc. ; Bob Webber, guitar & vocals ; Bob Raymond, bass ; Bob MacVittle, drums.

Narrated by Aida Farmer.

"Original cast recording" of the musical starring Glynis Johns, Len Cariou, Hermione Gingold ; Harold Hastings, conductor.

Philippe Entremont, piano ; National Philharmonic Orchestra, Okko Kamu, conductor.

Produced by Sunny Burke.

Production and sound by Bones Howe.

Read by the author ; music composed and conducted by Don Heckman ; notes by Kathleen Casey Shea on container.

Renata Scotto, soprano (Abigaille) : Elena Obraztsova, mezzo-soprano (Fenena) ; Veriano Luchetti, tenor (Ismaele) ; Matteo Manuguerra baritone (Nabucco) ; Nicolai Ghiaurov, bass (Zaccaria); Ambroaian Opera Chorus ; Philharmonia Orchestra, Riccardo Muti, conductor.

Temple University Concert Choir, Robert Page, director ; Arthur Harris, arranger.

7. Edition and history.

Based on: Modern Chinese reader, 2nd ed. Peking : Epoch Publishing House, 1963. First 30 lessons.

Compiled by instructors of the Chinese language special course for foreign students in Peking University.

Based on the book by William F. Brown ; screenplay by Joel Schumacher ; songs by Charlie Smalls.

English translation by Basil Creighton. New York : Holt, Rinehart and Winston, c1963.

Extracts from: The lion, the witch and the wardrobe/C.S. Lewis.

From: Fancies and goodnights. New York : Doubleday.

From 2 books: Babar and his children. New York, N.Y. : Random House, c1938 — Babar and Father Christmas/translated by Merle Haas. New York, N.Y. : Random House, c1940.

"Original motion picture soundtrack."

Recorded in 1953-54. Originally issued in this collection as Capitol T-1602 in 1961.

Recorded from an interview by Studs Terkel on radio station WFMT, Chicago, Ill.

Recorded in England.

Recorded in Powell Symphony Hall, St. Louis, Mo.

"Recording premiere of the first true classic organ in America, built by D.A. Flentrop in 1958 for the Busch-Reisigner Museum of Harvard University."

"A Tono (Zurich) production."

8. Material specific details.

This note is not used.

9. Added information about publication, distribution.

"Released under agreement with Deutsche-Harmonia Mundi, p1975."

"Selections are in the public domain."

Side 2 gives added information: New York : Capitol Records, p1977. Manufactured by Eva-Tone. Inserted in: National geographic, Jan. 1979, p. 24.

10. Added physical description.

Compact disc — Analog recording.

"Compatible with both stereo and SQ quad players."

Durations: cassette alone, 1 hour ; cassette and study guide, 2 hours.

Durations on container.

"Electronically re-recorded to simulate stereo."

In container, automatic sequence.

11. Accompanying material, added information.

Generically described accompanying material is added at the end of the physical description area. Accompanying material with a different or unique title or author is given in the note area. Accompanying material should be listed either as the last element in the physical description, or in the note area, but not in both. It is possible to give part of the accompanying material in the physical description area, and the remainder in the note area.

Accompanying books: New American Webster handy college dictionary / Albert and Loy Morehead. Rev. ed. New York, N.Y. : New American Library, c1973 — New American Roget's college thesaurus. Rev. ed. New York, N.Y. : New American Library, c1974 — How to achieve competence in English / Eric W. Johnson, New York, N.Y. : Bantam, c1975.

Booklet contains dance instructions by Michael Hermann.

Lyrics (12 p.) in guide.

Program notes / H. Krellman ; with English translation by R. Osborne, French translation by J. Fournier, and Italian translation by E. Neill and discography, laid in container.

Program notes in German, English, French and Spanish on container.

Program notes on container by Isaac Asimov.

Program notes by P.E. Stone, A. Raeburn, and G. Schuller, Latin text with English translation, discography, and bibliography (4 p.) bound in container.

Synopsis by H. Rosenthal ; libretto with English translation by G. Morris, laid in container.

12. Series.

Originally recorded in the series: Music for millions.

13. Dissertations

Recording of thesis (Ph.D.) — Northern Illinois University, 1987.

14. Audience and Restrictions.

For the audience level, the cataloger does not make a value judgement, but records what is given with the material being cataloged. The audience level note is used with educational material. Information about restrictions is also included in this note.

For primary grades.

In the public domain.

Copyright ends in 1986.

15. Reference to published descriptions.

Not used with music.

16. Other formats available.

Also available in digital recording.[5]

Also issued in digital recording.[6]

17. Summary.

This contains 75 words or less, does not need full sentences and is nonevaluative.

Summary: Story of good and evil portrayed through the characters of Aslam, the lion, centaurs, the White Witch, and humans.

Summary: The first black man to be chosen mayor of a major American city tells sociologist Kenneth Clark how he was elected and the problems yet to be overcome.

Summary: Presents the family as the most important factor in the individual's food habits. Defines the family within a culture; discusses socio-cultural variables of the family unit and, within the unit, factors which may affect the nutritional status and food habits of its members.

Summary: Selections from 60 common American birds are recorded to help the birdwatcher recognize birds in the field by their calls. Booklet describes the 60 birds and their songs in detail.

18. Contents.

Duration may be included here.

Contents: Ler sacre du printemps (32:10) — Four études for orchestra (8:54).

Contents: Straighten up and fly right / Mills-Cole (2:44) — Too young / Lippman-Dee (2:55) — It's only a paper moon / Arlen-Rose-Harburg (2:58).

Also contains: Krakowiak : grosses konzert-rondo F-dur op. 14.

19. Notes on publishers' numbers.

Used for sound recordings as Super Note 1.

20. Library specific information.

Ball State University's album lacks record 3.

21. "With" note. It is best to omit it entirely.[7]

A contents note and added entries can accomplish the same purpose.

APPENDIX B
ORDER OF PARTS FOR
CONSTRUCTING A UNIFORM TITLE
FOR SOUND RECORDINGS

1. The original title (25.3).[1]
A generic title is a substitute for a title in works without a unique title.
EXAMPLES of generic titles:

Concertos	(25.27B, collections 25.36B)
Lieder	(collections, 25.29H3)
Operas	(collections, 25.36B)
Piano music	(25.27B, collections, 26.36A(A2))
Selections	(25.35)
Sonatas	(25.27B, collections, 25.36B)
Symphonies	(25.27B; collections, 25.36B)
Trio sonatas	(25.27E)
Works	(25.34)

The generic terms should be in the plural.[2]
Examples of generic titles:

Ruggles, Carl.
[Works. 1980]
The complete music of Carl Ruggles [sound recording]
Beethoven, Ludwig van, 1770-1827.
[Quartets, strings, no. 1-6, op 18]
Die fruhen Streichquartette [sound recording] = The early string quartets . . .
Beethoven, Ludwig van, 1770-1827.
[Selections. 1959]
Symphonies and quintets of Beethoven . . .

2. Part, or section of the whole, is added. (25.6A)
The original title is first, followed by the name or number of the section.
EXAMPLE of *adding a number*:
Schumann, Robert
[Album fur die jugend. Nr. 30]
Pictures for the young [sound recording] . . .
EXAMPLE for *adding a name*:
Liszt, Franz, 1811-1886.
[Chants polonais. Mes joies]
EXAMPLES for adding to generic titles (which are in the plural):
Mahler, Gustav, 1860-1911.

[Symphonies, no. 6, A minor]
Symphonie Nr. 6 a-moll [sound recording] . . .
Tchaikovsky, Peter Ilich, 1840-1893.
[Concertos, piano, orchestra, no. 1, op 23]
Tchaikovsky concerto no. 1 [sound recording] . . .
3. Medium of performance is given. (25.29) (These terms will be
listed within 25.29)

25.29H2	=	choral music
25.36	=	collections of one type or in one medium
25.29C	=	combination of instruments
25.29E	=	groups of instruments
25.29D1	=	individual instruments
25.29D2	=	keyboard instruments
29.29J	=	medium indeterminate, not clearly defined
25.29F	=	orchestra
25.29G	=	solo(s) & accompanying ensemble
25.29H1	=	solo voices
25.29H3	=	songs, lieder

EXAMPLE of adding medium of performance for a uniquely title
work:
Thomson, Virgil, 1896-
[Portraits, piano (1981)]
EXAMPLE of adding medium of performance for a generically title
work:[3]
Shostakovich, Dmitrii Dmitrievich, 1906-1975.
[Concertos, piano, orchestra, no. 1, C minor]
Concerto no. 1 in C minor for piano and orchestra, op 35 . . .
Beethoven, Ludwig van, 1770-1827.
[Quintets, piano, oboe, clarinet, horn, bassoon, op. 16, E^b ma-
jor]
Lotti, Antonio, d. 1740.
[Trio sonatas, flute, viola da gamba, continuo, G major]
Sallinen, Aulis.
[Concertos, violoncello, orchestra, op. 44]
4. Add number of parts for particular instruments or voice to the
medium of performance (25.29A4).
EXAMPLE of number of parts added to the instruments in the uni-
form title:
Esercizi, voices (4)
11 hexachord vocalises.
Because the uniform title in this example is the main access point, it
is not in square brackets.

EXAMPLES of number of parts added to the instruments in the uniform title:[4]

Lasso, Orlando di, 1532-1594.

[Chansons, voices (4). Selections]

Dussek, Johann Ladislav, 1760-1812.

[Concertos, piano (2), orchestra, op. 63, B♭ major]

5. Other identifying elements. (25.31)

If they are available, a serial number, opus number, and/or key are included in the uniform title — in that order. A thematic index number or other identifying element may be given also.

EXAMPLES of adding other identifying elements to a generic title:[5]

Beethoven, Ludwig van, 1770-1827.

[Quartets, strings, no. 13, op. 130, B♭ major]

Boccherini, Luigi, 1743-1805.

[Quintets, flute, violins, viola, violoncello, G. 435, E♭ major]

6. Language. The name of the language is added when the work is a translation from an original language or is a liturgical text.

EXAMPLES for adding a language to a work with a unique title:

Hesse, Hermann, 1877-1962.

[Steppenwolf. English. Selections]

Polestrina, Giovanni Pierluigi da, 1525?-1594.

[Missa Papae Marcelli, Latin]

Hidalgo, Juan, d. 1685.

[Celos aun del aire. Libretto. English & Spanish][6]

EXAMPLE for adding a language to a generic title:

Brailoiu, Constantin, 1893-1958.

[Works. French & Romanian. 1967]

7. Altered work:

Alterations of musico-dramatic works (25.31B1-2)

Arrangements (25.31B4)

Librettos and song texts (25.31B5)

Vocal and chorus scores (25.32B3)

If the alterations made to a musical work produces a different title, the uniform title is constructed for the original work, with the altered title added in parenthesis.

EXAMPLES of adding a different title to the original, uniquely titled work:

Strauss, Johann

[Fledermaus (Gay Rosalinda). Selections]

Selections from Gay Rosalinda [sound recording] . . .

Some composers have given two different pieces the same title. In order for the cataloger to take the wording given by the composer for that one title, and differentiate this one title appropriately between two different works, which have the same title, the cataloger adds in parenthesis some distinguishing words.

Bach, Johann Sebastian, 1685-1750.
[Nun comm, der Heiden Heiland (Cantata), BWV 61]
8. Selections. (25.36C)

This means adding the term "Selections" to the uniform title.[7] Selections are added to a collective title when the pieces are not continuous. This term is also used when the work is an extract or abridgement of a larger work.

EXAMPLE of 12 pieces which are not continuous:
Rodgers, Richard, 1902-1979.
[Oklahoma. Selections]
Selections from Oklahoma and other standard hits
[sound recording] . . .

EXAMPLE of pieces from several different works:
Salieri, Antonio, 1750-1825.
[Orchestra music. Selections]

EXAMPLE of an extract:
Hesse, Hermann, 1877-1962.
[Steppenwolf. For madmen only. English. Selections]
Steppenwolf, for madmen only [sound recording] :
scenes from . . .

9. Sketches (25.30)

When cataloging the composer's sketches, formulate the uniform title for the completed work, and add (Sketches).

EXAMPLE for adding Sketches:
Gershwin, George
[Selections. (Sketches)]
Sketches from Gershwin's notebook [sound recording]. . . .[1]

10. Arrangements (25.31B2)

If the work is an arrangement, that is, it has been rewritten from the original medium to a new medium, *and* is entered under the original composer, then use the uniform title for the original work followed by a semicolon and add the term "arr."

EXAMPLES of adding arrangements to works with unique titles:[8]
Villa-Lobos, Heitor. [Bachianas brasileiras, no. 5. Aria; arr.]
Savinio, Alberto, 1891-1952.
[Chants de la mi-mort. Suite; arr.]

EXAMPLE of an arrangement for a work which has a generic title:[9]
Saint-Saens, Camille, 1835-1921.

[Études, piano, op. 52. No. 6; arr.]
11. Date is added.
    Analytical added entries (21.30M)
    Not added with "Selections" (25.35)
    Works (25.8)
A four digit date is added at the end of the uniform title in special instances:
    At the end of the uniform title "Works." because it is used so often;
    As the last element in an analytical added entry, that is, a tracing for a part within the item cataloged.

The date (in both of these instances) is copied from the publication, distribution area. Copyright symbols, question marks, brackets, and other symbols are removed. Open entries: use the beginning date given in the publication area. Uncertain dates have zeros added, in order to become a four digit date.

EXAMPLES of analytical added entries with the date at the end of the uniform title, in the tracing:
Brunhoff, Jean de, 1899-1937.
    [Babar en famille. English]
    Babar and his children ; Babar and Father Christmas [sound recording] / Jean De Brunhoff ; . . . New York, N.Y. (505 Eighth Ave., N.Y. 10018) : Caedmon, p1976.
    III. Brunhoff, Jean de, 1899-1937. Babar et le Pere Noel. English. 1976.

Explanation of III. above:

Brunhoff, Jean de, 1899-1937.	=	authority form for author
Babar et le Pere Noel	=	uniform title for story
English	=	Language of the translation
1976	=	date, taken from p1976 above[10]

Haydn, Joseph, 1732-1809.
    [Symphonies, H. I, 82, C major]
    Symphony no. 82 in C : l'ours = the bear ; Symphony no. 83 in G minor : la poule = the hen [sound recording] . . . —Minneapolis, Minn. (7500 Excelsior Blvd., Minneapolis, Minn. 55426) : International Arts, c1981.
    I. Haydn, Joseph, 1732-1890. Symphonies, H. I, 83, G minor. 1981.

Explanation of I. above:

Haydn, Joseph, 1732-1809.	=	authority form for author
Symphonies, H. I, 83, G minor	=	uniform title: Symphonies (which is generic and equals) Hoboken,[11] vol. One,[12] number 83, G minor
1981	=	date, taken from c1981 above[13]

Loewe, Frederick, 1904-1988
  [My fair lady. Selections]
  My fair lady / music of Lerner and Loewe. The king and I / music of Rodgers and Hammerstein [sound recording]. — New York, N.Y. : Richmond, [196-?].
  III. Rodgers, Richard, 1902-   . King and I. Selections. 1960.

Explanation of III. above:

Rodgers, Richard, 1902-	=	authority form for composer
King and I. Selections	=	uniform title, unique, plus Selections.
1960	=	date, taken from [196-?] above[14]

APPENDIX C
GLOSSARY OF TERMS USED
IN CATALOGING SOUND RECORDINGS
AND ACRONYMS AND TERMS USED
IN THIS MANUAL

AACR2. This is the acronym for *Anglo-American Cataloguing Rules*. 2nd ed. Chicago: American Library Association, 1978. Following the acronym there is generally a set of numbers, and this refers to the rule numbers used in this book. The rule interpretations, called LCRI for Library of Congress Rule Interpretations, also used the identical numbering pattern.

Accompanying material: "If the need is felt to give more information about accompanying material than can be given under option d [of 1.5E1] . . . , describe the material in a note and omit it from the physical description area. (In the second sentence of 6.7B11, the phrase 'not mentioned in the physical description area' modifies 'accompanying material,' not 'details.')" (MCB June '81)

Added entries for nonbook material: [Apply these guidelines in addition to 21.29 and 21.30:

1. Make added entries for all openly named persons or corporate bodies who have contributed to the creation of the item, with the following exceptions [these apply to films, etc., and not to sound recordings]
2. Make added entry headings for all corporate bodies named in the publication, distribution, etc., area.
3. Make added entries for all featured players, performers, and narrators with the following exceptions:
   a. [refers to motion pictures and videos]
   b. If there are many players (actors, actresses, etc.), make added entries under the headings for those that are given prominence in the chief source of information. If that cannot be used as a criterion, make added entries under the headings for each if there are no more than three.
4. Similarly, make added entries under the headings for persons in a production who are interviewers or interviewees, delivering lectures, addresses, etc., or discussing their lives, ideas, work, etc., and who are not chosen as the main entry heading." (CSB 13)

Also issued as: Means you don't have to own it.
Also available as: Means you do have to own it.

Analog sound recording: "A recording on which sound vibrations have been registered in a form analogous to the manner in which sound is perceived by the human ear; i.e., a mechanical, electrical, or magnetic fluctuation that follows the air pressure variations by which the human ear experiences sound." (CSB 30:27)

Analytics for sound recordings: "If a sound recording collection contains twenty-five or fewer musical works entered under two or more different headings, normally make up to fifteen entries according to [instructions are given]. Do not make any analytical added entries for sound recording collections

1. containing twenty-five or fewer works that would require more than fifteen analytical added entries;
2. containing pop, folk, ethnic, or jazz music;
3. containing recitals with an orientation toward performers(s) or instrument(s) rather than musical repertoire;
4. that are multipart items but incomplete at the time the collection is cataloged.

Without collective title:

If a sound recording collection contains no more than fifteen musical works entered under two or more different headings, enter the collection under the first work and make analytical added entries for the other works. Do not make analytical added entries for sound recording collections that are covered by the excluded categories in RI 21.7B." (CSB 28)

Arr. (when given in uniform title): "According to the definition in the AACR2 Glossary (Appendix D) an arrangement is defined as a work rewritten for a medium of performance different from that originally intended." (MCB Apr '85) A simplified arrangement in the same medium is not considered an arrangement by the cataloger. For a cataloger, it must be transformed into another medium of performance.

Audience level: Included for educational material.

Author of words: "In cataloging musical works that include words (songs, operas, musical comedies, cantatas, etc.) an added entry must be made in all cases for the author of the words, in accordance with rule 21.19A of the AACR2. It does not matter whether the author has collaborated with the composer or his text(s) has been taken up by the composer and set to music. Having taken care of the added entry for the author from the descriptive cataloger's viewpoint, we then turn to the usage guide for the most commonly used subdivisions in subject headings, which is published on pages xviii-lxxii of the *Library of*

Congress Subject Headings, 8th edition. Under "Musical Settings" we are told to use this form subdivision "under names of authors for musical scores in which the texts or a text of the author in question has been *set to music*." (MCB February '84)

Basso continuo: Use *"continuo* for a thorough bass part, with or without figures, realized or unrealized, whether it is named as basso continuo, figured bass, thorough bass, or continuo." (CSB 25)

Cadenzas: "Treat cadenzas as related works under this rule whether they are composed by the composer of the works into which they are to be interpolated or by someone else." (MCB)

CSB. This means *Cataloging Service Bulletin*. Available from: Library of Congress, Cataloging Distribution Service, Washington, D.C. 20541.

Chorus and Orchestra added entries: "If an added entry is needed on a sound recording for both the chorus and orchestra of an opera company, opera house, etc., make the added entry for the parent body alone. If an added entry is needed for the chorus alone or for the orchestra alone, make the added entry specifically for the body involved." (CSB 13)

Chorus score: "This term is used only for works originally for solo voice(s) and chorus with accompaniment. In order for this term to be used in the physical description area for a particular manifestation of a work, the item must omit the solo voice(s), at least in those portions of the work in which the chorus does not sing. In addition, if the accompaniment is originally for other than keyboard instrument it must be either arranged for keyboard instrument or omitted; if originally for keyboard instrument it must be omitted. (Understand "if any" to mean "omitted or.") This term is not used for works originally unaccompanied or for any manifestation of an accompanied work with the original accompaniment." (MCB June '81)

Clavichord in uniform title: "If the application of the subrules of 25.29D results in the separation of a composer's works between harpsichord or clavichord on the one hand and the piano on the other, choose the instrument for which the major portion of the works of a given type was intended and use that instrument name for all works of the type. If the "major" instrument is not apparent, use "keyboard instrument." (CSB 20)

Chorus score: A score of a vocal work showing only the chorus parts, with accompaniment omitted or arranged for keyboard instrument. (MCB Aug. '85. Note revisions to M and LCSH here.)

Close score: "A musical score giving all the parts on a minimum number of staves, normally two, as with hymns." (CSB 25)

Composer as performer: "If a composer is the main entry heading for a musical work and performs his or her own work(s), make an added entry to represent the performing function. If, however, the composer is represented not by the main entry heading but by a name-title added entry heading, then do not make the added entry to represent the performing function." (CSB 13)

Composition: "should be treated as a generic term per 25.27B." (MCB Mar '85)

"Concert piece, Little piece," etc., are considered distinctive titles. (CSB 14)

Condensed score: "A musical score giving only the principal musical parts on a minimum number of staves, generally organized by instrumental sections." (CSB 25)

Conductor part. See: Piano [violin, etc.] conductor part.

Continuo: "Use *continuo* for a thorough bass part, with or without figures, realized or unrealized, whether it is named as basso continuo, figured bass, thorough bass, or continuo." (CSB 25)

Contrabassoon. Use this term in uniform titles. (CSB 14)

Date of publication: "Do not add a date of publication, etc., to the uniform title "Selection" when this is used for collections of musical works by one composer (unless the uniform title is being used in an analytical added entry (cf. 21.30M)." (CSB 13)

Digital sound recording. "A recording in which sound vibrations have been registered by mechanically or magnetically encoding a series of numbers (digits) that completely describe the sound." (CSB 30:27)

Dixit Dominus: "Consider commonly used liturgical titles such as *Requiem, Te Deum, Salve Regina*, and *Dixit Dominus* to be generic terms. If a plural form is required, form one if possible by adding the letter *-s* to the last word of the title; if this is not convenient, consider the plural to be the same as the singular. Apply 25.29A2(a) and so do not normally include a statement of medium performance." (CSB 14)

Double string orchestra in uniform title: Don't use. Use [. . . , string orchestra] in the plural. (MCB Nov '82)

Edition 1. In the case of books and booklike materials, all those copies of an item produced from substantially the same type image, whether by direct contact or by photographic methods. 2. In the case of nonbook materials, all the copies of an item produced from one master copy and issued by a particular publishing agency or a group of such agencies. Provided the foregoing conditions are fulfilled, a change of identity of the distributing body does not constitute a change of edition. 3. In the case of manuscript items, a version of a manuscript with significant differences from other versions. See also Facsimile reproduction, Impression, Issue, Preprint. (CSB 33)

English horn. Use this term in uniform title. (CSB 14)

Elegy: "Based on the *Harvard Dictionary of Music* and other reference sources, [L.C.] decided to treat "Elegy" as a non-distinctive title and a type of composition for instrumental works. . . . [For works that are not instrumental works, L.C. has] treated their titles as distinctive. (MCB 8:86:9)

Excerpts: "For excerpts from one work, make a separate analytical added entry for each excerpt unless there are two or more excerpts numbered consecutively (25.6B1) or three or more unnumbered or nonconsecutively numbered excerpts (25.6B3). (Do not apply these provisions to sound recording collections of pop, folk, ethnic, or jazz music or to multipart collections that are not yet complete.)" (CSB 13)

Figured bass: "Use *continuo* for a thorough bass part, with or without figures, realized or unrealized, whether it is named as basso continuo, figured bass, thorough bass, or continuo." (CSB 25)

gmd. This means the general materials designation. This is explained in AACR2 1.1C.

Harpsichord in uniform title: "If the application of the subrules of 25.29D results in the separation of a composer's works between harpsichord or clavichord on the one hand and the piano on the other, choose the instrument for which the major portion of the works of a given type was intended and use that instrument name for all works of the type. If the "major" instrument is not apparent, use "keyboard instrument." (CSB 20)

Instrumental ensemble: This is used "as a statement of medium that is added to a title in a uniform title only if the medium is a group of diverse instruments not already provided for by other terms in the list." (CSB 18) "For an accompanying ensemble that has only one performer to a part, use an appropriate phrase for the group of instruments (e.g., "string ensemble," "wind ensemble," "instrumental ensemble") as a statement of medium that follows the statement for solo instruments in a uniform title." (CSB 11)

Keyboard instrument: "If the application of the subrules of 25.29D results in the separation of a composer's works between harpsichord or clavichord on the one hand and the piano on the other, choose the instrument for which the major portion of the works of a given type was intended and use that instrument name for all works of the type. If the "major" instrument is not apparent, use "keyboard instrument." (CSB 20)

"Little piece," etc., are considered distinctive titles. (CSB 14)

LCRI. This means the Library of Congress Rule Interpretations, which are given in the *Cataloging Service Bulletin*, published by the Library of Congress.

Main access. This means the main entry. See AACR2 21.1 for more information.

MCB. This means *Music Cataloging Bulletin*.

Melody or Melodies: "When a French work for solo voices and keyboard stringed instrument has the title *Melodie* or *Melodies*, do not translate the title into English, since the cognate words in English and other languages do not have the specific meaning of the French word. Consider the medium of performance to be implied by the title and do not include it in the uniform title (25.29A2(a)).

When a French work for solo voice without accompaniment or with accompaniment other than a keyboard stringed instrument alone has the title *Melodie* or *Melodies*, do not translate the title into English. Include the medium or accompaniment or a statement of the absence of accompaniment (25.29H3).

When the word *Melody* or *Melodie* or its cognate in another language (including French) is the title of any other work, consider it the name of a type of composition. Use the English form in the uniform title and include the medium of performance (25.29A1).") (CSB 14)

Motion-picture music: "For collections of music by a single composer for various motion pictures, use the uniform title "Motion-picture music" or "Motion-picture music. Selections" (without a statement of medium) instead of such uniform titles as "Orchestra music. Selections." (CSB 14)

Musical presentation statement (CSB 25): "A term or phrase found in the chief source of information of a publication of printed music or a music manuscript that indicates the physical presentation of the music (e.g., "score," "miniature score," "score and parts"). This type of statement should be distinguished from those that indicate an arrangement or edition of a musical work (e.g., "vocal score," "2-piano edition," "version with orchestra accompaniment," "chorus score").

Musical settings: "In cataloging musical works that include words (songs, operas, musical comedies, cantatas, etc.) an added entry must be made in all cases for the author of the words, in accordance with rule 21.19A . . . we then turn to the usage guide to the most commonly used subdivisions in subject headings . . . Under "Musical settings" we are told to use this form of subdivision . . . " (MCB Feb. '84)

NAR. This means the name authority records. These may be thought of as national, since they are available online with different library networks, and in microfiche.

No collective title: See 21.23D for main access point. (CSB 25)

Order of added entries. Give added entries in the following order:

1. Personal name;
2. Personal name/title;
3. Corporate name;
4. Corporate name/title;
5. Uniform title (all instances of works entered under title);
6. Title traced as Title-period.
7. Title traced as Title-colon, followed by a title;
8. Series

For arrangement within any one of these groupings, generally follow the order in which the justifying data appears in the bibliographic description. If such a criterion is not applicable, use judgment. (CSB 12)

Parallel data: "When succeeding statements of key, etc., are broken up in the source rather than grouped together by language, transcribe the statements so that all elements in one language are together. Treat the first group of elements in one language as part of the title proper and precede each one after the first by an equals sign. Thus

Concerto
D-Dur/D Major/Re Majeur
fur Horn unde Orchester
for Horn and Orchestra
pour Cor et Orchestre

would be transcribed as:
Concerto, D-Dur, fur Horn und Orchester = D major, for horn and orchestra = re majeur pour cor et orchestre. (CSB 26)

Part. See this manual, page 58.

Performing group. "This category emphasizes that the responsibility of a performing group must go beyond "mere performance, execution, etc." This means that the group must be responsible to a major degree for the artistic content of the work being performed. A typical example is an acting group that performs by means of improvisation. The group collectively "plans" the drama, that is, determines the broad outline of the plot, the nature of the characters, etc., in the absence of a written dialogue. The development of the drama proceeds entirely on the basis of improvised dialogue. The performance is recorded and it is the recording that is being cataloged. (CSB 25)

Piano [violin, etc.] conductor part. A performance part for a particular instrument of an ensemble work to which cues have been added for the other instruments to permit the performer of the part also to conduct the performance. (CSB 33)

Piano score: "can be used in the physical description area only for those works which have been reduced from their original *orchestral* version to a version for piano solo. . . . this definition should be interpreted in the narrower sense of applying to "orchestra scores" but not to "large choral works." (MCB Feb. '84) "The definition of 'piano' score" in the Glossary of AACR2 clearly limits its use to reduction of orchestral (or solo instrument(s) with orchestra) scores "to a version for piano, on two staves." A concerto reduction for solo instrument and piano would thus qualify as a score . . . " (MCB July '82)

Piece: "Is a generic title frequently used by different composers . . . while "Concert piece," "Little piece," etc., are considered distinctive titles." (CSB 14)

Plate number (Music). A numbering designation assigned to a publication by a music publisher, usually printed at the bottom of each page, and sometimes appearing also on the title page. It may include initials, abbreviations, or words identifying the publisher and is sometimes followed by a number corresponding to the number of pages or plates. See also Publisher's number (Music). (CSB 33)

Plectral instruments: replaced by "plucked instruments" in the list of terms for groups of instruments in uniform titles. (25.29E) (CSB 18)

Plucked instruments: to be used instead of "plectral instrument" in the list of terms for groups in uniform titles. (25.29E) (CSB 18)

Principal Performer: "In applying the rules and these interpretations, understand 'performer' to mean a person or corporate body whose performance is heard on the sound recording. When a person performs as a member of a corporate body, do not consider him or her as a separate person to be a performer. However, do not consider a conductor or accompanist to be a member of the body he or she conducts or accompanies. Likewise, if a person's name appears in conjunction with the name of a group (e.g., "J.D. Crowe and the New South"), do not consider him or her to be a member of the group.

For recordings containing works by different composers or writers, follow the guideline below in

1. deciding whether or not there are principal performers and
2. identifying the principal performers, if any.

The use of the term 'principal performer' in 21.23C-D can lead to confusion since the term implies a performer who is more important (or, in the words of footnote 5 on p. 314, given greater prominence) than other performers. This interpretation, however, would often produce undesirable results: it would make main entry under the heading for a performer impossible under 21.23C when there is only one performer or when there are only two or three performers who are given equal prominence. To avoid this difficulty, apply the following:

When two or more performers are named in the chief source of information, consider to be principal performers those given the greatest prominence there. If all the performers named in the chief source of information are given equal prominence there, consider all of them to be principal performers.

When only one performer is named in the chief source of information, consider that performer to be a principal performer.

When no performers are named in the chief source of information, consider that there are no principal performers.

In judging relative prominence on the basis of wording, layout, and typography, consider names printed in the same size and style of lettering and in association with one another to have equal prominence. When names appear in the same size and style of lettering but in different areas of the same source of information, consider those in a location implying superiority (e.g., a higher position) to have greater prominence. Do not consider names near the beginning of a list or sequence to have greater prominence than those near the end.'' (21.23C) (CSB 25)

Publisher's number (Music). A numbering designation assigned to a publication by a music publisher, appearing normally only on the title page, the cover, and/or the first page of music. The publisher's number may include initials, abbreviations, or words identifying a publisher. See also Plate number (Music). (CSB 33)

Requiem: "Consider commonly used liturgical titles such as Requiem, Te Deu, Salve Regina, and Dixit Dominus to be generic terms. If a plural form is required, form one if possible by adding the letter -*s* to the last word of the title; if this is not convenient, consider the plural to be the same as the singular. Apply 25.29A2(a) and do not normally include a statement of medium of performance.'' (CSB 14)

Salve Regina: "Consider commonly used liturgical titles such as Requiem, Te Deu, Salve Regina, and Dixit Dominus to be generic terms. If a plural form is required, form one if possible by adding the letter -*s* to the last word of the title; if this is not convenient, consider the plural to be the same as the singular. Apply 25.29A2(a) and do not normally include a statement of medium of performance.'' (CSB 14)

Score order: For classical symphonies, the order, reading from the top of the staff to the bottom, is first woodwind, second the brass and percussion, third the strings.

Selections: If this is used in formulating a uniform title it "is added to a collective uniform title [and] add it as the last element." (CSB 20) See also this manual, page 59.

Sketches: "For sketchbooks containing sketches for various composition or miscellaneous sketches, add "Sketches" in parentheses to the appropriate collective uniform title formulated under 25.35 or 25.36." (CSB 14)

Sound recording: *See* Analog sound recording, Digital sound recording. (CSB 30:27)

String ensemble: "For an accompanying ensemble that has only one performer to a part, use an appropriate phrase for the group of instruments (e.g., "string ensemble," "wind ensemble," "instrumental ensemble") as a statement of medium that follows the statement for solo instruments in a uniform title. (CSB 11)

Te Deum: "Consider commonly used liturgical titles such as Requiem, Te Deu, Salve Regina, and Dixit Dominus to be generic terms. If a plural form is required, form one if possible by adding the letter *-s* to the last word of the title; if this is not convenient, consider the plural to be the same as the singular. Apply 25.29A2(a) and do not normally include a statement of medium of performance." (CSB 14)

Thorough bass: Use *continuo* for a thorough bass part, with or without figures, realized or unrealized, whether it is named as basso continuo, figured bass, thorough bass, or continuo. (CSB 25)

Timpani: Use this term in uniform titles. (CSB 14)

Title connected to statement of responsibility: "When a title proper begins with a separable statement of responsibility that is omitted from the uniform title (cf. 25.3B), make an additional title added entry for the title without the initial statement of responsibility." (CSB 27)

Uniform title:

1. The particular title by which a work is to be identified for cataloging purposes.
2. The particular title used to distinguish the heading for a work from the heading for a different work.
3. A conventional collective title used to collocate publications of an author, composer, or corporate body containing several works or extracts, etc., from several works, e.g., complete works, several works in a particular literary or musical form." (CSB 18)

Uniform title added entry: "Do not make title added entries for uniform titles. There may, however, be instances in which a title added entry is the same as the uniform title (e.g., of paragraph 12 above).'' (CSB 27)

Vocal score: ''This term is used for works originally for chorus and/ or one or more solo voices with accompaniment. In order for this term to be used in the physical description area for a particular manifestation of a work, the item must include the solo voice(s) (if any). In addition, if the accompaniment is originally for other than keyboard instrument it must be either arranged for keyboard instrument or omitted; if originally for keyboard instrument it must be omitted.'' (Understand ''if any'' in the definition to mean ''omitted or.'') (MCB June '81)

Voice score: A score of a work for chorus and/or voices with the accompaniment omitted. (MCB Aug. '85. Note revisions to M schedule and LCSH here.)

Violoncello. Use this term in uniform titles. (CSB 14)

Wind ensemble: ''For an accompanying ensemble that has only one performer to a part, use an appropriate phrase for the group of instruments (e.g., ''string ensemble,'' ''wind ensemble,'' ''instrumental ensemble'') as a statement of medium that follows the statement for solo instruments in a uniform title.'' (CSB 11)

Work: See explanation at rule interpretation 25.26B.

From: CSB through 34.

  MCB through Nov. 1986

  MOUG through #31

APPENDIX D
REFERENCE BOOKS USEFUL
FOR CATALOGING SOUND RECORDINGS¹

American Society of Composers, Authors and Publishers. *ASCAP Biographical Dictionary* / compiled for the Society by Jacques Cattell Press. 4th ed. New York: R.R. Bowker, 1980. (ML 106 .U3 A51 1980)

Anderson, E. Ruth. *Contemporary American Composers: A Biographical Dictionary.* 2nd ed. Boston, Mass.: G.K. Hall. 1982. (ML 390.A54 1982)

Apel, Willi. *Harvard Dictionary of Music.* 2nd ed. Cambridge, Mass.: Belknap Press, 1969. Defines musical terms. (ML 100 .A64 1969)

Audio Video Market Place. New York: Bowker, c1984- . (LB 1043 .A86)

Baker, Theodore. *Baker's Biographical Dictionary of Musicians* / rev. by Nicolas Slonimsky. 7th ed. New York: Schirmer Books, 1984. (ML 105 .B16 1984)

Basic Music Library: Essential Scores and Books/ compiled by the Music Library Association, edited by Pauline S. Bayne. Chicago: American Library Association, 1978. (ML 113 .M8845 1978)

Billboard . . . International Buyer's Guide. New York, N.Y.: Billboard Publications, 1985. The record label names are translated into company names. This is issued biennially. (ML 18 .B5 1985)

British Library. Dept. of Printed Books. *The Catalogue of Printed Music in the British Library to 1980.* London: K. G. Saur, 1981- . (ML 18 .B5)

Cataloging Service Bulletin. Washington, D.C.: Library of Congress, 1978- . Available from: Cataloging Distribution Service, Library of Congress, Washington, D.C. 20541. Cost, about $20.00/year. Source of current rule interpretations to AACR2 by the Library of Congress.

Claghorn, Charles Eugene. *Biographical Dictionary of Jazz.* Englewood Cliffs, N.Y.: Prentice-Hall, 1982. (ML 205 .C59 1982)

Cohen, Aaron I. *International Discography of Women Composers.* Westport, Conn. : Greenwood Press, 1948. (ML 156.4 .W6 C6 1984)

Cohen, Aaron I. *International Encyclopedia of Women Composers.* New York: Bowker, 1981. (ML 105 .C7 1981)

Contemporary Authors. Detroit, Mich.: Gale, 1981- . (Z 1224 .C58 E156) (PN 771 .C61)

Dictionary of Contemporary Music/ John Vinton, editor. New York: E.P. Dutton, 1974. (ML 100 .V55 1974)

Dictionnaire des interpretes et de l'interpretation musicale au XXe siecle / [edite par] Alain Paris. Paris : R. Laffont, c1982. (ML 105 .D553 1982)

Duckles, Vincent Harris. *Music Reference and Research Materials: An Annotated Bibliography*. 3rd ed. New York, N.Y.: Free Press, 1974. A basic guide to music reference books. (ML 113 .D83 1974)

Dunning, John. *Tune in Yesterday: the Ultimate Encyclopedia of Old-Time Radio, 1925-1976*. Englewood Cliffs, N.J.: Prentice-Hall, 1976. (PN 1991.3 .U6 D8)

Feather, Leonard G. *The Encyclopedia of Jazz in the Seventies*. New York: Horizon Press [1976]. (ML 105 .F36)

Feather, Leonard G. *The Encyclopedia of Jazz in the Sixties*. New York: Horizon Press [1966]. (ML 105 .F35)

Gilder, Eric. *The Dictionary of Composers and Their Music: A Listener's Companion*. New, rev. ed. North Pomfret, Vt.: David & Charles, c1985. (ML 390 .G46 1986)

Helander, Brock. *The Rock Who's Who: A Biographical Dictionary and Critical Discography* . . . New York: Schirmer Books, c1982. (ML 102 .R6 H5 1982)

Heyer, Anna Harriet. *Historical Sets, Collected Editions, and Monuments of Music: A Guide to their Contents*. 3rd ed. Chicago, Ill.: American Library Association, 1980. < Richard Smiraglia says: "Fast way to locate complete works of particular composers; useful for locating composer's original titles when no thematic index is available. > (ML 113 .H53 1980)

Hounsome, Terry. *New Rock Record*. Rev. ed. New York, N.Y.: Facts on File, 1983. (ML 102 .R6 H64 1983)

The International Cyclopedia of Music and Musicians/ edited by Oscar Thompson. 11th ed. New York: Dodd, Mead, 1985. (ML 100 .T47 1985)

International Who's Who in Music and Musician's Directory / edited by Ernest Key. 10th ed. Cambridge, England: International Who's Who in Music, 1984. (ML 106 .G7 W441 1985)

Library of Congress Rule Interpretations. Oberlin, Ohio: Oberlin College Library, 1982- . Available from: Oberlin College Library, Oberlin, Ohio 44074. Cost, about $20.00/year. Loose-leaf service, cumulating the *Cataloging Service Bulletin* segment dealing with rule interpretations to AACR2.

McCorkle, Margit L. *Johannes Brahms: thematisch-bibliographis-*

ches Werkverzeichnis. Munchen : G. Henle, c1984. (ML 134 .B8 A3 1984)

Music Cataloging Bulletin. Canton, MA: Music Library Association, 1970- . Available from: Music Library Association, P.O. Box 487, Canton, MA 02021. Cost, about $20.00/year. Monthly. Gives cataloging decisions relating to music for AACR2, additions and revisions to M classification schedule (Library of Congress classification), subject heading changes relative to musical terms and works for the Library of Congress Subject Headings, current edition, and revised LC cards relative to music, which includes sound recordings.

Music Industry Directory: Formerly the Musician's Guide. 7th ed. Chicago, Ill: Marquis Professional Publications, 1983. (ML 13 .M506 1983) Descriptive listings of organizations and councils in the U.S. and Canada; competitions, awards and grants; education, including colleges and conservatories; resources, including music libraries, periodicals and book publishers; performances, including orchestras, operas, and festivals; professionals, including editors, critics and agents; trade and industry, including recording and music publishers.

Die Musik in Geschichte und Gegenwart. Kassel: Barenreiter-Verlag, 1949-79. (ML 100 .M92)

New Grove Dictionary of American Music/ edited by H.W. Hitchcock and Stanley Sadie. London: Macmillan, 1986. 4 v. (ML 100)

New Grove Dictionary of Music and Musicians / edited by Stanley Sadie. London: Macmillan, 1980. 20 v. (ML 100 .N48 1980)

The New Schwann Record & Tape Guide. Boston, Mass.: Schwann Record & Tape Catalogs, 1949- . Monthly listing of "in print" recordings by categories, and within categories, by composer, title and often by performer. "Record and Tape Price List" gives short form of manufacturer's name, with a 'see reference' if the name is a subunit of a larger firm and should be known under the larger firm's name. Sometimes copies are available free at local record stores. Another "Books in print" for sound recordings. (ML 156.2 .S385)

Nite, Norm N. *Rock on: the Illustrated Encyclopedia of Rock'n Roll, the Modern Years.* New York: Crowell, 1978. (ML 105 .N47)

Orovio, Helio. *Diccionario de la musica cubana: biografico y tecnico.* Cuidad de la Habana: Editorial Letras Cubanas, 1981. (ML 106 .C8 076 1981)

Papakhian, Arsen R. "The Frequency of Personal Name Headings in the Indiana University Music Library Card Catalogs." *Library Resources & Technical Services* 29(July/September):173-285.

Phonolog Reports. Los Angeles, Calif.: Phonolog Publishing Division, 1948-   . Expensive loose-leaf service. Good for identifying record labels, manufacturers, distributors, etc. Lists current recording artists. Another "Books in Print" for sound recordings. Available for consultation in larger record stores.

Reese, Gustave. *Music in the Middle Ages: With an Introduction on the Music of Ancient Times*. New York: Norton, 1968. (ML 172 .R32 M8 1968)

The Rolling Stone Encyclopedia of Rock & Roll / edited by Jon Pareles and Patty Romanowski. New York, N.Y.: Rolling Stone Press/ Summit Books, 1983. (ML 156.4 .R6 H68 1983)

Shestack, Melvin. *The Country Music Encyclopedia*. New York: Crowell [1974]. (ML 102 .C7 S5)

Smiraglia, Richard P. *Cataloging Music: A Manual for Use with AACR2*. 2nd ed. Lake Crystal, Minn.: Soldier Creek Press, 1986. Available from: Box 863, Lake Crystal, Minn. 56055 Cost, about $20.00. Cataloging examples are given for sound recordings and sheet music by a music librarian active in both cataloging and music associations. (ML 111 .S63 1983)

Smiraglia, Richard P. "Theoretical Considerations in the Bibliographic Control of Music Materials in Libraries." *Cataloging & Classification Quarterly* 5(Spring 1985):1-16.

Source Readings in Korean Music. Translated by Bang-song Songs. Seoul: Korean National Commission for UNESCO, 1980. (ML 342.1 .S65)

Southern, Eileen. *Biographical Dictionary of Afro-American Musicians*. Westport, Conn.: Greenwood Press, 1982. (ML 105 .S67 1982)

Stambler, Irwin. *Encyclopedia of Folk Country, and Western Music*. Rev. ed. New York, N.Y.: St. Martin's Press, 1982. (ML 102 .F66 S7 1982)

Stambler, Irwin. *Encyclopedia of Pop, Rock, and Soul*. New York, N.Y.: St. Martin's Press, 1977. (ML 102 .P66 S8 1977)

University of California. Berkeley. *Catalog of the Opera Collections in the Music Libraries, University of California, Berkeley [and] University of California, Los Angeles*. Boston, Mass.: G.K. Hall, 1983. (ML 136 .C152 .U523 1983)

Weidow, Judy. *Music Cataloging Policy in the General Libraries*. [Austin, Tex.]: University of Texas at Austin, General Libraries, 1984. (ML 111 .W4 1984) "Manual for music catalogers containing three major sections: an outline of general principles and guidelines for original cataloging of scores and sound recordings, including references to LC policy; input standards for books, scores and sound recordings cataloged on OCLC; and an appendix describing internal policies for authority work, handling monographic sets, and other special topics." (*MCB* March 1985)

Wursten, Richard B. "Review of Proposed Revision of 780 Music." *Cataloging & Classification Quarterly*, VI (Winter 1984): 57-66. "He notes that among [Dewey 780s] are its capacity for number-building, which allows for combination of medium of performance with any form, technique or tradition of music, as well as its emphasis on folk music and other traditions of music. Among its weaknesses are the lack of examples of better-known non-Western instruments, lack of number for familiar non-Western instrumental ensembles, the citation order established for vocal music which puts vocal form last, leaving shelf arrangement by medium . . . " *Music Cataloging Bulletin* 16(December 1985):6.

The Year in Rock: 1981-1982 / edited by John Swenson. New York, N.Y.: Delilah Books, 1981. (ML 3534 .Y4 1981)

APPENDIX E
THEMATIC INDEXES
FOR CATALOGING SOUND RECORDINGS

Listing of Thematic Catalogs to About 1971

Brook, Barry. *Thematic Catalogues in Music: An Annotated Bibliography including Printed, Manuscript, and In-preparation Catalogues, Related Literature and Reviews: an Essay on Definitions, History, Functions, Historiography and Future of the Thematic Catalogue.* Hillsdale, N.Y.: Pendragaon Press, 1972. (ML 113 .B86 1972)

Addenda

Updating of Barry Brook's Listing of Thematic Catalogs

ALBINONI
   Giazotto, Remo. *Tomaso Albinoni: Musico di Violino Dilettante Veneto.* Milan: Bocca, 1945. (ML 410 .A315 G5)
BACH, CARL PHILIPP EMANUEL
   Wotquenne, Alfred. *Thematisches Verzeichnis der Werke von Carl Philipp Emanuel Bach.* Wiesbaden: Breitkopf & Hartel, 1964. (ML 134 .B08 W46 1964)
BACH, JOHANN SEBASTIAN
   Schmieder, Wolfgang. *Thematisch-systematisches Verzeichnis der Musikalischen Werke von Johann Sebastian Bach, Bach-Werke-Verzeichnis (BWV).* Leipzig: Breitkopf & Hartel, 1950. (ML 134 .B1 S3)
   Wohlfarth, Frank. *Drei meister der Tomkunst.* Hamburg: Freie Akadamie der Kunste in Hamburg, 195-? (ML 390 .W84) Wohlfarth's is not the thematic catalog for Bach, but Wohlfarth's index numbers will continue to be applied when necessary.
BACH, WILHELM FRIEDMANN
   Falck, Martin, *Wilhelm Friedmann Bach: sein Leben und seine Werke mit thematischen Verzeichnis seiner Kompositionen.* Leipzig: Kahnt, 1919. (ML 410 .B17 F2 1919)
BEETHOVEN
   Kinsky, Georg and Halm, Hans. *Das Werk Beethovens: thematisch-bibliographisches Verzeichnis seiner samtlichen vollendeten Kompositionen.* Munchen: G. Henle, 1955. (ML 134 .B4 K4)

BENDA
Lee, Douglas A. *Franz Benda (1709-1786), a Thematic Catalogue of his Works.* New York, N.Y.: Pendragon Press, 1984. (ML 134 .B442 A2 1984)

BOCCHERINI
Gerard, Yves. *Catalogue of the Works of Luigi Boccherini.* London: Oxford University Press, 1969. (ML 134 .B63 G5)

BULL
John Bull: Keyboard Music I[-II]. Edited by John Steele, Francis Cameron and Thurston Dart. 2 vols. London: Stainer and Bell, 1960-1963. (In: Musica Britannica, vols. 14 and 19.) (M 2 .M635)

BUXTEHUDE
Karstadt, Georg. *Thematisch-systematisch Verzeichnis der musikalischen Werke von Dietrich Bustehude.* Wiesbaden: Breithopf & Hartel, 1974. (ML 134 .B95 K3)

CHARPENTIER
Hitchcock, H. Wiley. "Charpentier, Marc-Antoine." In: *New Groves' Dictionary of Music and Musicians.* 1980. Vol. 4, pages. 162-176. (ML 100 .N48 1980)

CLEMENTI
Tyson, Alan. *Thematic Catalogue of the Works of Muzio Clementi.* Tutzing: Hans Schneider, 1967. (ML 134 .C585 T9)

COPERARIO
Charteris, Richard. *John Coprario, a Thematic Catalogue of his Music.* New York, N.Y.; Pendragon Press, 1977. (ML 134 .C65 A15)

CROUBELIS, SIMON DALL
The Symphony in Denmark. New York: Garland, 1983.

EYBLER
Hermann, Hildegard Luise Appelbaum. *Thematisches Verzeichnis der Werke von Joseph Eybler.* Munchen: E. Katzbichler, 1976. (ML 134 .E95 A2 1976)

FERRABOSCO, THE ELDER
Charteris, Richard. *Alfonso Ferrabosco the Elder (1543-1588): A Thematic Catalogue of his Music.* New York, N.Y.: Pendragon Press, 1984. (ML 134 .F34 A13 1984)

FREDERICK II, KING OF PRUSSIA
Spitta, Philipp. *Zur ausgabe der compositionen Friederichs des Grossen, Musikalische Werke.* Leipzig: Breitkopf & Hartel, 1890. From: *Vierteljahrschrift fur wissenschaft/* herausgegeben von Friedrich Chrysander, Philipp Spitta und Guido Alder. Leipzig: Breitkopf und Hartel, 1885-1894. 10 v. Vol. for 1890 contains this article.

GABRIELI
Kenton, Egon. *Life and Works of Giovanni Gabrieli*. [S.1.]: American Institute of Musicology, 1967. (ML 410 .G11 K4 1967)
GARCIA, JOSE MAURICIO NUNES
Mattos, Cleofe Person de. *Catalogo Tematico das Obras do Padre Jose Mauricio Nunes Garcia*. Rio de Janiero: Ministerio da Educacao e Cultura, 1970.
GASMANN
Hill, George R. *A Thematic Catalog of the Instrumental Music of Florian Leopold Gassmann*. Hackensack, N.J.; J. Boonin, 1976. (ML 134 .G2 A17)
GRIFFES
Anderson, Donna K. *The Works of Charles T. Griffes: A Descriptive Catalog*. Ann Arbor, Mich.: UMI Research Press, 1983. (ML 134 .G85 A73 1983)
HANDEL
Handel-Handbuch: Gleichzeitig Supplement zu Hallische Handel-Ausgabe (Kritische Gesamtausgabe) / hrsg. von Kuratorium der Georg-Friedrich-Handel-Stiftung von Walter Eisen u. Margaret Eisen. Kassel: Barenreiter, c1978- . (ML 134 .H16 A19 1978)
These are used for types of composition, excluding op. 2-7.
Bell, A. Craig. *Handel Chronological Thematic Catalogue*. Darley: Grain-Aig Press, 1972. (ML 134 .H16 A15) No longer used.
HAYDN
Hoboken, Anthony van. *Joseph Haydn: Thematisch-bibliographisches Werkverzeichnis*. 3 vols. Mainz: B. Schott's Sohne, 1957-1978. (ML 134 .H272 H6) v.1 Instrumental works v.2 Vocal works v.3, Index, Addenda, etc.
HINDEMITH
"Since the items in op. 11, op. 25, and op. 31 were not conceived or published as a set, and since reference sources (cf. New Grove) do not assign collective titles to these opera, treat each item of each opus as a separate work, e.g. [Sonatas, violin, piano, op. 11, no. 2, E♭], [Sonatas, viola, piano, op. 11, no. 5, F]. The result of this treatment will be advantageous in that the numerous Hindemith sonatas (except those with distinctive titles) will be arranged in one sequence according to the medium of performance." (MCB January '86)
Also see the comment in the National Authority Records.
HOFFMEISTER
Hoffmeister, Franz Anton. *Two symphonies, them. Index*. D1, G5 / Roger Hickman. In: *The Symphony, 1720-1840*. New York: Garland, 1984. Series B. vol. 5. (Folio M 1001 .H72 Op 9 No. 1 1984)

MOZART
Kochel, Ludwig Ritter von. *Chronologisch-thematisches Vrzeichniss [sic] sammtleicher Tonwerke W.A. Mozarts*. 6 Aufl. Wiesbaden: Breitkopf & Hartel, 1964. (ML 134 .M9 K55 1964)

NOVOTNY, FERENC
Somogyi, Dorottya. *The Symphony in Hungary* . . . 1984. In: *The Symphony, 1720-1840*. New York: Garland, 1984. Series B. vol. 12. (Folio M 1001 .N936 S1 1984)

PEZEL
Wienandt, Elwyn Arthur. *Johann Pezel, 1639-1694: a Thematic Catalogue of his Instrumental Works*. New York, N.Y.; Pendragon Press, 1983. (ML 134 .P618 A35 1983)

PLEYEL
Benton, Rita. *Ignace Pleyel: a Thematic Catalogue of his Compositions*. New York, N.Y.: Pendragon Press, 1977. (ML 134 .P74 A13)

PURCELL
Zimmerman, Franklin B. *Henry Purcell, 1659-1695: an Analytical catalogue of his Music*. London: Macmillan, 1963. (ML 134 .P95 Z4)

QUANTZ
Kohler, Karl-Heinz. "Die Triosante bei den Dresdener Zeitgenossen Johann Sebastian Bachs." Jena, 1956. (Thesis (doctoral) — Friedrich-Schiller-Universitat at Jena, 1956)

RACHMANINOFF
Threlfall, Robert and Norris, Geoffrey. *A Catalog of the Compositions of S. Rachmaninoff*. London: Scholar Press, 1982. (ML 134 .R12 T5 1982)

RYBA
Nemecek, Jan. *Jakub Jan Ryba: Zivot a dilo*. Praha: Statni Hudebni Vydavaltelstvi, 1963. (ML 410 .R48 N4 1963)

SCARLATTI
Kirkpatrick, Ralph. *Domenico Scarlatti*. 6th corrected printing. Princeton, N.J.: Princeton University Press, 1970. (ML 410 .S221 K5)

SCHUBERT
Deutsch, Otto Erich. *Schubert: Thematic Catalogue of All his Works in Chronological Order*. London: Dent, 1951. (ML 134 .S38 D44)

SOLER, ANTONIO, 1729-1783.
Marvin, Frederick. *Soler's Sonatas for piano*. London: 1957- .

STRAUSS, RICHARD, 1864-1949.
Muller von Asow, E.H. (Erich Hermann). *Richard Strauss, Thematisches Verzeichnis*. 1974. 3v. See: Trenner, Franz. *Richard Strauss: Werkverzeichnes*. Wien: Doblinger, c1985. Based on the above.

TARTINI
Dounias, Minos. *Die Violinkonzerte G. Tartinis*. Wolfenbuttel: Museler Verlag, 1966. (ML 410 .T18 D5 1966)

TORELLI
Giegling, Franz. *Giuseppe Torelli: ein Beitrag zur Entwicklungsgeschichte des italienischen Konzerts*. Kassel: Barenreiter, 1949. (ML 410 .T68 G5 1949)

VIOTTI
White, Chappell. *Giovanni Battista Viotti (1755-1824), A Thematic Catalogue of His Works*. New York: Pendragon Press, c1985. For thematic-index numbers used in uniform titles for instrumental works.

VIVALDI
Ryom, Peter. *Verzeichnis der Werke Antonio Vivaldis*. Kleine Ausg. Leipzig: Deutscher Verlag fur Musik, 1974. (ML 134 .V7 R954)
Ryom, Peter. *Antonio Vivaldi: Table de Concondances des Oeuvres (RV)*. Kobenhavn: Engstrom & Sodring, 1973. (ML 134 .V7 R96 1973)
Younghold, Philip. "Antonio Vivaldi: Uniform Titles for Instrumental Works." Music OCLC Users Group *Newsletter*, No. 20 (November 1983), p. 7-13.
Younghold, Philip. "Antonio Vivaldi: Uniform Titles for Instrumental Works." Music OCLC Users Group *Newsletter*, No. 31 (November 1986), p. 11-18. (Changes since the above)

VOGLER
Schafhautle, Karl Emil von. *Abt Georg Joseph Vogler*. Augsburg: M. Huttler, 1888. 1979 reprint ed. (ML 410 .V88 1979)

WAGENSEIL
Scholz-Michelitsch, Helga. *Das Klavierwerk von Georg Christoph Wagenseil: Thematischer Katalog*. Wien; Groz: Bohlau in Kommission, 1966. (ML 134 .W08 S4 1966)

WEISS
Klima, Josef. *Silvius Leopold Weiss: Kompositionen fur die Laute: Quellen-und Thermenverzeichnis*. Wien: J. Klima, 1975. (ML 134 .W44 A2 1975)

WILLIAMS

Kennedy, Michael. *A Catalogue of the Works of Ralph Vaughan Williams*. Rev. ed. London; New York: Oxford University Press, 1982. (ML 134 .V3 K4 1982)

NEW THEMATIC CATALOG LISTINGS

Music Cataloging Bulletin. Canton, MA: Music Library Association, 1970- . Available from: Music Library Association, P.O. Box 487, Canton, MA 02021. Cost, about $20.00/year.

How to Locate Information When No Thematic Catalog is Available or Establishing Titles of First Editions

Necessary Duplication from Reference Books

Anderson, E. Ruth. *Contemporary American Composers: A Biographical Dictionary*. 2nd ed. Boston, Mass.: G.K. Hall. 1982. (ML 390.A54 1982)

American Society of Composers, Authors and Publishers. *ASCAP Biographical Dictionary*/ compiled for the Society by the Jaques Cattell Press. 4th ed. New York: R.R. Bowker, 1980. (ML 106 .U3 A5 1980)

Baker, Theodore. *Baker's Biographical Dictionary of Musicians*. 7th ed. New York: Schirmer Books, 1984. (ML 105 .B16 1984)

Cohen, Aaron I. *International Encyclopedia of Women Composers*. New York: Bowker, 1981. (ML 105 .C7 1981)

Dictionary of Contemporary Music/ John Vinton, editor. New York: E.P. Dutton, 1974. (ML 100 .V55 1974)

Duckles, Vincent. *Music Reference and Research Materials: An Annotated Bibliography*. 3rd ed. New York, N.Y.: Free Press, 1974. A basic guide to music reference books. (ML 113 .D83 1974)

Feather, Leonard G. *The Encyclopedia of Jazz in the Sixties*. New York: Horizon Press [1966]. (ML 105 .F35)

Feather, Leonard G. *The Encyclopedia of Jazz in the Seventies*. New York: Horizon Press [1976]. (ML 105 .F36)

Gilder, Eric. *The Dictionary of Composers and Their Music: A Listener's Companion*. New, rev. ed. New York: Holt, Rinehart and Winston, c1985. (ML 113 .G4 1985)

Heyer, Anna Harriet. *Historical Sets, Collected Editions, and Monuments of Music: A Guide to their Contents*. 3rdc ed. Chicago, Ill.: American Library Association, 1980. < Richard Smiraglia says:

''Fast way to locate complete works of particular composers; useful for locating composer's original titles when no thematic index is available. > (ML 113 .H53 1980)

The International Cyclopedia of Music and Musicians/ edited by Oscar Thompson. 10th ed. New York: Dogg, Mead, 1975. (ML 100 .T47 1975)

New Grove Dictionary of Music and Musicians/ edited by Stanley Sadie. London: Macmillan, 1980. 20 v. (ML 100 .N48 1980)

Repertoire International des Sources Musicales. Internationales Quellenlexikon der Musik. Kassel, 1954- .

Stambler, Irwin. *Encyclopedia of Folk, Country, and Western Music*. Rev. ed. New York, N.Y.: St. Martin's Press, 1982. (ML 102 .F66 S7 1982)

Stambler, Irwin. *Encyclopedia of Pop, Rock, and Soul*. New York, N.Y.: St. Martin's Press, 1977. (ML 102 .P66 S8 1977)

COMPLETE SET OF CATALOG CARDS

This Appendix shows what the cards in a manual file will look like for a main entry with an extensive set of tracings. The following examples appear in this manual as Example 4.6.

```
Respighi, Ottorino, 1879-1936.
  [Pini di Roma]
  The pines of Rome ; The fountains of Rome
[sound recording] / Respighi. -- New York :
Columbia, c[196-?]
  1 sound disc : analog, 33 1/3 rpm, mono. ; 12
in.
    Columbia: MS 6001.                          Note Super 1
    Symphonic poems.                            Note 1
    The Philadelphia Orchestra, Eugene Ormandy, Note 6
conductor.
    1. Symphonic poems. I. Ormandy, Eugene, 1899-
     . II. Respighi, Ottorino, 1879-1936. Fontane
di Roma. III. Philadelphia Orchestra. IV. Title.
```

Example F.1. This is the Main Entry.

```
SYMPHONIC POEMS.
Respighi, Ottorino, 1879-1936.
  [Pini di Roma]
  The pines of Rome ; The fountains of Rome
[sound recording] / Respighi. -- New York :
Columbia, c[196-?]
  1 sound disc : analog, 33 1/3 rpm, mono. ; 12
in.
    Columbia: MS 6001.                          Note Super 1
    Symphonic poems.                            Note 1
    The Philadelphia Orchestra, Eugene Ormandy, Note 6
conductor.
    1. Symphonic poems. I. Ormandy, Eugene, 1899-
     . II. Respighi, Ottorino, 1879-1936. Fontane
di Roma. III. Philadelphia Orchestra. IV. Title.
```

Example F.2. This is the subject tracing.

```
  Ormandy, Eugene, 1899-        .
Respighi, Ottorino, 1879-1936.
  [Pini di Roma]
  The pines of Rome ; The fountains of Rome
[sound recording] / Respighi. -- New York :
Columbia, c[196-?]
  1 sound disc : analog, 33 1/3 rpm, mono. ; 12
in.
  Columbia: MS 6001.                            Note Super 1
  Symphonic poems.                              Note 1
  The Philadelphia Orchestra, Eugene Ormandy,   Note 6
conductor.
  1. Symphonic poems. I. Ormandy, Eugene, 1899-
  . II. Respighi, Ottorino, 1879-1936. Fontane
di Roma. III. Philadelphia Orchestra. IV. Title.
```

Example F. 3. This is the first added entry.

```
  Respighi, Ottorino, 1879-1936.
    Fontane di Roma.
Respighi, Ottorino, 1879-1936
  [Pini di Roma]
  The pines of Rome ; The fountains of Rome
[sound recording] / Respighi. -- New York :
Columbia, c[196-?]
  1 sound disc : analog, 33 1/3 rpm, mono. ; 12
in.
  Columbia: MS 6001.                            Note Super 1
  Symphonic poems.                              Note 1
  The Philadelphia Orchestra, Eugene Ormandy,   Note 6
conductor.
  1. Symphonic poems. I. Ormandy, Eugene, 1899-
  . II. Respighi, Ottorino, 1879-1936. Fontane
di Roma. III. Philadelphia Orchestra. IV. Title.
```

Example F.4. This is the second added entry.

```
  Philadelphia Orchestra.
Respighi, Ottorino, 1879-1936.
  [Pini di Roma]
  The pines of Rome ; The fountains of Rome
[sound recording] / Respighi. -- New York :
Columbia, c[196-?]
  1 sound disc : analog, 33 1/3 rpm, mono. ; 12
in.
  Columbia: MS 6001.                            Note Super 1
  Symphonic poems.                              Note 1
  The Philadelphia Orchestra, Eugene Ormandy,   Note 6
conductor.
  1. Symphonic poems. I. Ormandy, Eugene, 1899-
  . II. Respighi, Ottorino, 1879-1936. Fontane
di Roma. III. Philadelphia Orchestra. IV. Title.
```

Example F.5. This is the third added entry.

```
    The pines of Rome.
Respighi, Ottorino, 1879-1936.
  [Pini di Roma]
  The pines of Rome ; The fountains of Rome
[sound recording] / Respighi. -- New York :
Columbia, c[196-?]
  1 sound disc : analog, 33 1/3 rpm, mono. ; 12
in.
  Columbia: MS 6001.                            Note Super 1
  Symphonic poems.                              Note 1
  The Philadelphia Orchestra, Eugene Ormandy,   Note 6
conductor.
  1. Symphonic poems. I. Ormandy, Eugene, 1899-
   . II. Respighi, Ottorino, 1879-1936. Fontane
di Roma. III. Philadelphia Orchestra. IV. Title.
```

Example F. 6. The fourth and last added entry

The latest included here is from *Cataloging Service Bulletin* 34.

1.0H (CSB 25) Items with several chief sources of information

Rule change

1) In cataloging an item comprising different works and with no chief source of information pertaining to the whole item, treat the chief source of information as if they were a single source. Common examples of this situation are books containing a number of works with title pages for each (see 1.1G2) and sound discs with a different label on each side (see 6.0B1).

1.1A2 (CSB 11)

Note that the second paragraph of this rule includes a provision for transposing data to their proper positions.[1] For example, if a title proper appears following a subtitle in the source, transpose the title proper to the first position in the title and statement of responsibility area (cf. also the schemas in 1.9D). Thus, 1.1E2 is simply a further ruling to record other title information as it appears, but only *after* one has transposed the title proper according to 1.1A2. Rule 1.1F3[2] is the specific rule for transposing a statement of responsibility to its proper position if possible.

1.1B3 (CSB 15)

The following interpretation below applies to sound recordings only:

If the chief source shows the name of an author or the name of a performer before the titles of individual works and there is doubt whether the publisher, etc., intended the name to be a collective title proper or a statement of responsibility, treat the name as the title proper.[3]

Exception: If the works listed are musical compositions and the name is that of the composer of the works, treat the name as a statement of responsibility in cases of doubt.

If the chief source being followed is the label of a sound recording and the decision is to treat the name as a title proper, but one name appears on the label or one side and another name on the second side, transcribe the two names as individual titles (separated by a period-space).[4]

1.1B10 (CSB 18)

If the chief source of information bears both a collective title and the titles of individual works, give the collective title as the title proper and give the titles of the individual works in a contents note (see 1.7B18).[5]

Three notable stories
Contents: Love and peril / the Marquis of Lorne — To be or not to be / Mrs. Alexander — The melancholy hussar / Thomas Hardy.

Six Renoir drawings
Contents: La danse a la campagne — Les deux baigneuses — Pierre Renoir — Enfants jouant a la balle — Baigneuse assise — Étude d'une enfant.

1.1C (CSB 11)
For material currently cataloged by the Library of Congress, apply only the following general material designations [gmd]s:

    filmstrip
    kit
    microform
    motion picture
    slide
    sound recording
    transparency
    videorecording

Do not apply any of the options that permit specific materials designations to be shortened when they are repetitious of GMDs (e.g., 6.5B1)

1.1D2 (CSB 11)
For items issued in the United States, record all parallel titles appearing on the chief source.

1.1E5 (CSB 25)
Rule change:
1. [Add as the last sentence of the second paragraph:]
    Precede the parallel statement(s) by an equals sign.
2. [change the second example to read:]
    Variations of a Czech love song [GMD] : for piano solo and woodwind choir = pour piano soliste et ensemble de bois.
Option decision
Generally apply the optional provision of the rule.

Single Other Title Information
If there are two or more titles that are parallel but other title information for only one of them, transcribe the other title informa-

tion directly after the corresponding title, no matter the actual order in the source.

1.1F1 (CSB 13)

In determining what statement to record in a statement of responsibility, bear in mind that the objective is to record only those statements that are of bibliographic significance — significant from the point of view of the intellectual and artistic content of an item. (In many cases such names are also likely candidates to be searched under in a catalog when looking for the particular item with which they are associated.)

Guidelines for Recording Statement of Responsibility

To achieve the objective stated above, observe the following guidelines:

Include in statements of responsibility the names of those whose contributions are judged to be of bibliographic significance if such names appear prominently. Judge bibliographic significance as follows:

a) *Editors*. Bibliographic significance in this context encompasses that portion of the definition of the term editor in the glossary stating that the editorial labor includes " . . . revision (restitution) of elucidation of the text, and the addition of an introduction, notes, and other crucial matter."

Human walking / Verne T. Inman, Henry J. Ralston, Frank Todd ; edited with a preface by Jean C. Liberman

Cross-country skiing : racing techniques and training tips / by Sigi Maier and Toni Reiter ; translated by Mark Goldman ; edited by Don A. Metivier.

Excluded from this category, and therefore not candidates for transcription, are credits for "in-house" editors, editorial supervisors, publications editors, managing editors, photo-editors, sponsoring editors, and the like.

b) *Others*. Bibliographic significance in this context equates to the definition of statement of responsibility in the glossary, namely " . . . persons responsible for the intellectual or artistic content of the item . . . or performance of the content of the item." *Excluded* from this category, and therefore not candidates for transcription, are statements of technical credits, often performed by in-house staff and members of publishing firms, such as

> book designer
> consultant

cover and page designer
cover artist
cover designer
cover photographer
designer
graphic designer
layout designer
page make-up
production manager
. . . . other material omitted.

1.1G1 (CSB 11)

Most such titles should be recorded as they appear (cf. "Le prince" example in 1.1G2). Generally restrict the application of this rule to cases in which the secondary titles do not appear in the same source as the predominant title.

1.1G2 (CSB 25)

Rule change:

If, in an item lacking a collective title, no one part predominates, either describe the item as a unit or make a separate description for each separately titled part, linking the separate description with a note (see 1.7B21).

If describing the item as a unit, record the titles of the individually titled parts in the order in which they are named in the chief source of information or in the order in which they appear in the item if there is no single chief source of information. Separate the titles of the parts by semicolons if the parts are all by the same person(s) or emanate from the same body (bodies), even if the titles are linked by a connecting word or phrase. If the individual parts are by different persons or emanate from different bodies, or in case of doubt, follow the title of each part by its responsibility, and full stop followed by two spaces.

Clock symphony : no. 101 ; Surprise symphony : no. 94 [gmd] / Haydn[7]

Lord Macaulay's essays ; and, Lays of ancient Rome [gmd]

Saudades do Brasil : suite de danses pour orchestre / Darius Milhaud. Symphonie concertante pour trompette et orchestre / Henry Barraud [gmd][8]

Le prince / Machiavel. Suivi de L'anti-Machiavel de Frederic II [gmd]

(at head of title: Machiavel)

(Title: Le prince, suivi de L'anti-Machiavel de Frederic II)

As instructed in 1.0H, treat multiple sources of information as if they were one source.

Punctuation

The final sentence of this rule specifies that two spaces are to follow a period. Instead, see the rule interpretation for 1.0C and apply that, which means following the period with *one* space.

Multiple Sources

If there is no single chief source of information for a single part item and it is not possible to say which work is first, second, etc., transcribe them in English alphabetical order.

For materials such as books that normally confine the source for the title and statement of responsibility to one location within the item, make a note to explain the situation when there is no single chief source for the single part item (e.g . . . , "no collective t.p. Titles transcribed from individual title pages.").

Other Title Information

If a single statement of other title information applies to all the titles listed, record it after all the titles if all the titles are by the same person(s) or body (bodies). Precede the statement by a space-colon-space. Otherwise, record it in a note.

source: Party party // Girl friends // two short novels by // Ronni Sandroff

title . . . area: Party party ; Girlfriends : two short novels / by Ronni Sandroff

source: Henry Esmond // Thackeray // Bleak House // Dickens // Two novels

title . . . area: Henry Esmond / Thackeray. Bleak house / Dickens.

note area: "Two novels."

Statements of Responsibility

If a single *subsequent* statement of responsibility applies to all the titles listed, record it after the final *first* statement of responsibility if possible. Precede the subsequent statement by a space-semicolon-space.

History of the elementary school contest in England / Francis Adams. The struggle for national education / John Morley ; [both] edited, with an introduction, by Asa Briggs

1.4B1 (CSB 33)

Rule change

For unpublished materials, see 1.4C8 and 1.4D8.

1.4C3 (CSB 23)

If a place of publication and the name of its larger jurisdiction(s) (e.g., country, state, or similar designation) appear together in the sources from which they are being transcribed (e.g., title page, cover, etc.), transcribe all that appear. Do this even if the place does not need to be identified or is clearly the best known one of that name.

source: New York, New York
transcription: New York, N.Y.

source: Washington, D.C.
transcription: Washington, D.C.

source: Taipei, Taiwan, China
transcription: Taipei, Taiwan, China

If a place of publication and the name of its larger jurisdiction do not appear together, add the name of the larger jurisdiction whenever the place is definitely obscure. Also add the name of the larger jurisdiction when there is more than one place of the same name and the one in the item being cataloged is not the best known. Give the appropriate qualifier according to the provisions of chapter 23. (*Note*: Make a quick judgment in the matter of adding the name of the larger jurisdiction; in any case of doubt, do not add the name. Also, do not attempt any consistency in the transcription of the same place in the publication, etc., area from one record to another.)

source: Cambridge
transcription: Cambridge [Cambridgeshire]

source: Feldkirchen
transcription: Feldkirchen [Austria]

1.4C7 (CSB 15)

Give the address of a publisher, etc., following the name of the place of publication, etc., only for a monograph cataloged according to chapter 2 or chapter 5[9] that meets these three conditions:

    a. it was issued by a U.S. publisher, distributor, etc., whose address is given in the item being cataloged;

    b. it was issued in the current three years;

    c. it does not bear an ISBN or ISSN.

Do not apply 1.4C7 if two or more publishers, distributors, etc., are being recorded in the publication, etc., area. *Exception*: If one of the entities is a U.S. distributor for a monograph published outside the U.S., give the address of the U.S. distributor if the item meets these four conditions:

    a. the U.S. distributor is the only entity being recorded with the distributor's place of publication;

    b. the U.S. distributor's address is given in the item;

c. the item was issued in the current three years;

d. the item lacks an ISBN or ISSN.

Apply 1.4C7 also to items in which the name of the publishers, distributor, etc., is unknown and the name of the U.S. manufacturer is being given in the publication, etc., area (1.4G1) if the monograph meets these three conditions:

a. the manufacturer's address is given in the item;

b. the item was issued in the current three years;

c. the item lacks an ISBN or ISSN.

When applying 1.4C7, routinely repeat the name of the city in the address. For street addresses, abbreviate such words as "street," "avenue," "place," etc., according to normal usage. Omit unnecessary elements from the address (e.g., the name of the building when the street address or post office box is given). Do not bracket any of the elements given in the address.

1.4C8 (CSB 33)

Rule change

Do not record a place of publication, distribution, etc., for unpublished items (manuscripts, art originals, naturally occurring objects that have not been packaged for commercial distribution, unedited or unpublished film or video materials, stock shots, non-processed sound recordings, etc.). Do not record a place of publication, distribution, etc., for unpublished collections (including those containing published items but not published as collections). Do not record s.l. in either case.

1.4D1 (CSB 25) Name of publisher, distributor, etc.

Publisher not named

For an item that does not name a publisher in imprint position but a corporate body is named at the head of title, regard the corporate body named at the head of title as the publisher. Transpose its name to publisher position in the publication, etc., area unless the item contains information indicating that the corporate body is not the publisher or casting doubt on this assumption. (If the body has been recorded in the title and statement of responsibility area, apply 1.4D2).

If the item does not name a publisher, in the absence of evidence to the contrary, assume that the copyright holder named in the copyright statement is the publisher if it is a corporate body known as a publishing entity. Consider other corporate bodies as well as persons named only as copyright holders as publishers only if the particular case makes the inference very plausible. When recording, as publisher, an entity that is named only in a copyright statement, do not bracket the name if the copyright statement appears in a prescribed source for the publication, etc., area.

Government Printers

When a government printer or government printing office is named on the item and there is no evidence that its functions are not that of a publisher or distributor, record it as the publisher. If, however, another body also appears on the item and the government printing office is named only in a less prominent position unaccompanied by a statement of printing or distribution, the likelihood is greater that it functions as a printer and that the body is the publisher.

University Presses

Consider university presses as publishers unless there is clear evidence to the contrary.

Privately Printed Works

For cataloging purposes, treat privately printed works as published works even if they have been distributed only to a very limited group (e.g., a keepsake for dinner guests or a Christmas greeting for friends). Treat the person or body issuing the item, whether a commercial publisher, a private press, or a person or group for whom it may have been printed, as the publisher. If it is stated in the item that it has been privately printed, this fact may be expressed in a note, usually quoted. (*Note*: Private presses should be considered publishers of the items they print if there is no evidence to the contrary in the item or in reference sources consulted.)

1.4D2 (CSB 34)

Rule change

If the shortest form of the name of the publisher, distributor, etc., is in more than one language or script, record the form that is in the language or script of the title proper. If this criterion does not apply, record the shortest form in the language or script that appears first.

Optionally, give the shortest form in each language or script. Precede each parallel statement by an equals sign. If the shortest form is the same in all languages or scripts, give it only once.

> : Editions du peuple = Commoner's Pub.
>
> : Host

NOT: Host & Sons Forlag - Host & Son Publisher

Option Decision

Do not apply the optional provision of the rule.

Omissions

When the name of a publisher, etc., is part of a hierarchy, for commercial publishers only omit parts of the hierarchy that are not needed to identify the publishing entity.

source: National Archives & Records Service // General Services Administration
transcription: National Archives & Records Service, General Services Administration

source: Lexington Books // D.C. Heath
transcription: Lexington Books

Terms of Incorporation, etc.

If "Inc.," "Ltd." etc., appear after a serial title being recorded as a publisher, etc., retain it. Also retain these elements when they follow foreign words/names that the cataloger is unable to interpret sufficiently.

1.4D8 (CSB 33)

Rule change

Do not record the name of a publisher, distributor, etc., for unpublished items (manuscripts, art originals, naturally occurring objects that have not been packaged for commercial distribution, unedited or unpublished film or video materials, stock shots, nonprocessed sound recordings, etc.). Do not record the name of a publisher, distributor, etc., for unpublished collections (including those containing published items but not published as collections). Do not record s.n. in either case.

1.4F1 (CSB 33)

Rule change

1. [Revise the first sentence to read:]
    For published items, give the date of publication, distribution, etc., of the edition named in the edition area.

2. [Add as a new paragraph following the examples:]
    For unpublished items, see 1.4F9. For unpublished collections, see 1.4F10.

1.4F5 (CSB 25) Date of publication, distribution, etc.

Rule change

The Joint Steering Committee for Revision of AACR has approved the following addition as a second example in rule 1.4F5 in the printed text of AACR2:

[1980, p1975

Optional Decision

Apply the optional rule whenever the copyright date of the *whole* item is different from the date of publication, etc. Ignore a copyright date that applies to only part of the item (e.g., only the prefactory material; some but not all the works in the collection). Nevertheless, for works of mixed responsibility (i.e., situations covered by 21.8), with copyright dates only for the separate contribution (or for only some of the contributions), treat these copyright dates as applying to the whole item for the purpose of applying 1.4F5 and 1.4F6. If the dates vary, consider the latest date to apply to the whole item.

If a copyright date is being recorded, transcribe copyright dates other than a phonogram copyright date preceded by a lowercase "c"; transcribe the phonogram copyright date preceded by a lowercase "p."

1.4F9 (CSB 33)

Rule change

Do not record a date for naturally occurring objects that have not been packaged for commercial distribution. For other unpublished items (manuscripts, art originals, unedited or unpublished film or video materials, stock shots, nonprocessed sound recordings, etc.), record the date of production (creation, inscription, manufacture, recording, etc.).

1.4F10 (CSB 33)

Rule change

Record the date or inclusive dates of unpublished collections (including those containing published items but not published as collections).

1.5B1 (CSB 25)

Rule change

[. . . add the following examples]

25 identical maps

50 identical sets of 10 slides

1.5B4 (CSB 33)

Rule change

If the item being described has a playing time, give that playing time as follows:

a. if the playing time is stated on the item, give the playing time as stated.

1 sound cassette (40 min.)

1 film loop (3 min., 23 sec.)

2 sound discs (1 hr., 30 min.)

b. optionally, if the playing time is neither stated on the item nor is readily ascertainable, give an approximate time.

1 piano roll (ca. 7 min.)

2 film reels (ca. 90 min.)

c. optionally, if the parts of a multipart item have a stated uniform playing time or an approximate uniform playing time, give the playing time of each part as stated followed by the word each. Otherwise, give the total duration.

31 sound cassettes (60 min. each)
11 sound cassettes (ca. 30 min. each)
2 videoreels (Ampex 7003) (50 min.)
Option decisions
The Library of Congress does not apply the first option. The second option is applied on a case-by-case basis.
1.5C1 (CSB 30)
[Change 4th example to:]
1 sound disc (20 min.) : analog, 33 1/3 rpm, mono.
1.5D1 (CSB 30)
[Change 4th example to:]
1 sound disc (56 min.) : digital, stereo. ; 4 3/4 in.
1.5D2 (CSB 33)
Rule change
Optionally, if the item is in a container, name the container and give its dimensions after the dimensions of the item or as the only dimensions.

12 paperweights : glass ; each 12 cm. diameter in box, 40 × 50 × 8 cm.

1 stone : malachite ; in box, 12 × 9 × 18 cm.

Option decision
Apply the option on a case-by-case basis.
1.5E1 (CSB 29) Accompanying material
1. Usually make a separate entry for material that either is not issued at the same time as the main work or shows an important difference in titles or statements of responsibility from those appearing in the main work.
2. Do not apply multilevel description to any item.
3. Generally record in a note material of the following types:
   a. The item is clearly of little bibliographic importance.
   b. Although the item might be eligible for method 4), it is best described by a less general terminology than that used under method 4).
   c. The item is best mentioned in a note because the title on the item is more a description than a true title.
4. Generally record material at the end of the physical description when the item satisfies all the *following conditions*:
   a. It is issued at the same time and by the same publisher as the main work and essentially is of use only in conjunction with the main work.
   b. It is by the same author as the main work or makes no mention of an author or, if it is by a different author, the name of

the work makes unnecessary any note or added entry for this different author.

c. The title is a general term (e.g., "teacher's manual") or is otherwise dependent on the title of the main work or lacks a title (e.g., "plates"). (When recording material at the end of the physical description, always use a generic term in English.)

Catalog separately all supplements, etc., to serials except for indexes that may be noted (according to 12.7B17) or supplements, etc., that may be noted informally according to method c). *EXCEPTION*: Describe in a note supplements that are usable only in conjunction with the main work.

Apply the optional provision of the rule on a case-by-case basis.

1.7A3 (CSB 22) Forms of notes

When nonroman data (including quotations) are being recorded in the note area, give them in romanized form in all cases, including those cards that contain nonromanized elements in the body of the entry.

When a note begins with a formal introductory term such as "contents," "credits," or "summary," do not use all caps in any case; instead, use upper and lower case as illustrated in AACR2.

1.7A4 (CSB 22) Notes citing other editions and works

Rule change

Notes relating to items reproduced. In describing an item which is a reproduction of another (e.g., a text reproduced in microform; a manuscript reproduced in book form; a set of maps reproduced as slides), give the notes relating to the reproduction and then the notes relating to the original. Combine the notes relating to the original in one note, giving the details in the order of the areas to which they relate.

Form of citation

In citing a serial in a note on bibliographic record for a serial, apply LCRI 12.7B. In other situations, when citing another work or another manifestation of the same work, in general give the uniform title for the work if one has been assigned to it. Otherwise, give its title proper.

Translation of: Odyssey.

not Translation of: Odysseia.

If the work being cited is entered under a name heading that differs from the main entry heading on the work being cataloged and the difference is not apparent from information given in the body of the entry, add the name after the title (uniform title or title proper). Use the name in the form that appears in whatever source is at hand. (For personal names, approximate the form required by 22.1-22.3 if there is no such source at hand or if the form in the source at hand is unsatisfactory for any reason.) Separate the name from the title by a space-slash-space.

Adaptation of: Kipps / H.G. Wells.

Rev. ed. of: Guide to reference books / Constance M. Winchell. 8th ed. 1967.

Continues: General catalouge of printed books. Five year supplement, 1966-1970 / British Museum.

Notes citing other editions and works

When a revised edition (other than a revised translation, cf. 25.2B) of a work is being cataloged and

1. it has a different title from that of the previous edition or,
2. it has a different choice of entry from that of the previous edition (for reasons other than the change to AACR2), e.g., 21.12B,

link the new edition with the immediately preceding edition by using AACR2 style for connecting notes on both AACR2 and non-AACR2 records.

. . . . .additional material omitted from 1.7A4.

1.7B2 (CSB 30)

Generally restrict the making of language and script notes to the situations covered in this directive.[10] (*Note*: In this statement, "language" and "language of the item" mean the language or languages of the content of the item (e.g., for books, the language of the text; "title data" means title proper and other title information.)

If the language of the item is not clear from the transcription of the title data, make a note naming the language whether or not the language is named after a uniform title. Use "and" in all cases to link two languages (or the final two when more than two are named). If more than one language is named, give the predominant language first if readily apparent; name the other languages in alphabetical order. If a predominant language is not apparent, name the languages in alphabetical order. For the form of the name of the language, follow *Library of Congress Subject Headings*. (*Exception*: Use "Greek" for classical Greek and modern Greek. If, however, the item is a translation from classical Greek into modern Greek, use "Modern Greek" in the note. If the item includes text in both, use "Classical Greek" and "Modern Greek" in the note.)

For some "dialects" that cannot be established as subject headings, a specific language will be used in the note area only. (See LCRI 25.5D for the use of language names in uniform titles.)

Articles chiefly in French; one article each in English and Italian.

Arabic and English.

Text in Coptic and French; notes in French.

. . . . additional material from 1.7B2 omitted.

1.7B4 (CSB 22) Variations in title

A note may be essential to show a variation from the chief source title appearing elsewhere in the item. Although the source may contain more than one title, record in a note only the needed variant title, not titles already given in the description. (Always include in a note the source of the variant.)

. . . . additional material from 1.7B4 omitted.

1.7B6 (CSB 14)

In general, when recording a name in a statement of responsibility in a note, give the name in the form it appears in whatever source is at hand. If there is no such source, or if the form in the source is unsatisfactory for any reason, approximate the form required by 22.1-22.3 (for personal names) or 24.1-24.3 (for corporate names).

Do not routinely record in a note the name of the person or body chosen as the main entry heading if the name does not appear in the body of the entry or the note area for another reason.

1.7B16 (CSB 12)

When formulating a note under this rule, introduce the note with "Issued also . . . " (e.g., "Issued also as . . . ," "Issued also in . . . ," "Issued also on . . . ").

1.7B 20 (CSB 12)

For monographs, routinely make notes on any special features or imperfections of the copy being described. Carefully distinguish such copy-specific notes from other kinds of notes that record information valid for all copies of an edition, introducing the copy-specific notes with the phrase "LC copy . . . ," "LC set . . . ," or "LC has . . . : as appropriate.

LC copy imperfect; all after leaf 44 wanting.

LC set incomplete: v. 12 wanting.

LC set lacks slides 7-9.

LC has v. 2, 3-5, and 7 only.

LC has no. 20, signed by author.

LC has no. 145.

1.7B21 (CSB 22) "With" notes

The "with" note is appropriate *only* in the following case: two or more works issued independently have been subsequently placed together under one cover or comparable packaging. For two or more works that have been issued together in one cover or other packaging, create one bibliographic record, applying either 1.1G or 1.10.

For each item listed in a "with" note, give the title proper (or uniform title if one has been assigned), the statement of responsibility, and the entire publication, distribution, etc., area. If there are more than two works, cite all the other works in the record for the first work; in the records for succeeding works, cite only the first work. Use ISBD punctuation, except omit the period-space-dash-space between areas.

> With: The Bostonian Ebenezer. Boston : Printed by B. Green & J. Allen, for Samuel Phillips, 1698 – The cure of sorrow. Boston : Printed by B. Green, 1709. Bound together subsequent to publication.

If the works are too numerous to be listed in the "With" note, make an informal note such as the following:

> No. 3 in a vol. with binder's title: Brownist tracts, 1599-1644.

1.7B22 (CSB 18) Combined notes (see 1.7A4) relating to the original
Rule change

> Facsim. of: A classification and subject index for cataloguing and arranging the books and pamphlets of a library. Amherst, Mass. : [s.n.], 1976 (Hartford, Conn. : Case, Lockwood & Brainard). 44 p. ; 25 cm.

1.10B (CSB 30)

> [Change 2nd example to:]
> 3 v. : ill. 30 cm.
> *Note*: Sound disc (12 min. : analog, 45 rpm, mono. ; 7 in.) in pocket at end of v.3

1.10C2 option b) (CSB 30)

> [Change physical description in 2nd example to:]
> 1 sound cassette (15 min.) : analog, mono.

2.5E1. (CSB 30)

> [Change 3rd example to:]
> 27 p. : ill. ; 21 cm. + 1 sound disc (25 min. : analog, 33 1/3 rpm, mono. ; 12 in.)

5.1B1 (CSB 26)
Rule change

> 5.1B1. Record the title proper as instructed in 1.1B. If a title con-

sists of the name(s) of one or more types of composition[11] and one or more of the following statements — medium of performance, key, date of composition, and/number — record those elements as the title proper.[12]

> Rhapsody
> Songs & folk music
> Violin-Sonaten 1, 2, 3
> String quartet 5
> Sonate en re majeur, opus 3, pour violin
> Scherzo for two pianos, four hands
> Symphony no. 3, A major, opus 56
> String quintet no. 2, A major, op. 18
> Zwei Praeludien und Fugen fur Orgel, op. posth. 7
> Musik fur Saiteninstrumente, Schlagzeug und Celesta
> Duoa piese pentru Orchestra
> Prelude and fugue in A minor
> Sinfonia I (1970)
> VIII. Symphonie c-Moll

In all other cases, [13] treat statements of medium of performance, key, date of composition, and number as other title information (see 5.1E).

> Die Meistersinger von Nurnberg
> Sinfonia mazedonia
> Little suite
> Easter fresco
> Georgia moon
> Gigi
> 3 D.H. Lawrence love poems
> Hymne a la joie
> Charles Aznavour presente ses plus grands succes
> The vocal score and libretto of The merry widow
> The Beatles song book
> 1952 electronic tape music

In case of doubt,[14] treat statements of medium of performance, key, date of composition, and number as part of the title proper.

Serial Numbers

Transcribe as part of the title proper a serial number (whether it appears as arabic or roman numerals or spelled out) which appears in conjunction with the title but without the designation "no." or its equivalent, regardless of the nature of the title.

> Antiphony II : variations on a theme of Cavafy

NOT Antiphony : II : variations on a theme of Cavafy.[15]

Multiple parallel data

When succeeding statements of key, etc., are broken up in the source rather than grouped together by language, transcribe the statements so that all elements in one language are together. Treat the first group of elements in one language as part of the title proper and precede each one after the first by an equals sign. Thus,

Concerto
D-Dur/D Major/Re Majeur

fur Horn und Orchester
for Horn and Orchestra
pour Cor et Orchestre

would then be transcribed as

Concerto, D-Dur, fur Horn und Orchester = D major, for horn and orchestra = re majeur, pour cor et orchestre

(Record all the parallel elements; do not apply the provisions for omission in 1.1D2.)

Adopt the following solutions for data that are other title information or statements or responsibility and that are only *partially* repeated from language to language. For such a problem with a statement of responsibility, rule 1.1F11 provides a solution in the second paragraph ("If it is not practicable . . . ") by saying to give the statement that matches the language of the title proper and to omit the other statement(s).

. . . [Czech title proper] Revidoval — Revidiert von Antonin Myslik

. . . / revidoval Antonin Myslik

There is no comparable "If it is not practicable . . . " provision in the rule for other title information, yet the same difficulty of transcription arises with *partial* repetition of other title information. Nonetheless apply the same idea to other title information.

Sonata a velocita pazzesca
per   for
cembalo

The transcription would be

Sonata a velocita pazzesca : per cembalo

If no real match in languages is possible, then give the first of the language forms, matching at least the other title information with the statement of responsibility if possible.

Chief source

Gregor Joseph Werner
Concerto per la camera a 4
fur   for
Violincello & Piano
Herausgegeben und bearbeitet von Edited and arranged by
Richard Moder

Transcription

Concerto per la camera a 4 : fur Violoncello & Piano / Gregor Joseph Werner ; herausgegeben und bearbeitet von Richard Moder

5.1D1 (CSB 25)

Rule change

If the title proper includes statements of medium of performance, key, date of composition, and/or number (see 5.1B1) in two or more languages or scripts, record these elements in the order in which they appear in the chief source of information, preceding each parallel set of statements by an equals sign.[16]

> Konzert Nr. 1 fur Klarinette und Orchester, Es-Dur [GMD] = E^b -major = mi^b -majeur

> Sonata a 3, en mi mineur, pour 2 violons our hautbois (flutes) et basse continue [GMD] = e-Moll, fur 2 Violinen oder Oboen (Floten) und Generalbass = in E. minor, for 2 violins or oboes (flutes and thorough-bass)

5.2B4 (CSB 34)

Rule change

Optionally, give the parallel statements, each preceded by an equals sign.

Option Decision

Do not apply the optional provision of the rule.

5.4F1 (CSB 33)

Rule change

Record the date of publication, distribution, etc., of a published music item as instructed in 1.4F.

5.5E1 (CSB 30)

[Change 2nd example to:]

1 score (vii, 32 p.) ; 28 cm. + 1 sound tape reel (60 min. : analog, 7 1/2 ips, mono. ; 7 in., 1/2 in. tape)

6.0B1 (MCB February '86)

For sound recordings containing two works of the same type by one composer without a collective title on the label(s), do not consider as a collective title a title on the container or accompanying material that is made up of the name of the type plus one or more of the following identifying elements for the two works: serial number, opus number, thematic index number, key.

On container:

Piano concertos no. 25, K. 503, no. 26, K. 537

Do not transcribe as collective title

On container:

Sonatas no. 4, op. 7, and no. 11, op 22

Do not transcribe as collective title

On container:

Symphonies nos. 88 and 104 (London)

Do not transcribe as collective title

BUT: *On container*:

The violin concertos / Serge Prokofiev

Transcribe as collective title

On container:

Les deux sonates pour violoncelle et piano

Transcribe as collective title

On container:

Ballets / Igor Stravinsky

(Contains Apollo and Orpheus)

Transcribe as collective title

6.1B1 (CSB 33)

Rule change

1. [Substitute the following as the second sentence:] For data to be included in titles proper for music items, see 5.1B1.
2. [Add as the last examples:]

    [Address to high school students, discussing good writing]

    [Recording of W.B. Yeats reading "The lake isle of Innisfree"]

6. 1G2 (CSB)

Rule change

[Add the following as the last example in rule 6.1G2]

Dreamboat / Linzer ; [performed by] Limmie & Family Cookin'. Made in heaven / Levine, Russell Brown ; [performed by] Limmie & Family Cookin' [GMD]

Label side A: Dreamboat

(Linzer)

Limmie & Family Cookin'

Label side B: Made in heaven

(Levine-Russell Brown)

Limmie & Family Cookin'

6.4C (CSB 13)

Apply the option stated in 1.4C7 for adding the full address of a publisher, distributor.

6.4C1 (CSB 33)

Rule change

[Revision of first sentence]

Record the place of publication, distribution, etc., of a published sound recording as instructed in 1.4C.

6.4C2 (CSB 33)

Do not record a place of publication, distribution, etc., for a non-processed sound recording.[17]

6.4D4 (CSB 33)

Rule change

Do not record the name of a publisher, distributor, etc., for non-processed sound recordings.

6.4F2 (CSB 33)

Rule change

If the date of recording appears on a published sound recording, give it in a note.

6.4F3 (CSB 33)

Rule change

Give the date of recording of a nonprocessed sound recording as instructed in 4.4B1.[18]

6.5B1 (MCB December '83)

For multipart items, give only the number of physical units (e.g., discs) in the physical description area. If the number of containers or discographic units (often called "volumes") differs from the number of physical units, give this information in notes (cf. CD 6.7B10, CD 6.7B18).[19]

6.5B2 (CSB 33)

Rule change

Record the playing time of the item as instructed in 1.5B4.

1 sound disc (50 min.)

1 sound tape reel (ca. 90 min.)

3 sound cassettes (4o min. each)

Interpretation

When the total playing time of a sound recording is not stated on the item but the durations of its parts (sides, individual works, etc.) are, if desired add the stated durations together and record the total, rounding off to the next minute if the total exceeds 5 minutes.

Precede a statement of duration by "ca." only if the statement is given on the item in terms of an approximation. Do not add "ca." to a duration arrived at by adding partial durations or by rounding off seconds.

If no durations are stated on the item or if the durations of some but not all the parts of a work are stated, do not give a statement of duration. Do not approximate durations from the number of sides of a disc, type of cassette, etc.

6.5C1 (CSB 30)
[Alter the 1st, 3rd, and 5th details to:]
  type of recording
  groove characteristics (analog discs)
  number of tracks (tapes)
6.5C2[20] (CSB 30)
[Delete and substitute:]
Type of recording. Give, for a disc or tape, the type of recording, i.e., the way in which the sound is encoded on the item being cataloged.
  1 sound disc (45 min.) : analog
  1 sound disc (56 min.) : digital
  1 sound cassette (90 min.) : analog
Give, for a sound track film, the type of recording (either *optical* or *magnetic*) or the name of a unique recording system (e.g., *Phillips-Miller*).
  1 sound track film reel (10 min.) : magnetic
  1 sound track film reel (15 min.) : Phillips-Miller
6.5C3 (CSB 30)
[Change 1st paragraph and example to:]
Playing speed. Give the playing speed of an analog disc in revolutions per minute (rpm).
  1 sound disc (45 min.) : analog, 33 1/3 rpm
[Add, as 2nd paragraph]
Give the playing speed of a digital disc in metres per second (m. per sec.) if it is other than 1.4 metres per second.
[Change 2nd example to:]
  1 sound tape reel (16 min.) : analog, 7 1/2 ips
Do not give the playing speed if it is standard for the item (e.g., 1-7/8 inches per second for a tape cassette).
  1 sound cassette (120 min.) : analog, 15/16 ips, mono.
6.5C4 (CSB 30)
[Change "a disc" to "an analog disc," and change example to:]
  1 sound disc (7 min.) : analog, 78 rpm, microgroove

6.5C7 (CSB 33) Number of sound channels.
  Rule change
     1. [Replace the first sentence with the following:]
        Give the number of sound channels, if the information is readily available, using one or more of the following terms as appropriate:
          mono.
          stereo.
          quad.
     2. [Add to the examples:]
        2 sound discs (66 min.) : 33 1/3 rpm, mono., stereo.[21]
6.5C8 (CSB 30)
  [Change example to:]
     1 sound cassette (60 min.) : analog, stereo., Dolby processed
6.5D2. (CSB 30)
  [Delete example and substitute:]
     1 sound disc (20 min.) : analog, 33 1/3 rpm, stereo. ; 12 in.
6.5D5 (CSB 30)
  [Change example to:]
     1 sound cassette (85 min.) : analog, 3 3/4 ips, mono. ; 7 1/4 × 3 1/2 in, 1/4 in. tape
6.5D6 (CSB 30)
  [Change example to:]
     1 sound tape reel (60 min.) : analog, 7 1/2 ips, mono. ; 7 in., 1/2 in. tape
6.5E1 (CSB 30)
  [Change example to:]
     1 sound disc (50 min.) : analog, 33 1/3 rpm, stereo ; 12 in. + 1 pamphlet (11 p. : col. ill. ; 32 cm.)
6.7B10 (CSB 30)
  [Add, between "all" and "discs" in the 3rd line, "analog" and add to the examples under *"Discs"*:]
     Compact disc
     Analog recording
        (For a digital disc made from an analog original)
     Digital recording
        (For an analog disc made from a digital original)
  [Add to the example under *Tape*:]
     Digital record
        (For an analog tape made from a digital original)

6.7B7 (CSB 33) Edition and history
Rule change
[Add as the second paragraph and example:]
For nonprocessed sound recordings, give the available details of the event.

Recording of speech given at the University of Kentucky Academic Library Institute, Lexington, Ky., May 24, 1984.

6.7B18 (MCB December'83)
For multipart items, when the number of discographic units (often called "volumes" by publishers) differs from the number of physical units (e.g., discs) or containers, include when necessary the number of physical units or containers in the contents note (cf. RI 2.7B18(3)(6b)).[22]

Contents: 1. Vom 6. Sonntag bis zum 17. Sonntag nach Trinitatis (6 discs) — 2. Vom 18. bis zum 27. Sonntag nach Trinitatis (6 discs) . . .

6.11 (CSB 33) Nonprocessed sound recordings
Rule change
[Delete this rule. Its provisions are now covered by rules 6.1B1, 6.4C2, 6.4D4, 6.4F3, and 6.7B7.]

8.5E1 (CSB 30)
[change 2nd example to:]
40 slides : col. + 1 sound disc (30 min. : analog, 33 1/3 rpm, mono. ; 12 in.

10.5E1 (CSB 30)
[Change 2nd example to:]
1 hand puppet : red and blue ; 20 cm. long + 1 sound disc (20 min. : analog, 33 1/3 rpm, mono. ; 12 in.)

13.5A (CSB 30)
[Change first part of 6th example to:]
Bob Wills and his Texas Playboys [gmd]. — side 4 of 2 sound discs (ca. 17 min.) : analog, 33 1/3 rpm, stereo. ; 12 in.

13.5 (CSB)
[Change first part of 7th example to:]
Nonbook materials (NBM) [gmd] / Ronald Hagler. — on side B of tape 2 of 3 sound cassettes : analog, mono.

13.5A (CSB 30)
[Change first part of 2nd example to:]
American folklore [gmd] / co-ordinated for the Voice of America by Tristram Coffin. — Washington : United States Information Agency [production company] — sound tape reels : analog, 7 1/2 ips, mono. ; 7 in. — (Forum series)

21.7B (CSB 25) Category E Performing group

This category emphasizes that the responsibility of a performing group must go beyond "mere performance, execution, etc." This means that the group must be responsible to a major degree for the artistic content of the work being performed. A typical example is an acting group that performs by means of improvisation. The group collectively "plans" the drama, that is, determines the broad outline of the plot, the nature of the characters, etc., in the absence of a written dialogue. The development of the drama proceeds entirely on the basis of improvised dialogue. The performance is recorded and it is the recording that is being cataloged.

Sound recordings

If a sound recording collection contains twenty-five or fewer musical works entered under two or more different headings, normally make up to fifteen entries according to the following instructions:

1. If one heading is represented by one work, make an analytical added entry for the work.
2. If one heading is represented by one excerpt from one work, make an analytical added entry for it (25.32A).
3. If one heading is represented by two or more consecutively numbered excerpts from one work, make one analytical added entry (25.32B).
4. If one heading is represented by two unnumbered or nonconsecutively numbered excerpts from one work, make an analytical added entry for each excerpt (25.32B).
5. If one heading is represented by three or more unnumbered or nonconsecutively numbered excerpts from one work, make one analytical added entry (25.32B).
6. If one name heading is represented by two works, make an analytical added entry for each work (25.33).
7. If one personal name heading is represented by three or more works, make an analytical added entry using an appropriate collective uniform title (e.g., "Selections." "Piano music. Selection") (25.34-25.36).

Do not make any analytical added entries for sound recording collections

1. containing twenty five or fewer works that would require more than fifteen analytical added entries;
2. containing pop, folk, ethnic, or jazz music;[23]
3. containing recitals with an orientation towards performer(s) or instrument(s) rather than musical repertoire;[24]

4. that are multipart items but incomplete at the time the collection is cataloged.

21.7C (CSB 28) without collective title.

Sound recordings

If a sound recording collection contains no more than fifteen musical works entered under two or more different headings, enter the collection under the first work and make analytical added entries for the other works. Do not make analytical added entries for sound recording collections that are covered by the excluded categories in LCRI 21.7B.[25]

21.23A (CSB 25) One work

Rule change

[Add caption]

21.23A One work

Added Entries

For a sound recording covered by 21.23A or 21.23B, make whatever added entries are prescribed by the rules under which the choice of main entry for the work or works recorded was made (e.g., for a joint author or composer under 21.6C1; for an arranger under 21.18B; for a librettist under 21.19A), as well as any others provided for under 21.29.

Chief source of information:

L'ELISIR D'AMORE — Highlights
   (Donizetti; Romani)

Music by Donizetti; libretto by Romani, based on Le philtre *by Eugene Scribe)*

Main entry under the heading for Donizetti as composer 21.23A, 21.19A)

Added entries under the headings for Romani and for Scribe's *Le philtre* (21.19A)

21.23B (CSB 25) Two or more works by the same person(s) or body (bodies)

Rule change

[Add caption]

21.23B Two or more works by the same person(s) or body (bodies)

Added entries

See LCRI 21.23A.

21.23C (CSB 25) Works by different persons or bodies.

Collective title

Rule change

If a sound recording containing works by different persons or bodies has a collective title, enter it under the heading for the person or body represented as principal performer.[26]

(Information about PRINCIPAL PERFORMER appears two pages later in this manual)

Pieces of the sky

(Songs by various composers performed by Emmylou Harris)

Main entry under the heading for Harris

All that jazz

(Pieces by several composers performed by Fats Waller)

Main entry under the heading for Waller

Bonaparte's retreat

(Folk tunes and songs by various hands performed by the band of the Chieftains)

Main entry under the heading for the Chieftains

Elisabeth Schumann

(Arias and Lieder by various composers sung by Elisabeth Schumann with various orchestras, conductors, and pianists accompanying)

Main entry under the heading for Schumann

Adrian Ruiz plays Neils Gade and Christian Sinding

(Two works by Gade and 6 by Sinding performed by Ruiz)

Main entry under the heading for Ruiz

If there are two or three persons or bodies represented as principal performers, enter under the heading for the first named and make added entries for the others.

Great tenor arias

(Arias by various composers sung by Carlo Bergonzi with the Orchestra of the Accademia di Santa Cecilia, Rome)

Main entry under the heading for Bergonzi

Added entry under the heading for the orchestra

Dancer with bruised knees / Kate & Anna McGarrigle

(Songs by the McGarrigle sisters and others performed by the sisters)

Main entry under the heading for K. McGarrigle

Added entry under the heading for A. McGarrigle

Irish rebel songs

(Sung by Mike Barret and Joe Kiernan)

Main entry under the heading for Barrett

Added entry under the heading for Kiernan

If there are four or more persons or bodies represented as principal performers, or no principal performers, enter under title.[27]

Music of nineteenth century England
    (Several pieces performed by various groups and singers)
    Main entry under title
Five centuries of music in Reims
    (Seven pieces by various composers performed variously by
    individual singers and performers and by choirs and orchestras)
    Main entry under title

Principal Performer

In applying the rules and these interpretations, understand "performer" to mean a person or corporate body whose performance is heard on the sound recording. When a person performs as a member of a corporate body, do not consider him or her as a separate person to be a performer. However, do not consider a conductor or accompanist to be a member of the body he or she conducts or accompanies. Likewise, if a person's name appears in conjunction with the name of a group (e.g., "J.D. Crowe and the New South"), do not consider him or her to be a member of the group.

For recordings containing musical works by different composers or writers follow the guidelines below in (1) deciding whether or not there are principal performers and (2) identifying the principal performers, if any.

The use of the term "principal performer" in 21.23C-D can lead to confusion since the term implies a performer who is more important (or, in the words of footnote 5 on p. 314, given greater prominence) than other performers. This interpretation, however, would often produce undesirable results: it would make main entry under the heading for a performer impossible under 21.23C when there is only one performer or when there are only two or three performers who are given equal prominence. To avoid this difficulty, apply the following:

When two or more performers are named in the chief source of information, consider to be principal performers those given the greatest prominence there. If all the performers named in the chief source of information are given equal prominence there, consider all of them to be principal performers.[28]

When only one performer is named in the chief source of information, consider that performer to be a principal performer.

When no performers are named in the chief source of information, consider that there are no principal performers.

In judging relative prominence on the basis of wording, layout, and typography, consider names printed in the same size and style of lettering and in association with one another to have equal prominence. When names appear in the same size and style of lettering but in different areas of the same source of information, consider these in a location implying superiority (e.g., a higher position) to have greater prominence. Do not consider names near the beginning of a list or sequence to have greater prominence than those near the end.

Chief source of information

> **JESS WALTERS SINGS**
> **CLASSIC FOLK SONGS**
> Jess Walters, baritone
> Hector Garcia, guitar

Main entry under the heading for Walters as principal performer

Chief source of information

> Joan Sutherland
> **SONGS MY MOTHER TAUGHT ME**
> Songs by Dvorak, Mendelssohn, Massenet,
> Gounod, Delibes, Grieg, Liszt, and others
> Richard Bonynge
> The New Philharmonia Orchestra

Main entry under the heading for Sutherland as principal performer

Chief source of information

> **SONATAS OF J.S. BACH & SONS**
> **JEAN-PIERRE RAMPAL**, Flute
> **ISAAC STERN**, Violin
> **JOHN STEELE RITTER,**
> Harpsichord and Fortepiano
> **LESLIE PARNAS**, Cello

Main entry under title; Rampal, Stern, Ritter, and Parnas are principal performers

Chief source of information

> **MUSIC OF CHABRIER AND MASSENET**
> Detroit Symphony Orchestra
> Paul Paray

Main entry under the heading for the orchestra
Added entry under the heading for Paray
(The orchestra and Paray are principal performers)

Chief source of information

> **LAS VOCES DE LOS CAMPESINOS**
> Francisco Garcia and Pablo and Juanita Saludada sing corridos
> about farm workers and their union

Main entry under the heading for Garcia

Added entries under the headings for P. Saludado and J. Saludado

(Garcia and the Saludados are principal performers)

Chief source of information

SARAH BERNHARDT & THE COQUELIN BROTHERS

(Dramatic readings performed by Sarah Bernhardt, Constant Coquelin, and Ernest Coquelin)

Main entry under the heading for Bernhardt

Added entries under the headings for C. Coquelin and E. Coquelin

(Bernhardt, C. Coquelin, and E. Coquelin are principal performers)

Chief source of information

SONGS OF THE WOBBLIES
With Joe Glazer

(Sung by Glazer, with instrumental ensemble)

Main entry under the heading for Glazer as principal performer

Chief source of information

Serge Cassel
POESIES ET PROSE FRANCAISES

(Various poems and prose selections read by Serge Cassel)

Main entry under the heading for Cassel as principal performer

Chief source of information

SOUTHERN CLAWHAMMER BANJO
(No performers named)

Main entry under title

(No principal performers)

21.23D (CSB 25) Works by different persons or bodies. No collective title.

Rule change

If a sound recording containing works by different persons or bodies has no collective title and is to be cataloged as a unit (see 6.1G), follow one of the instructions below.

1. If the works are of a type in which the participation of the performers goes beyond that of performance, execution, or interpretation (as is commonly the case in "popular," rock, and jazz music), enter under the heading for the person or body represented as principal performer.

I want to make you smile / Bill Medley ; [sung by]

Kenny Rogers. Coward of the county / R. Bowlings, B.E.
Wheeler ; [sung by] Kenny Rogers

Main entry under the heading for Rogers

If there are two or three persons or bodies represented as principal performers, enter under the heading for the first and make added entries for the others.

All my love / Jolson, Akst, Chaplin ; Freddy Martin and his orchestra ; vocal refrain by Clyde Rogers and the Martin Men. When the white roses bloom in Red River Valley / Paul Herrick, Allie Wrubel ; Freddy Martin and his orchestra ; vocal refrain by Stuart Wade and the Martin Men

Main entry under the heading for Martin

If there are four or more persons or bodies represented as principal performers or no principal performers, enter under the heading appropriate to the first work named.

Ko Ko Mo / Forest, Haven ; the Harmonaires with Bob Murray Orchestra. Tweedle dee / Scott ; Joni Downs and the Starliners. Ballad of Davy Crockett / Blackburn, Burns ; Heck Johns and the Pioneers. How important can it be? / Benjamin, Weiss ; Joan Forest with Jay Weston Orchestra

Main entry under the heading of Forest

2. If the works on the recording are of a type in which the participation of the performer(s) does not go beyond that of performance, execution, and interpretation (as is commonly the case in the classical and other "serious" music), enter under the heading appropriate to the first work and make added entries for the other works as appropriate (cf. 21.7C).

Sinfonia in G minor, op. 6, no. 6 / Johann Christian Bach. Symphony in G / Michael Haydn. Cassation in D. K. 62a / Wolfgang Amadeus Mozart

(All works performed by Dennis Russell Davies conducting the Saint Paul Chamber Orchestra)

Main entry under the heading for Bach

Added entries (name-title) under the headings for Haydn and Mozart

Added entries under the headings for Davies and the orchestra

Concerto grosso no. 1 for string orchestra with piano obbligato / Bloch. Spirituals : for string choir and orchestra / Gould

(The first work performed by Rafael Kubelik conducting the Chicago Symphony Orchestra; the second work performed by Antal Dorati conducting the Minneapolis Symphony Orchestra)

Main entry under the heading for Bloch

Added entry (name-title) under the heading for Gould

Added entries under the headings for Kubelik, the Chicago Symphony Orchestra, Dorati, and the Minneapolis Symphony Orchestra

The Pied Piper / Robert Browning. The hunting of the Snark / Lewis Carroll

(Both poems read by Boris Karloff)

Main entry under the heading for Browning

Added entry (name-title) under the heading for Carroll

Added entry under the heading for Karloff

I look back ; Wistfull ; Service of all the dead ; A child's grace ; This glittering grief ; The ouselcock / Herbert Elwell. String quartet no. 7 / John Verrall. Spatials ; Sonata no. 2 ; Spektra / George Walker.

(Ellwell songs performed by Maxine Makas, soprano, and Anthony Makas, piano; Verral work performed by the Berkshire Quartet; Walker works performed by the composer on the piano)

Main entry under the heading for Elwell

Added entry (name-title) under the heading for Verrall

Added entries under the headings for M. Makas, A. Makas, the Berkshire Quartet, and Walker.

Principal Performer

See LCRI 21.23C

21.28A (MCB December '83)

LIBRETTOS

In order for a libretto to qualify for entry "under the heading appropriate to the musical work" (footnote 7), a reference to the libretto's musical setting must appear in the chief source of information or in the foreword or other prefatory matter of the publication.[29]

21.29 (CSB 12)

Order of added entries. Give added entries in the following order:

1. Personal name;
2. Personal name-title;
3. Corporate name;
4. Corporate name-title;
5. Uniform title (all instances of works entered under title);
6. Title traced as Title-period;
7. Title traced as Title-colon, followed by a title;
8. Series

For arrangement within any one of these groupings, generally follow the order in which the justifying data appears in the bibliographic description. If such a criterion is not applicable, use judgment.

21.29 (CSB 13) and 21.30 (CSB 13)

In making added entries for audiovisual materials, follow the general rules in 21.29, and apply, in addition to those in 21.30, the following guidelines: [some omitted that did not pertain to sound recordings]

1. Make added entry headings for all corporate bodies named in the publication, distribution, etc., area.
2. Make added entries for all featured players, performers, and narrators with the following exceptions:

   . . .

   a) If there are many players (actors, actresses, etc.), make added entries under the headings for those that are given prominence in the chief source of information. If that cannot be used as a criterion, make added entries under the headings for each if there are no more than three.
3. Similarly, make added entries under the headings for persons in a production who are interviewers or interviewees, delivering lectures, addresses, etc., or discussing their lives, ideas, work, etc., and who are not chosen as the main entry heading.

21.29D (CSB 34)

Make added entries for all performers named on a sound recording (persons or corporate bodies) with the following exceptions:

1. Do not make an added entry for a person who functions entirely or primarily on the item being cataloged as a member of a corporate body represented by a main or added entry. Do not consider a conductor or accompanist to be a member of the body he or she conducts or accompanies.[30] If a person's name appears in conjunction with the name of a group, determine whether the corporate name includes this personal name. If the conclusion is that the corporate name does not include the person's name, do not consider the person a member of the group; if the conclusion is that it does include the person's name, consider the person to be a member of the group.[31]
2. If both the chorus and the orchestra of an opera company, opera house, etc., participate in a performance and both are named, along with the name of the parent body, make only a single added entry under the heading for the parent body.
   On recording:
   Bolshoi Theater Orchestra and Chorus
   Added entry under the heading for the theater
3. When a featured performer is accompanied by an unnamed group that, if it had a name, would be given an added entry as a

corporate body, do not make added entries for the individual members of the group. Do not, however, apply this exception to jazz ensembles, even if one or more of the performers is given greater prominence than the others, i.e., normally make added entries for all the individual performers (except any who are covered by exceptions (4) and (5) below) in such cases.

4. Do not make an added entry for a performer who participates in only a small number of the works in a collection or for a performer whose role is minor (e.g., an announcer on a radio program).

5. Do not make an added entry for a performer who receives main entry heading as principal performer under 21.23C.

6. If there are many performers performing the same function (e.g., singers in an opera, actors in a drama), make added entries only for those who are given prominence over the others in other places on the sound recording (e.g., the container, the program booklet, etc.) or, if that criterion does not apply, for those performing the most important function (e.g., singing the principal roles, acting the principal parts).

Chief source of information (labels):

> L'ELISIR D'AMORE — Highlights
> (Donizetti; Romani)
> Spiro, Malas, Maria Casula, Joan Sutherland,
> Luciano Pavarotti, Dominic Cossa
> with the Ambrosian Opera Chorus
> and the English Chamber Orchestra
> conducted by
> Richard Bonynge

Container:

> Donizetti
> L'ELISIR D'AMORE Highlights
> JOAN SUTHERLAND, LUCIANO PAVAROTTI
> Dominic Cossa, Spiro Malas, Maria Casula
> Ambrosian Opera Chorus, English Chamber Orchestra
> RICHARD BONYNGE
> Added entries under the headings for Sutherland,
> Pavarotti, Bonynge, the chorus, and the orchestra

If a composer is the main entry heading for a musical work and performs his or her own work(s), make an added entry to represent the performing function.[32] If, however, the composer is represented not by the main entry heading but by a name-title added entry heading, then do not make the added entry to represent the performing function.

21.30F. (MCB November '86)
ELECTRONIC OR COMPUTER MUSIC STUDIOS
For recordings of electronic or computer music, make an added entry for the studio or studios where the music was realized, when the item being cataloged identifies the studio or studios. If more than three studios were involved, however, make no such added entries.

(MCB March '85)
Make an added entry for any person mentioned in the title proper or other title information of a bibliographic record for a musical work or collection. Exception: do not make an added entry if the person's relationship to the item is purely a subject relationship.

> Liszt, Franz
>> Praludium und Fuge uber den Namen Bach . . .
> Added entry: Bach, Johann Sebastian

21.30G (MCB March '85)
When an instrumental work or collection is based on, inspired by, etc., one or two individual literary works, make a related-work added entry or entries (cf. RI 21.30M) for the literary work or works. (For vocal works based on literary works, see 21.19A.)

> Tchaikovsky, Peter Ilich
>> [Romeo et Juliette (Fantasy-overture)]
>> Romeo und Julia : Fantasie-Ouverture nach Shakespeare
> Added entry: Shakespeare, William. Romeo and Juliet

When an instrumental work or collection is based on, inspired by, etc., three or more literary works by the same author, or an author's oeuvre in general, make an added entry for the author.

> Henze, Hans Werner
>> [Royal winter music. No. 1]
>> Royal winter music. First sonata on Shakespearean
>>   characters . . .
> Added entry: Shakespeare, William

When a musical work is based on, inspired by, etc., one or more works by an artist, or an artist's oeuvre in general, make an added entry for the artist.

> Mussorgsky, Modest Petrovich
>> [Kartinki s vystavki]
>> Pictures at an exhibition . . .
>> Note: Suite based on paintings and drawings by Victor
>>   Hartmann.
> Added entry: Hartman, Viktor Aleksandrovich

21.30J (MCB April '84))[33]
Generally make added entries for nicknames, etc., of musical works

that are transcribed as other title information. Exception: Do not make an added entry for a word or words that customarily are not used alone to identify the work. Transcription: Symphony in B minor no. 8 : (The unfinished symphony . . .
Title a.e.: I. Title: Unfinished symphony.

Transcription: Symphony no. 8 in B. minor : (Unfinished) . . .
No title a.e.

Transcription: Sinfonie Nr. 41 C-Dur KV 551 : (Jupiter-Sinfonie) . . .
Title: a.e.: I. Title: Jupiter-Sinfonie.

Transcription: Symphony no. 41 in C major, K. 551 : "Jupiter" . . .
No title a.e.

22.1B (CSB 34)
. . . . [much is omitted]
Rule application
Treat a music composer as an author and determine the name from the form found in the chief source for the published music.[34] If no form in the published music is in the composer's language, determine the name from reference sources of the composer's country of residence or activity. If the name is not listed in these reference sources, use the name found in the published music.

22.3A (CSB 33) Fullness
If the forms of an author's name vary in fullness from one work to another in the same language and the AACR2 form for the heading has not yet been determined, apply the following:

1. If the form found on the item being cataloged agrees with the form used for the heading on existing records in the catalog, accept this form as AACR2. (The "catalog" referred to here is the file against which the cataloging and searching is being done.)

2. If the form found on the item being cataloged does not agree with the form already in use, choose as the AACR2 form the form found in 80% of the author's works (counting forms appearing in both main and added entries). (The form found in the chief source of a person's thesis is taken into account when choosing the form to be used in the heading.)

When calculating the 80%, do it quickly and use common sense. This means

1. count the forms if there are no more than approximately 15 records or

2. if there are more than approximately 15, browse through the

file, looking for an obvious case of predominance. If nothing is obvious, sample the file (every 3rd, 5th, 10th, etc., record, depending on the length of the file).

When there is no commonly found form (defined above), choose the fullest form as the AACR2 form. (When determining the fullest form for a person who uses both forename initials and forenames, make no distinction between initials and forenames, e.g., "B.E.F. Pagen" is fuller than "Bernard Edward Pagen."

Note: Equating the predominant form or the commonly found form with the form found in 80% of the person's works applies only to 22.3A; no such formula has been assigned to "predominant form" or "commonly found form" in the other rules.

Headings already coded "AACR2" or "AACR2 compatible"

If an established heading is already coded "AACR2" and subsequently received items show forms in the chief source that vary in fullness, change the established heading to the form found in 80% of the author's works if it differs from the form used in the heading.

If an established heading is already coded "AACR2 compatible" because it varies in fullness from the AACR2 form, generally do not reconsider the heading.

Variant forms within one item

If the name of an author appears in two or more forms in one work, apply the following:

1. If the name appears in two or more sources, once in the chief source and one or more times in other sources, choose the form appearing in the chief source.

title page: T.B. Smith
verso of t.p.: T. Basil Smith III
heading: Smith, T.B. (T. Basil)

2. If the name does not appear in the chief source but does appear once in another prominent source (cf. 0.8) and one or more times in other sources, choose the form appearing in the prominent source.

verso of t.p.: R.J. Gottschall
page 239: Robert J. Gottschall
heading: Gottschall, R.J. (Robert J.)

3. In all situations not covered by (1) or (2) above, choose the fullest form of name.

verso of t.p.: Victoria Galofree Neuto
page 1 of cover: Victoria Galofre
heading: Galofre Neuto, Victoria

Note: Do not choose for the heading a form appearing in the following sources if the name appears prominently elsewhere in the item: (1) the copyright statement: (2) the colophon for items published in the Soviet Union.

24.4B (CSB 18) Names not conveying the idea of a corporate body . . . [much is omitted]

Performing Duets

For performing duets, do not add a general designation qualifier if the name contains two surnames (with or without forenames or forename initials) or if the name contains two forenames.

Performing Groups

In dealing with performing groups, apply the following:

1. If the name contains a word that specifically designates a performing group or a corporate body in general (e.g., Band, Consort, Society) or contains a collective or plural noun (e.g., Ramblers, Boys, Hot Seven), do not add a designation to the name.
2. If the name is extremely vague, consisting primarily of single, common words (e.g., Circle, Who, Jets) or the name has the appearance of a personal name (e.g., Jethro Tull), add a designation to the name.[35]
3. If the name falls between the above categories (e.g., Led Zeppelin, Jefferson Airplane, Road Apple, L.A. Contempo), add a designation to the name.
4. If there is doubt whether a designation should be added, add it.

Use the designation "(Musical group)" unless special circumstances (such as a conflict) require a more specific term.

. . . [more is omitted]

25.3A (CSB 11)

If a uniform title begins with an article (definite or indefinite) and is in the nominative case (for inflected languages), delete the article in all cases, even when the uniform title is entered under a name. . . .

25.26B (MCB January '84)

"Beethoven wrote 16 string quartets and they are serially numbered 1-16. Brahms wrote 3 string quartets and they are serially numbered 1-3. The first question that the cataloger must ask himself when cataloging these works is, "Are these works, with the same title and the same medium of performance, consecutively numbered?" If the answer is *Yes*, he then determines that he is dealing with the first definition of "work" on p. 474 ("a work that is a single unit in-

tended for performance as a whole") in order to apply rules
25.31A2 through 25.31A5. The result would be such examples as:
Beethoven . . .
    [Quartets, strings, no. 2, op. 18, no 2, G major]
Brahms . . .
    [Quartets, strings, no. 2, op. 52, no. 2 A minor]
A more complicated case would be Beethoven's 32 piano sonatas
which are also consecutively numbered 1-32. There are examples
here where the serial number (25.31A2) does not match the serial
number within the opus number (25.31A3):
Beethoven . . .
    [Sonatas, piano, no. 16, op. 31, no. 1, G major]
For the Beethoven [Trios, strings . . .], Paganini [Caprices, violin,
op. 1] and Corelli [Sonatas, violin, continuo, op. 5] the answer to
the cataloger's first question is *No*; i.e., Beethoven wrote 4 string
trios (a 5th is called "Serenade") but they are not consecutively
numbered; Paganini wrote 24 Caprices within his op. 1; and Corelli
wrote 12 violin sonatas within his op. 5. The cataloger therefore
determines that he is dealing with the third definition of "work" on
p. 474, and each of the Trios (within op. 9), each of the Caprices,
and each of the Sonatas becomes a *part*. Rule 25.32A is applied and
the net results are the examples:

Paganini . . .

[Caprices, violin, op. 1. No. 20]

Corelli . . .

[Sonatas, violin, continuo, op. 5. No. 4]

Beethoven . . .

[Trios, strings, op. 9. No. 1]

plus others, such as:

Beethoven . . .

[Trios, strings, op. 3, E♭ major]

Onslow, Georges

[Quartets, strings, op. 8. No. 1]

25.27B (CSB 14)
    Footnote 9 lists three categories of titles that are to be treated as
"titles consisting solely of the name of one type of composition":
    1. titles that consist of a name of a form;
    2. titles that consist of a name of a genre;
    3. titles that consist of a generic term frequently used by different
       composers. The third category (and the third category only)
       should be evaluated with the final sentence of the footnote in

mind also. This will be particularly true when the common term is accompanied by some modifier other than a medium or a numeral. One should consider that all modifiers other than a medium or a numeral make the phrase a distinctive title — no matter how common sounding it is. For example "Piece" is a generic term frequently used by different composers, but "Concert piece," "Little piece," etc., are considered distinctive titles.

When a French work for solo voice and keyboard stringed instrument has the title *Melodie* or *Melodies*, do not translate the title into English, since the cognate words in English and other languages do not have the specific meaning of the French word. Consider the medium of performance to be implied by the title and do not include it in the uniform title (25.29A2(a)).

When a French work for solo voice without accompaniment or with accompaniment other than a keyboard stringed instrument alone has the title *Melodie* or *Melodies*, do not translate the title into English. Include the medium or accompaniment or a statement of the absence of accompaniment (25.29H3).

When the work *Melody* or *Melodies* or its cognate in another language (including French) is the title of any other work, consider it the name of a type of composition. Use the English form in the uniform title and include the medium of performance (25.29A1).

Consider commonly used liturgical titles such as *Requiem, Te Deum, Salve Regina*, and *Dixit Dominus* to be generic terms. If a plural form is required, form one if possible by adding the letter *s* to the last word of the title; if this is not convenient, consider the plural to be the same as the singular. Apply 25.29A2(a) and do not normally include a statement of medium of performance.

When cataloging the first occurrence of a work of a particular type by a composer
  1. If the composer is deceased, search reference sources to determine whether the composer wrote more than one work of the type, and use the singular or plural form in the uniform title according to the information found.
  2. If the composer is living, use the singular form in the uniform title unless the work being cataloged bears a serial number (including 2); in that case use the plural form on the assumption that the composer has written or intends to write more works of the type.

When cataloging the second occurrence of a work of a particular type by a composer, if the singular form has been used in the uniform title for the first work of the type, revise that uniform title to use the plural form.

Note that the medium of performance is not a criterion in the application of this provision of the rule; if a composer wrote one piano sonata and one violin sonata, he or she wrote two sonatas and the plural form must be used.

25.29A1 (MCB September '85)

Do not apply this rule to title consisting of two words each of which alone would be the name of a type of composition, when the combination of the two words produces a distinctive title (cf. RI 25.27B, first paragraph).

[Humoreske-bagatteller]

not [Humoreske-bagatteller, piano . . .]

Note, however, that "trio sonata" (cf. 25.27E) and "chorale prelude" are each the name of *one* type of composition.

25.29A2 (CSB 33)

Rule change

1. [Revise the fourth example to read:]
   Songs, Lieder, etc.

   (implied medium: solo voice(s) with accompaniment for keyboard stringed instrument or, if in a "popular" idiom, solo voice(s) with instrumental and/or vocal accompaniment)

2. [Revise subsection b) to read:]
   or b) the work consists of a set of compositions for different media, or is one of a series of compositions with the same title but for different media.

25.29A3 (CSB 33)

Rule change

1. [Revise category c) to read:]
   c) the order of other instruments in score order
2. [Add below c):]
   d) continuo.
3. [Add as the last example:]
   [Trio sonata, flute, bassoon, continuo . . .]

25.29C. (CSB 33) Standard combinations of instruments.

Rule change

[Replacement for the third paragraph in rule 25.29C]

For works entitled "Trio," "Quartet," or "Quintet" that are for combinations other than those listed above, record the full statement of medium even if more than three different instruments must be recorded. For the order of instruments, see 25.29A3.

25.29D (CSB 20) Individual instruments

Use the following instrument names: violoncello, English horn, contrabassoon, and timpani.

If the application of the subrules of 25.29D results in the separation of a composer's works between harpsichord or clavichord on the one hand and piano on the other, choose the instrument for which the major portion of the works of a given type was intended and use that instrument name for all works of the type. If the "major" instrument is not apparent, use "keyboard instrument."

25.29D4 (CSB 25)

Rule change

Use *continuo* for a thorough bass part, with or without figures, realized or unrealized, whether it is named as basso continuo, figured bass, thorough bass, or continuo.

25.29E (CSB 18) Groups of instruments

Rule change

. . . replacement of "plectral instruments' with "plucked instruments" in the list of terms for groups of instruments . . .

25.29G (CSB 11)

For an accompanying ensemble that has only one performer to a part, use an appropriate phrase for the group of instruments (e.g., "string ensemble," "wind ensemble," "instrumental ensemble") as a statement of medium that follows the statement for solo instruments in a uniform title.

25.29H3 (CSB 33) Songs, Lieder, etc.

Rule change

[Revision of the first sentence]

If works other than those in a "popular" idiom have the title Songs, Lieder, etc., and are accompanied by anything other than a keyboard stringed instrument alone (see 25.29A2), add the name of the accompanying instrument(s) and acc.

25.29J (CSB 33) Medium indeterminate.

Rule change

[addition of a last example]

Weelkes, Thomas

[Madrigals, voices (5-6)]

Madrigals of 5 and 6 parts, apt for the viols and voices . . .

25.30 (CSB 14)

For sketchbooks containing sketches for various compositions or miscellaneous sketches, add "Sketches" in parentheses to the appropriate collective uniform title formulated under 25.35 or 25.36.

[Selections (Sketches)]

[Instrumental music. Selections (Sketches)]
[Piano music. Selections (Sketches)]
[Sonatas, piano. Selections (Sketches)]
Symphonies, no. 7-9 (Sketches)]

25.31A1 (CSB 11)

When adding a serial number, opus or thematic index number, or key to a title that consists solely of the name(s) of type(s) of composition or to a title that conflicts, generally use English terms and arabic numbers. Abbreviate both English and non-English terms in accord with Appendix B and transcribe numbers in accord with Appendix C.

25.31A5 (MCB October '83)

For twentieth-century works, include the key in the uniform title if it is part of the composer's original title (25.27A) or the first-edition title used as a substitute for the composer's original title (CD 25.27A) (before the deletion of the elements such as key under 25.26A).

25.31B1 (MCB December '85)

For works with titles not consisting of the name of a type of composition which have serial numbers associated with them (whether the numbers appear as arabic or roman numerals or spelled out, and whether or not they are preceded by the designation "no." or its equivalent), apply 25.29A1(d) to 25.31B1 and omit the medium of performance when a better file arrangement would result.

[Antiphony, no. 2]
Antiphony II : variations on a theme of Cavafy . . . [36]

When cataloging the first work received in such a sequence, it may, however, be advisable to defer the use of a uniform title until another work in the sequence is received, since it will then be easier to see what numbering pattern is being followed. When the second work is cataloged, the bibliographic record(s) for the first will have to be revised to add the uniform title.

25.32 (CSB 33) Parts of a musical work.

Cancel; covered by LCRI 25.32C.

25.32A1 <[R]ule 25.32A1 completely contradicts rule 25.6A1, and must be used in the latter's place, in accordance with rule 25.25. MCB August '86>

Rule change (CSB 33)

Use, as a uniform title for a separately published part of a musical work, the title of the whole work followed by the title or other verbal designation and/or number of the part, as instructed below. If the part has a distinctive title, make a name/title reference from the heading for the composer and the title of the part.

a. If each of the parts is identified only by a number, use the number of the part being cataloged.
Brahms, Johannes
[Ungarische Tanze. No. 5]

b. If each of the parts is identified only by a title or other verbal designation, use the title or other verbal designation of the part being cataloged.
Verdi, Giuseppe
[Aida. Celeste Aida]
x Verdi, Giuseppe. Celeste Aida
Beethoven, Ludwig van
[Symphonies, no. 1, op. 21, C. major. Andante canabile con moto]

c. If each of the parts is identified both by a number and by a title or other verbal designation, use the title or designation of the part being cataloged.
Mozart, Wolfgang Amadeus
[Cosi fan tutte. Come scoglio]
(Each aria has a number, e.g., No. 14 for Come scoglio, as well as a title)
x Mozart, Wolfgang Amadeus. Come scoglio
If each of the parts is identified both by a number and by a title or other verbal designation, and the title or designation is the same for all of the parts, use the number of the part being cataloged.
Vivaldi, Antonio
[Estro^{37} armonico. N. 8]
(Each part has the title Concerto as well as a number)

d. If each of the parts is identified by a number, and some of the parts are also identified by a title or other verbal designation, use the number of the part being cataloged, followed by the title or designation when there is one.
Schumann, Robert
[Album fur die Jugend. Nr. 30]
Schumann, Robert
[Album fur die Jugend. Nr. 2. Soldatenmarsch]
x Schumann, Robert. Soldatenmarsch

e. If the part being cataloged is part of a larger part that has a distinctive title, include the title of the larger part in the uniform title. Omit the designation of the larger part if it is not distinctive. However, if an indistinctive designation of the larger part is required to identify the smaller part, include that designation.

Praetorius, Hieronymus
  [Opus musicum. Cantiones sacrae. O vos omnes]
  x Praetorius, Hieronymus. O vos omnes
Handel, George Frideric
  [Messiah. Pifa]
  not Messiah. Part 1. Pifa
Verdi, Giuseppe
  [Traviata.[38] Atto3°. Preludio]
Handel, George Frideric
  [Suites de pieces. 1ᵉʳ v. No. 5. Air]

Interpretation

When selecting the title of a part of a musical work, follow 25.26A and 25.27A but not 25.27B.

When the number of a part of a work is used in the uniform title of the part, precede the number by the abbreviation "No." ("No," "Nr.," "N.," etc.) when such an abbreviation, or the corresponding word, appears with the numbers of the parts in the source on which the uniform title is based. Give the abbreviation in the language of the first element of the uniform title.

Brahms, Johannes
  [Ungarische Tanze. Nr. 5]

25.32A2 (CSB 33)

Rule change

  1. [Revise the examples to read:]
     Cima, Giovanni Paolo
       [Concerti ecclesiastici. Sonata, brasses, violin, continuo]
     Cima, Giovanni Paolo
       [Concerti ecclesiastici. Sonata, cornett, violin, continuo]
  2. [Add as the second paragraph and examples:]

When the title or other verbal designation of the part is used in the uniform title and two or more parts have the same title or designation, and making additions as instruction in the paragraph above is not appropriate, add the number of the part in the set, enclosed in parentheses.

Milan, Luis
  [Maestro.[39] Pavana (No. 23)]
Milan, Luis
  [Maestro. Pavana (No. 24)]

Milan, Luis
[Maestro. Fantasia del primero tono (No. 1)]
Milan, Luis
[Maestro. Fantasia del primero tono (No. 40)]
Interpretation
When the number of the part is used as an addition for the purpose of distinguishing between two or more parts with the same title, precede it by the English abbreviation "No." in all cases.
25.32B1 (CSB 33)
Rule change
1. [Revise the third example to read:]
Schubert, Franz
[Impromptus, piano, D. 899. No. 2]
Deux impromptus, op. 90, nos 2 et 4 . . .
Added entry under: Schubert, Franz. Impromptus, piano, D. 899. No. 4
2. [Add as the last example:]
Wagner, Richard
[Ring[40] des Nibelungen. Rheingold.[41] Selections]
25.32B1 (MCB March '85)
When evidence is lacking as to whether an "original cast" recording of a musical comedy or an "original sound track" recording of a motion picture score contains all the music, do not add "Selections" to the uniform title.[42]
25.32B2 (MCB March '86)
ALTERNATIVE INSTRUMENTS: Do not consider to be an arrangement
1. a work composed before 1800 for a baroque, Renaissance, or other early instrument (viola da gamba, recorder, etc.) which is edited for or performed on a contemporary instrument;
2. a work for a melody instrument which is edited for or performed on an alternative instrument specified by the composer or in early editions, preferable the first — provided the key is unchanged and the notation has not been significantly changed.
Bach, Johann Sebastian
[Sonatas, viola da gamba, harpsichord, BWV 1027-1029]
Sonatas for cello and piano, BWV 1027, 1028, 1029
[sound recording] . . .
Subject entry: Sonatas (Violoncello and piano)
Kuhlau, Friedrich
[Sonatas, violin, piano, op. 79. No. 1]

Sonate en fa majeur pour flute & piano, op. 79, no. 1 . . .
(Originally for violin or flute and piano)
Subject entry: Sonatas (Flute and piano—Scores and parts.)
25.32C (CSB 33)

Rule change

Add to the uniform title for a single part or for several parts of a musical work elements as instructed in 25.31B2, 25.31B3, 25.31B5, 25.31B6, 25.31B7, when appropriate.

Wagner, Richard
[Ring[43] des Nibelungen. Walkure.[44] Libretto. English & German]

Bach, Johann Sebastian
[Weihnachts-Oratorium. 1.-2. Theil. Vocal score. English & German]

Handel, George Frideric
[Messiah. He shall feed His flock; arr.]

25.35 (CSB 13)

Do not add a date of publication, etc., to the uniform title "Selections" when this is used for collections of musical works by one composer (unless the uniform title is being used in an analytical added entry (cf. 21.30M)).

25.35 (MCB May '86)

Substitute the following for the examples under no. 1, i.e., Chopin-Godowsky:

Chopin, Frederic
[Piano music. Selections]
Waltzes ; and, Scherzos . . .
Added entries: Chopin . . . Waltzes, piano
　　　　　　　　Chopin . . . Scherzos, piano

(CSB 34)

If a sound recording collection contains three, four, or five musical works entered under a single personal name heading, enter the collection under the collective uniform title appropriate to the whole item. Make name-title analytical added entries for each work in the collection. For excerpts from one work, make a separate analytical added entry for each excerpt unless there are two or more excerpts numbered consecutively (25.6B1) or three or more unnumbered or nonconsecutively numbered excerpts (25.6B3)

Do not apply these provisions to the following sound recording collections:

    1. a collection whose contents consist of all a composer's works of a particular type or of a particular type for a particular medium of performance (26.36B);

2. a collection made up of a consecutively numbered group of works (25.36C);
3. collections of pop, folk, ethnic, or jazz music;
4. multipart collections that are not yet complete.

25.36 (CSB 20) < This rule applies to more than sound recordings. >

Works of various types for one broad or specific medium and works of one type for one specific medium or various media.

Subdivisions

For collections of vocal works or texts of vocal works, add "Vocal scores," "Chorus scores," "Librettos," "Texts," and/or name of language to any collective uniform title provided by 25.36A or 25.36B. (*Note.* Use "Texts" if the collection contains both librettos and other texts set to music.)

[Operettas. Vocal scores]
[Operas. Librettos. English & Italian]
[Masses. Latin]
[Vocal music. Texts. Polyglot]

25.36A (CSB 33)

Rule change

[Replacement for fifth example in the second paragraph]
[Piano music, pianos (2)]

25.36B (CSB 14)

For collections of music by a single composer for various motion pictures, use the uniform title "Motion-picture music" or "Motion-picture music. Selections" (without a statement of medium) instead of such uniform titles as "Orchestra music. Selections."

25.36C (CSB 20)

If the term "Selections" is added to a collective uniform title, add it as the last element.[45]

[Songs. English & German. Selections]
[Operas. Librettos. English & Italian. Selections]
[Vocal music. Texts. Polyglot. Selections]
[Masses. Latin, Selections]
[Operettas. Vocal scores. Selections]

25.4A3 (CSB 33) Titles of parts cataloged under the title of the whole work

Rule change

[Additional examples]
   Verdi, Giuseppe
    Celeste Aida
     See
   Verdi, Giuseppe
    Aida. Celeste

Schumann, Robert
  Soldetenmarsch
    See
Schumann, Robert
  Album fur die Jugend. Nr. 2. Soldatenmarsch

Appendix Notes

Appendix A

1. The other notes follow in the normal pattern (LCRI 6.7B19).
2. See the example: *Million dollar memories* for this.
3. LCRI 6.7B6.
4. This is not consistent with cataloging rules for motion pictures.
5. This means the library owns both formats.
6. This means the library does NOT own this format, but the cataloger knows it is available.
7. LCRI 1.7B21.

Appendix B

1. For early works, the title under which it is known in modern reference sources will be used . . . (25.4.) A part may be entered under its own name if it is a complete entity in its own right. For example, the set entitled: *Great Books of the Western World*, would be cataloged under the name of the set. Books in the set have individual authors and titles, and could be cataloged under their own author and titles, for example, *Aristotle's Republic*. But one chapter in *Aristotle's Republic* would never be cataloged by itself, because it is not considered a separate entity in its own right, but rather is considered an integral part of the book. If a uniform title were needed for the chapter, the uniform title would begin with the book's title, then give the part, or chapter, identification. (See 25.27A, 25.27F and examine: LCRI 26.6A.)

EXAMPLES for a unique title for a work written since 1500:
Loewe, Frederick, 1904-1988
[My fair lady. Selections]
My fair lady [sound recording / Richard Hayman and . . .

Bach, Johann Sebastian, 1685-1750.
[Auf Christi Himmelfahrt allein]
2. Unless the composer is deceased and known to have written only one piece in this form. See 25.27B and the LCRI 25.27B.
3. Generic titles are in the plural.

4. Generic titles are in the plural.

5. A generic title is written in the plural.

6. See 25.5D for works in two languages, where the cataloger names both languages, and for works in three or more languages, where the term "Polyglot" is used. The order of specifying the language is also given in this section.

7. It is possible to use the term "Selections" as the leading term in the uniform title, and this is listed in the first section of this Appendix.

8. These are entered under the name of the original composer.

9. This is entered under the original composer.

10. In the place, publisher, date area.

11. The thematic index for Haydn.

12. Of the Hoboken index.

13. In the place, publisher, date area.

14. In the place, publisher, date area.

Appendix D

1. There is some duplication here with Appendix E: Thematic Indexes, "How to locate information when no thematic catalog is available."

Appendix G

1. *Black Man in America*, Example 8.7, illustrates this.

2. Which also refers to 1.1B2.

3. *Ink Spots* is an example.

4. Mozart, Example 4.8, shows this in the tracing.

5. See Herb Alpert and the Tijuana Brass, Example 2.10.

6. See Haydn, Example 4.7 and 4.8.

7. See Haydn, Example 4.7 and 4.8.

8. See Mozart, Example 4.8.

9. LCRI for 6.4C says to "Apply the option stated in 1.4C7 for adding the full address of a publisher, distributor, etc."

10. See *Modern Chinese*, Example 8.12.

11. In other words, a generic title.

12. For examples, see: Mozart, Example 4.8, Haydn, Example 4.7, and Paine, Example 4.1.

13. For unique titles.

14. Consider the title as generic.

15. See 25.31B1 also.

16. See Haydn, Example 4.7.

17. Nonprocessed sound recordings are noncommercial recordings, generally existing in unique copies.

18. "Give the date or inclusive dates of the manuscript or manuscript collection unless it is already included in the title (as with letters and legal documents). Give the date as a year or years, and optionally the month and day (in the case of single manuscripts), in that order.

19. CD means Cataloging Decision, and is indicated in this chapter by the words *"Rule change:"*.

20. Additional comments are provided in *Music Cataloging Bulletin* 15(May 1984):3.

21. While this is in *CSB* 33, it appears to be an old style, so apply this cautiously until more information is available.

22. RI means "Rule interpretation" and is given in this chapter as the material from *CSB*.

23. See *Ink Spots*, Example 2.4.

24. See Petri, Example 4.9.

25. See Mozart, Example 4.8.

26. With *All purpose folk dances*, Example 7.4, the person was named first. With *Glorious sound of Christmas*, Example 7.2, the orchestra was named first. The catalog record is different in each case because the information was transcribed the way it appeared on the label.

27. See *Christmas Sound of Music*, Example 7.3.

28. See *A Little Night Music*, Example 9.4.

29. See *Il Trovatore*, by Verdi, Example 4.4.

30. See *All Time Favorites*, Example 2.19.

31. See *Sugarloaf*, Example 2.16.

32. See *Ink Spots*, Example 2.4.

33. This appears a bit unusual. Could this not be done better with cross references in the authority file?

34. See Verdi, Example 4.4.

35. See "Ace," Example 2.15, and "Sugarloaf," Example 2.16.

36. See 5.1B1 also.

37. LCRI wrote L'estro, but LCRI 25.3A calls for deleting the initial articles.

38. LCRI wrote La traviata but LCRI 25.3A calls for deleting the initial articles.

39. LCRI wrote El maestro, but LCRI 25.3A calls for deleting the initial articles.

40. LCRI wrote Der Ring . . . , but LCRI 25.3A calls for deleting the initial articles.

41. LCRI wrote Das Rheingold, but LCRI 25.3A calls for deleting the initial articles.

42. See *The Wiz*, Example 5.8, *Cross and the Switchblade*, Example 5.1, and *A Little Night Music*, Example 9.4.

43. LCRI wrote Der Ring, but LCRI 25.3A calls for deleting the initial articles.

44. LCRI wrote Die Walkure, but LCRI 25.3A calls for deleting the initial articles.

45. See Lewis' *Prince Caspian*, Example 6.3, as well as Bond's *Paddington for Christmas*, Example 6.2.

Index